Effective Real Estate Sales and Marketing

3rd Edition

DATE DUE

			llege
			d, ABR,
			PRO, GRI

Demco, Inc. 38-293

THOMSON
✶
SOUTH-WESTERN

Australia · Brazil · Canada · Mexico · Singapore · Spain · United Kingdom · United States

THOMSON
SOUTH-WESTERN

Effective Real Estate Sales and Marketing, 3rd Edition
Johnnie Rosenauer and John D. Mayfield

VP/Editorial Director:
Jack W. Calhoun

VP/Editor-in-Chief:
Dave Shaut

Executive Editor
Scott Person

Assoc. Acquisitions Editor:
Sara Glassmeyer

Developmental Editor:
Arlin Kauffman
LEAP Publishing Services, Inc.

Sr. Marketing Manager:
Mark Linton

Assoc. Marketing Communications Manager:
Sarah Greber

Content Project Manager:
Kelly Hoard

Director of Professional Marketing:
Terri Coats

Manager of Technology, Editorial:
Vicky True

Sr. Technology Project Editor:
Matt McKinney

Manufacturing Coordinator:
Charlene Taylor

Production House:
Interactive Composition Corporation

Printer:
Globus Printing
Minster, OH

Art Director:
Linda Helcher

Internal and Cover Designer:
Bethany Casey

Cover Images:
© Digital Vision
Digital Stock Corp

Library of Congress Control Number:
2006904141

For more information about our products, contact us at:
Thomson Learning Academic Resource Center
1-800-423-0563

Thomson Higher Education
5191 Natorp Boulevard
Mason, OH 45040
USA

Dedication

On a professional level, I dedicate this book to the many wonderful people who have come into my world through the Texas Real Estate Teachers Association (TRETA). On a personal level, I offer it as a token of my love and appreciation to the Lady Danell, my Little Princess Jessica Alene, and the Dino Boy Corban Walker.

Johnnie Rosenauer

Contents

Preface   ix

Part I   The Planning Stage—Getting Yourself Ready to Sell   1

Chapter 1   An Overview of Sales and Marketing   3

Marketing and Sales: Definitions and Differences   3
  Factors Influencing the Marketing Concept   4
Overview of the Sales Process   5
  Selling Defined   6
  Marketing, Sales, and the Uniqueness of Real Estate   7
Traits of a Successful Salesperson   8
  Identifying What We Sell   10
Advantages and Disadvantages of Selling Real Estate   11
Professionalism   13
Summary   22
  Review Questions   22
  Discussion Questions   22
  Situation   23

Chapter 2   The Technology of Real Estate Sales and Marketing   25

An Overview of Technology   25
Developing a Technology Budget   26
Computer Needs   26
Cellular Phones/Smart Phones   28
Digital Photography   29
Software   30
  Contact Management   31
  Database Needs   32
  Calendar Tasks/Needs   32
  Desktop Publishing   32
  Accounting and Bookkeeping   32

PDF (Portable Document Format) Software   33
  Word Processing   33
  Presentation Software   33
  Photo Editing Software   34
  Specialty Programs   34
Web Sites   35
Putting It All Togethe   36
Summary   37
  Review Questions   37
  Discussion Questions   38

Chapter 3   Defining Your Marketplace   39

Selling Your Knowledge   39
Deciding Where to Work   39
Gaining Market Knowledge   41
  Establishing Boundaries   41
  Schools   42
  Houses of Worship   43
  Public Facilities   43
  Public Services   43
  Commercial Facilities   43
  Government Structure   44
  Real Estate Developments   44
Knowing Your Marketplace History   45
  Keeping Up with Activity   45
  Keeping Up with Appreciation   46
Summary   49
  Review Questions   49
  Discussion Questions   49
  Situation   50

Chpter 4   Personal Management   51

Self-Discipline   51
Personal Motivaton   51

Keep Setbacks in Perspective   52

Expect Problems and Attempt to
Minimize Them   52

Remember Victories   52

Give Yourself Some Time Away   52

The BIKE Approach   52

Time Management   54

Guidelines to Improve Time
Management   54

Goal Setting   57

Goals Must Be Personal   57

Goals Must Be in Writing   57

Goals Must Be Flexible and Subject to
Review   58

Goals Must Be Measurable   58

Challenging Yet Realistic Goals   59

Summary   60

Review Questions   60

Discussion Questions   60

Situation   61

**PART II   The Marketing Stage—
Putting Your Knowledge
to Work   63**

**Chpater 5   Developing a Prospecting
System   65**

Applying Your Knowledge   65

Suspect or Prospect?   65

How Prospecting Works   66

Developing a System   66

The Satisfied Customer   67

Centers of Influence   67

Farming   70

For Sale By Owners and Expired
Listings   76

Open House   78

Summary   80

Review Questions   80

Discussion Questions   81

Situation   81

**Chapter 6   The Listing
Presentation   83**

Listings   83

The Importance of Listings   83

Exposure in a Marketplace   84

Generating More Business   84

The Stability of a Listing   84

Other People Working for
the Agent   86

Guidelines for Making a Listing
Presentation   86

Plan for the Presentation   86

Explain the Agent's Role   88

Explain the Seller's Role   88

The Listing Presentation Kit   90

Contents of Kit   92

Summary   95

Review Questions   95

Discussion Questions   95

Situation   96

**Chpter 7   Advertising and the
Communications
Process   99**

Communicating with the Consumer   99

How People Learn   99

Communication   100

Communication Barriers   101

Advertising   102

Advertising to Attracting Sellers and
Buyers   102

Enhancing Your Agency's Image   102

Exposure in the Marketplace   103

Educating the Public   103

Satisfying the Seller   103

Types of Advertising   103

Classified Advertising   105

Headings Attract Readers   105

The Body Gives the Facts   105

The Conclusion Brings Action   106

Effective Ad Techniques   107
    Monitoring Ad Results   107
    Ad Location   107
    Concise Wording   107
    Conveying the Right Image   108
    Reverse Advertising   109
General Guidelines for Ad Writing   111
Other Media   112
Summary   114
    Review Questions   114
    Discussion Questions   115
    Situation   115

Chapter 8   Telephone Techniques   117

People Contact   117
Receiving Incoming Calls   118
    Prepare for the Calls Beforehand   118
    Be Aware of Telephone Image   119
Placing Calls   124
    Plan Calls in Advance   124
    Identify Yourself and Clear Time to Talk   125
    State Purpose of Call   125
    Don't Waste Time on Hold   126
    Give a Timetable for Return Calls   126
General Telephone Techniques   126
    Keep in Touch   126
    Handle Messages with Care   127
    Return Calls   127
    Don't Tie Up the Lines   127
    National Do Not Call Registry   127
    Practice, Practice, Practice   128
Summary   129
    Review Questions   129
    Discussion Questions   130
    Situation   130

Chapter 9   The Qualifying Process   133

What Is Qualifying?   133
Why Does an Agent Qualify?   134
    Time Savings   134
    Client Relations   135
    Buyer-Property Match   135
    Increasing Confidence   135
When Does an Agent Qualify?   135
How Does an Agent Qualify?   136
    Avoid Insulting Suspects   136
    Explain-and-Request Method   136
Areas of Investigation   137
    Qualifying Issues Checklist   137
Qualify versus Afford   142
Buying Motives   145
Summary   146
    Review Questions   146
    Discussion Questions   147
    Situation   147

Chapter 10   Presenting the Property   149

Role of Showing in the Sales Process   149
Why Showing Is Necessary   149
    To Sell   150
    For Involvement   150
    To Point Out Features and Benefits   151
    Further Qualifying   151
Some Showing Guidelines   152
    Preview the Property   152
    Plan the Showing   153
Summary   162
    Review Questions   162
    Discussion Questions   163
    Situation   163

PART III   The Closing Stage: Making the Sale and Keeping It Together   165

Chapter 11   Handling Objections and Closing   167

Why People Object   167
    Slowing Things Down   167
    Gaining or Maintaining Control   168
    Misunderstanding   168
    Hiding the Real Reason   168
    Valid Objections   169
Five Steps for Handling Objections   169
Closing   172
    Buying Signals   172
    Closing Techniques   175
    Guidelines for Closing   178
Summary   183
    Review Questions   183
    Discussion Questions   184
    Situation   184

Chapter 12   Presenting the Offer and Negotiating Counteroffers   185

Presenting the Offer   185
    Plan the Presentation   185
Contact the Seller   187
Work to Maintain Control   187
    Bring the Seller Up-to-Date on the Marketplace   187
    Personalize the Offer   188
    Answer All of the Seller's Questions   189
    Close the Sale   189
    Keep Cool!   190
Negotiating Counteroffers   190
    Keeping Personalities Out of the Negotiations   90
    Deal Only with the Differences   190

Concentrate on Real Needs   191
Zero In on the Offer   191
Attempt to Balance the Differences   191
Remain Positive   192
Summary   194
    Review Questions   194
    Discussion Questions   195
    Situation   195

Chapter 13   Keeping the Sale Together   197

The Salesperson's Responsibilities   197
    Review the Earnest Money Contract   197
    Process the Earnest Money   198
    Help the Parties Fulfill Terms of Agreement   198
    Keep Everyone Informed   199
    Be Prepared to Close   201
    Follow Up after Closing   202
The Sales Process Revisited   202
Summary   206
    Review Questions   206
    Discussion Questions   207
    Situation   207

Chapter 14   Broker Selection and Legal Awareness   209

What to Look for in a Broker   209
    Hiring the Best Broker   210
Legal Awareness   213
    Fair Housing   213
    Equal Credit Opportunity   214
    Truth in Lending   214
    Anti-Trust   215
    Deceptive Trade Practices   215
Summary   218
    Review Questions   218
    Discussion Questions   218
    Situation   219

About the Authors

Johnnie Rosenauer is a Professor and Program Coordinator of Real Estate at San Antonio College. Educationally he holds a BBA in Marketing and Real Estate from Texas State University, a MA in Higher Education and Management from The University of Texas at San Antonio. He was awarded a Doctorate in Education from Texas A&M University in the field of Adult Education. Dr. Rosenauer also serves as Director of the Raul S. Muguia Learning Institute at San Antonio College, an institute devoted to helping college teachers be more effective in the classroom. For the last several years, Dr. Rosenauer has also been a faculty member in the Graduate School at the University of Texas at San Antonio in the Adult and Higher Education Program.

Licensed as a real estate broker in Texas for over thirty years, he has an active real estate brokerage and consulting practice, specializing in farm and ranch and developmental properties. A Life Member of the Texas Real Estate Teacher's Association, he was awarded the Don Roose Excellence Award in 2002. He proudly served a number of years for TRETA as a Lead Instructor for the Certified Real Estate Instructor (CREI) program. A frequent speaker and writer, Johnnie has numerous books and professional articles to his credit.

A 4th generation rancher in Frio County south of San Antonio, he breeds and raises registered American Quarter Horses and carries out intense game management practices on his and other area ranches, focusing on raising high quality whitetail deer.

Johnnie is married to Danell Mackey Rosenauer, originally from Sayre Oklahoma, whose family has also farmed and ranched for many generations in western Oklahoma. The Rosenauers have two children, Jessica Alene and Corban Walker.

John Mayfield received his real estate license at the age of 18 in 1978. John was one of the first sales associates in his board of REALTORS® to reach the Missouri Association of REALTORS® Million Dollar Club. John achieved this award during a time when interest rates were record highs. John has been a practicing broker since 1981 and he owns and manages three offices in Southeast Missouri, and manages over 35 real estate agents. John has taught pre- and post-license real estate courses since 1988. John has earned the ABR®, ABRM, CRB, e-PRO®, and GRI designations throughout his real estate tenure.

John is an avid real estate speaker and trainer. John is a GRI instructor for The Missouri Association of REALTORS® and the Arkansas Association of REALTORS®. John was one of the featured speakers at the 2004 National Association of REALTORS® convention in Orlando, FL. He is the author of two books, *5 Minutes to a Great Real Estate Sales Meeting* and *5 Minutes to a Great Real Estate Letter* by Thomson Learning, and these books were listed in the TOP 10 Broker Resources by the Council of Real Estate Brokerage Managers (CRB), February 2005. John is also one of the contributing editors to the "Sales Coach" section for REALTOR® Magazine Online, and is a real estate writer for Hewlett Packard's Web site. John is also active on a local, state, and national level for the REALTORS® Association. John is also an NAR Director for the state of Missouri.

John and his wife, Kerry, have two children, Alyx and Anne. They also own and run a "Pick Your Own" Blueberry and Blackberry Farm (Liberty Farms) in Southeast Missouri.

Introduction

The first part of this book helps you get yourself ready to sell. This begins with a broad overview of sales and marketing that shows you the "big picture" of the sales process. The book offers a flow chart of how we see the sale developing in hopes that by seeing this macro perspective, you can then understand how the smaller pieces of selling fit together. Besides a definition of selling, we describe some of the traits or characteristics of successful salespeople. We also attempt to remind you of what you are actually selling . . . starting with yourself. Finally, we review the plusses and minuses of being in real estate sales.

Chapter 2 deals with the technology of real estate sales. Understanding how to use these powerful tools to your advantage is an important achievement. After all, they are supposed to be helping, not hurting us in our business.

In Chapter 3, we look at the very important aspect of defining your marketplace. None of us can know every aspect of the business, so it is important to know a great deal about your specific target market.

Chapter 4 focuses on personal management and time management. Real estate agents need to make good use of their time, and planning your day is a critical and essential part of making the most of your real estate career. The BIKE approach is discussed to help your reach your goals.

In Chapter 5, we look at why prospecting is a major area real estate professionals must develop if they want longevity in their real estate careers. We will also look at various prospecting ideas and systems, such as working your center of influence (COI), farming new areas, and corresponding with prospects. The chapter also focuses on ways to meet new prospects, including holding open houses and working expired listings.

The listing presentation is an important task for every real estate professional. Why are listings important? Gathering information and helping to set a competitive price will all be examined in Chapter 6.

Chapter 7 focuses on advertising and the communications process. How consumers learn and ways to attract buyers and sellers through advertising as well as enhancing your image in the marketplace will be discussed in this chapter.

In Chapter 8, you'll learn about telephone techniques and different opportunities the real estate professional receives from incoming phone calls. Preparing for calls in advance is important, as is understanding how your image is portrayed during the phone conversation. We'll also look at ways to identify yourself and how to obtain the caller's identity.

The qualifying process is the focal point for the real estate professional and today's consumer in Chapter 9. When does an agent begin to qualify and how do you qualify? These are just two questions that will be addressed in this chapter. We'll also look at formulas for VA and FHA qualifying along with the analysis of what a person qualifies for and what the buyer can really afford. A review of motives buyers may process during the home-buying process is also an important part of this chapter.

Presentation of the property is the focus in Chapter 10. You'll learn about the real estate agent's role during the sales process and why it is important. Showing guidelines are covered as well as ways the agent can prepare the prospective buyers in making an informed decision during the home-buying process.

In Chapter 11, we'll focus on handling objections and the real estate closing. We'll look at some of the various reasons misunderstandings arise during the real estate transaction and how the real estate professional can work with these issues to make the process easier for all parties.

In Chapter 12, we consider presenting the offer and negotiating counteroffers. We will discuss ways to bring the seller up-to-date on the marketplace as well as personalizing the offer. Helping to keep personalities separate during the negotiating process is also covered. You'll also learn about a good counteroffer plan.

Chapter 13 includes finalizing the sale along with reviewing the contract, processing the earnest money, and knowing the buyer's and seller's role through the closing. Keeping a good closing checklist, ways to keep everyone informed, and avoiding last-minute surprises are an integral part of Chapter 13.

Chapter 14 covers broker selection and legal awareness aspects of the real estate industry. The chapter covers what to look for when interviewing brokers and explores the interview process. We'll also look at anti-trust issues and fair housing laws that all real estate professionals must be aware of in their day-to-day careers.

Acknowledgements

Putting together a text has always been an exciting but demanding effort for me. It is gratifying to work again on my "first" book, but difficult to know what to change for improvement and what to leave alone because it is good as is. I could not have accomplished this task without the help of some wonderful people. The folks at Thomson have been very good to me for a number of years and I appreciate their support. Sara Glassmeyer has been a great Acquisitions Editor. The belief in the product exhibited by Mark Linton and the Marketing Team all represent the type of encouragement that most authors desire. Thanks to Arlin Kauffman for all of his assistance throughout the project. My sincere thanks to John Mayfield as well for his work on the technology aspects of this book. John is a master at putting technology and real estate practice together. Thank you, Mayfield Team! At the San Antonio college level, my sincere thanks to Angelica Gutierrez for her wonderful administrative help. She is a lifesaver for a backwoods cowboy Aggie like me. My bosses at the college have always encouraged me to grow and develop. Vernell Walker, Business Department Chair, and Dr. Robert Zeigler, President, are great friends and fantastic supervisors whose work ethic and standards are superior in every way. Their confidence in and support of me is gratefully acknowledged.

Certainly it is important to thank the students through the years in my college classes and training programs who have allowed me to practice on them with the material found here. And the buyers, sellers, and licensees that I have interacted with in the many transactions, mostly successful and pleasant, and a few not so successful or pleasant, have caused me to learn a great deal.

While all of the abovementioned individuals deserve what credit is offered them, and even more, I alone assume responsibility for any errors found in this book. It is our unified hope that you will enjoy and learn from what is presented here.

PART I

THE PLANNING STAGE—GETTING YOURSELF READY TO SELL

An Overview of Sales and Marketing

Key Terms

- Code of Ethics and
  Standards of Practice
- Flow chart
- Four Ps
- Marketing
- Professionalism
- Selling

Marketing and Sales: Definitions and Differences

You probably have heard people say, "I'm in marketing. I do _____," "I'm in sales. I do _____," or "I'm a sales consultant." These labels could be describing nearly the same function, as the roles can be closely related. Depending on your business, however, these two terms may or may not be synonyms.

The difference in *sales* and *marketing* can be illustrated by the **Four Ps**, an idea originally conceived by E. Jerome McCarthy. According to Dr. McCarthy, marketing involves the right *product* at the right *price* at the right *place* with the right *promotion*.[1] For many people involved in real estate, sales is a part of promotion, but it is only one portion. Figure 1.1 shows the typical relationship between marketing and its groupings.

According to the American Marketing Association, **marketing** is "the performance of business activities that direct the flow of goods and services from producer to consumer or user."[2] If you add the common-sense idea that people buy only goods and services that meet some sort of need, then this definition may be restated in simpler terms: Marketing is the group of activities that meets people's needs and wants through the exchange of things of value.

The first reaction of many salespersons is that these same elements are involved in the sales process.

---

[1] Adapted from E. Jerome McCarthy, *Basic Marketing*, 7th ed. (Homewood, Ill.: Richard D. Irwin, 1981).

[2] Committee on Tenns, *Marketing Definitions: A Glossary of Marketing Terms* (Chicago: American Marketing Association, 1960).

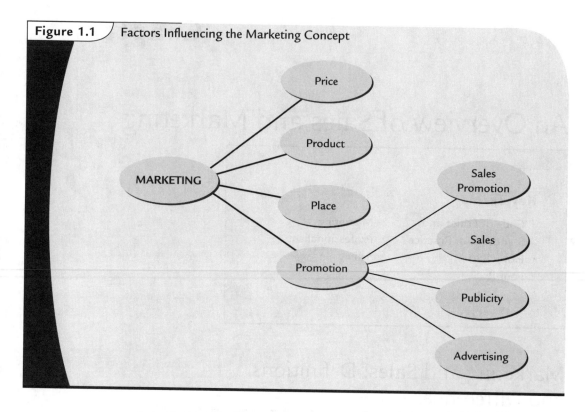

Figure 1.1   Factors Influencing the Marketing Concept

A simple example illustrates how the aspects of marketing and sales work together but are somewhat different. Brad Boyd is an experienced real estate broker with his own firm. One morning, Kyle and Jennifer Cunningham walk into his office. They have read ads from his company and noticed a For Sale sign on a local house; so they decide to visit Boyd's office. As potential first-time homebuyers with a two-year-old child, the Cunninghams want to be close to schools, parks, and shopping. Their combined income is well within the range to afford most of the homes within the area they prefer. After a brief interview with them, Brad selects three listings and takes Kyle and Jennifer on an inspection of the homes. The first is too large, the third is too expensive, but the second is very close to what they are seeking. The couple makes an offer, and eventually a compromise is reached on price. They get the necessary financing, the title is conveyed, the family moves in, and they all are very satisfied with the experience.

This simple example cuts a few corners, but it demonstrates the overall process. The Cunninghams find the kind of house they wanted (the product), in the location they wanted (place), for what they can afford to pay (price). Boyd's services are advertised to them (promotion), and they respond by visiting the office.

Factors Influencing the Marketing Concept

The preceding example points out the relationship of the Four Ps, but don't overlook the differences between marketing and sales. Boyd knows where to find the kinds of homes that customers like the Cunninghams would want before he meets them. In other words, he knows the market. By the time they come into his office, he has general information about the kind of property they probably would want. Most of this knowledge comes from marketing. Simply stated, Brad Boyd knows how to match people's needs with conditions in the marketplace.

The sales side of Boyd's activity comes into play when he has to meet the needs of a specific person or persons. During the interview, Brad determines the couple's particular needs and wants. They might have inherited a large amount of money, or they might want a house with a large lot and be willing to live in a smaller house. The variations are endless, but a practitioner can't know the customer until the customer has approached him. This is when he becomes a salesperson.

Sales activity relates to here and now with a particular consumer. Marketing is broad based, more general, and long-term in perspective.

Overview of the Sales Process

Let's begin with an overview of the entire sales process, by providing definitions of selling and professionalism. We also will discuss the positive and negative aspects of a sales career and how marketing and selling interrelate.

The sales process is explained in the **flow chart** shown in Figure 1.2. This plan offers a logical, easy-to-follow progression from start to finish. The chart represents a sort of pictorial job description for the salesperson.

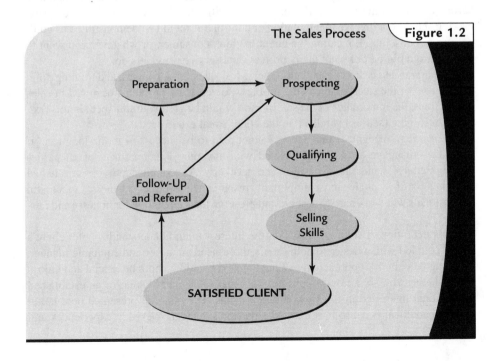

The Sales Process   Figure 1.2

Selling Defined

Selling is defined in many ways. Through the years, salespeople have been stereotyped as cheats, thieves, and scoundrels. Others have held them up as valued professional service providers, whereas still other viewpoints are more moderate and somewhere in between. For purposes of this text, **selling** is *the basic art of influencing other people to help them make decisions that solve problems to benefit all parties.* This definition contains a number of key words and phrases that deserve to be explored further.

Basic to every human civilization is the exchange of goods and services. Traders and merchants (sometimes referred to by other names) are depicted in the histories of all societies. For business to occur, someone must sell something. It can be as fundamental as a skilled hunter trading meat to a more competent leather worker for clothing.

Art forms vary from artist to artist. Likewise, much variation exists in selling styles. What works well for one person may not for another. This is true from salesperson to salesperson and from client to client. This text is not designed to teach the reader one best way but will attempt to offer ideas and approaches that increase the chances of success. Remember that all the techniques presented here must be adapted to at least three factors: the individual salesperson, the specific consumers in a particular transaction, and the overall selling environment at that particular time. Most of the material should be considered flexible and not as hard and fast rules, except, of course, for laws and/or professional ethics.

Influencing decisions implies that the effective salesperson will definitely affect another person's decisions. The first influence should be in the area of demonstrating a sincere desire to help. If the prospective buyer or seller perceives the salesperson as a hazard or threat rather than a helper, no sale will occur. This influence on decision making should not involve manipulation or control but should be demonstrated as guidance and counseling. Educating the client, patient, consumer, or whatever you want to call them is a big part of what many professional service providers do.

Solving problems is the salesperson's goal. Most sales texts, courses, and training point out the role of the salesperson as the problem solver. If no problems occurred in sales transactions, the importance of the salesperson would be greatly diminished. In this text, problem solving (selling) is related to the client's real estate needs.

To benefit all recognizes that agents cannot plan to be successful in the long term if they take advantage of people associated with any sale. Fair treatment of all parties and high ethical standards of business are necessary. A recommendation by a satisfied customer is the single most important resource for future business; successful professionals will work hard to deserve and preserve their reputation for honesty and fairness.

This definition of selling focuses on the interest in and understanding of a client's needs, coupled with a desire to help satisfy those needs in a fair and equitable manner. If you agree with this approach to selling, this text should be both beneficial and enjoyable, whether you are a novice considering a real estate sales career or an established professional interested in a review and new ideas. The material presented here is not highly theoretical because it is derived from the practical, everyday experiences and observations of many highly successful real estate salespeople, managers, and trainers and is based on ideas and techniques proven effective in the field.

Marketing, Sales, and the Uniqueness of Real Estate

Now you are beginning to see how sales and marketing fit together. On the broad scale, sales is only one part (although a critical one) of the entire marketing process. In some industries, the role of a salesperson is different than it is in other industries. In real estate, for example, the salesperson rarely has anything to do with the actual development or construction of the property. Generally, the salesperson is not an employee of either the buyer or the seller. In truth, the agent usually is self-employed. The unique position of a real estate salesperson is more one of a go-between, attempting to serve as an interpreter (and sometimes a buffer) of and between the two main parties.

At times, potential legal controversy develops about the true role of the salesperson in terms of working for (being the agent of) a buyer or a seller. However, generally, one person is a client (usually the seller), and the other is a customer. The salesperson has an obligation to treat both honestly. For real estate salespersons, there is usually someone they work *with* and someone they work *for*. Fiduciary duties become a factor for the real estate person to consider carefully. Some of the guides needed to carry out this obligation are state or national laws. Others are the local practices developed by the local board of REALTORS®, and still other guidance is provided by the particular brokerage company with which the salesperson associates. Stay well within the boundaries of doing what is right and you'll have less concern about being criticized about your actions. A current copy of the *National Association Code of Ethics* is included in this book for your reference.

Another interesting characteristic of real estate sales and marketing is that many duties are placed upon the shoulders of the salesperson or agent. Although you can expect some support from your broker and others involved in the sale, such as lenders and title company people, the main focus is on the agent. The real estate agent may receive praise and appreciation for a job well done but also the blame if things go wrong.

Because a salesperson really is offering knowledge of real estate and its transfer plus the energy to get the job done, there is no physical product that can be shown to a potential buyer or seller as there is in other fields. Therefore, successful and professional real estate salespeople are very confident and competent in their ability to explain exactly what they have to offer. We are, for the most part, professional service providers.

Buyers and sellers often choose agents not so much on tangible factors (such as comparing one piece of furniture to another) as on intangible ones. When asked why they picked one agent over others, buyers and sellers often say they had a better "feel" about the one they selected. This feel in part comes from the agent's ability to explain clearly what he or she can do for the other person.

Trends & ISSUES

According to The *National Association of REALTORS® 2004 Profile of Homebuyers and Sellers*, more consumers used real estate agents because a friend, family member, or coworker recommended one.

Thinking about this referral trend as a future stream of income, what are some ways new real estate professionals can capture a piece of the real estate market by using their friends, family members, and coworkers?

From a technology standpoint, real estate agents need to know and understand how to use a computer database for mail merging correspondence to friends and close acquaintances. Several software databases and contact managers are available for real estate professionals. A few websites you might look into include the following:

- http://www.topproducer.com
- http://www.frontrange.com
- http://www.act.com
- http://www.microsoft.com (Excel, Access, and Outlook are three programs available from Microsoft.)

Traits of a Successful Salesperson

Through 30 years of teaching, training, writing about, and practicing real estate, I've been asked a frequent question. Worded a variety of ways, the key components are pretty much the same. What does it take to be a success in real estate sales? The following characteristics are not based upon any sophisticated research methodology (see Figure 1.3). The list represents a combination of what I have read and observed through the last three decades of immersion in the real estate industry. As you consider these traits, note that they all can be developed; there aren't many "born" salespeople. Certainly some people are predisposed to be successful in certain areas, no matter what the field. I have trained enough salespeople to know that genetics can play a role in the interest and ability in certain circumstances, but there is no guarantee of consistently predicting the success or failure of any individual, based upon anything except personal desire and development. I've chosen the acronym CRAFT to help you remember the proposed traits. Add to them as you see fit, but all of these are "keepers" in the list:

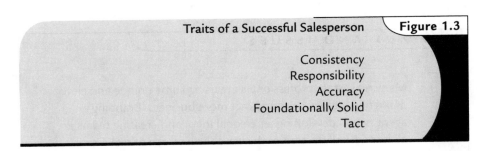

Traits of a Successful Salesperson   Figure 1.3

Consistency
Responsibility
Accuracy
Foundationally Solid
Tact

- **Consistency:** More long-term benefit comes from someone who is willing to "keep after it" than someone who is focused and motivated today but disinterested and discouraged tomorrow. The idea of 10 percent or less inspiration and 90 percent or more perspiration is credited to Thomas Edison, the brilliant inventor. The same is true in real estate salespeople.

- **Responsibility:** Much of a person's success, from a long-term perspective, is based upon that person's willingness to take charge of his or her own life. Certainly we all need and deserve support from our managers, trainers, brokers, and so on; however, a huge part of an individual salesperson's rewards must ultimately come from personal initiative. There are no guarantees of success in life, simply opportunities to succeed. "If it's meant to be, it's up to me" is a good motto for real estate agents.

- **Accuracy:** Although the "horseshoes and hand grenades" mentality works in some situations in life when "close enough" is acceptable, that is not true for real estate selling! Salespeople cannot reasonably be expected to know everything exactly; however, they must acknowledge when something such as seller's closing cost or monthly payment amount is a best guess estimate. What is a few hundred square feet of living area in a home or few hundred dollars a month of debt service among friends? It's everything! Successful people make every effort to be as accurate as possible in all their research and calculations to provide the best possible professional service.

- **Foundationally Solid:** A person must first become well grounded in the real estate industry and then stay well grounded. Back to the basics is a common theme in much of the sales and marketing literature, and it seems prudent to never leave the basics. Advance, grow, and risk, but don't forget the firm foundation that will allow you to weather the general downturns and personal slumps that are inevitable in a lengthy career in this industry.

- **Tact:** One definition of tact centers on the ability to suggest to folks that they go jump in the lake in such a way that they look forward to the dive. Some people seem more adept at handling other people's issues successfully. The salesperson's role as a professional service provider requires an ability to deal with varying viewpoints and conflicts. Salespeople are measured on their ability to perform, but they must perform in a manner that does not alienate people from them personally or from the industry in general.

Trends AND ISSUES

Many real estate professionals are using some unique and clever marketing ideas today to attract more business. Branding an agent name, developing a personal logo, and creating teams are all just a small fraction of the ways the new age of real estate marketing is unfolding. For example, Cheri Peterson of Prudential Alliance in St. Louis, Missouri, details the following in a May 2004 interview from *REALTOR® Magazine Online* by Haley M. Hwang:

> *"Then one day someone said, 'Cheri, figure out a niche—make it something you enjoy doing and incorporate it into your business,' so I went out and took a picture on my Harley," Peterson says. She had business cards made with the photo, which shows her sitting on her prized bike wearing a white T-shirt, blue jeans, and a visor. She also placed the photo on a giant billboard on I-94 in St. Charles County.*
>
> *Peterson says that, in the beginning, there were some snickers from other real estate practitioners about her Harley niche. "I came up with this idea and everyone made fun of me and thought that it was stupid," she says. But her business took off and she had the last laugh.*
>
> *In 2003, Peterson closed 124 transactions with $20 million in sales volume. She has three assistants who work with her, and she is in the top 2 percent of all of Prudential's sales associates nationwide.*

Visit http://www.HobbsHerder.com to learn how other real estate professionals are thinking creatively to market themselves.

Identifying What We Sell

Effective real estate sales and marketing has a lot to do with the product of property, and it has a great deal to do with other things that we must sell in addition to, and often before, the property itself. Following are some of the issues you must resolve/sell successfully to succeed in this business. You may choose to add more to this list, but the aspects found here are necessary.

- **Yourself:** The first thing you have to sell and keep sold is you. If a consumer does not like or trust you, the rest of the process is dead in the water most of the time. Whether you are liked or trusted can be influenced by the kind of respect you convey, how pressured the consumer feels in your presence, and how you introduce yourself in that critical first impression stage. Remember, if the consumer is not sold on you, it is very hard to be sold on what you are selling. This does not mean the buyer or seller must want to adopt or be adopted by you, but rather you have created an environment of comfort so the sale can proceed forward.

- **Service:** Rarely do real estate salespeople own the products they are selling. By definition, they are mostly in the brokerage business. This means they buy/sell or lease/rent on behalf of other parties. Most customers or clients, either as buyers or sellers, landlords or tenants, will be asking this key question: What can you do for me? If you cannot competently and confidently articulate your ability to offer top-quality service, your sales possibilities will be diminished if not lost completely.

- **Logic:** Relative to many other consumer goods, real estate is an expensive and complex product to buy or sell. As a professional service provider, you must be able to educate the people you deal with as to why certain things are the way they are. Because real estate purchases are not everyday occurrences for most consumers, effective salespeople understand that they must routinely educate the people they deal with. Certainly, when representing someone in a transaction, salespeople are called upon to offer advice, counsel, and strategies in a manner that shows calm and rational thinking. You must provide something for consumers to "hold on to" during the potentially long and difficult time periods before a sale can actually consummate after a decision is made to buy or sell property.

- **Emotion:** For most people, the logical side needs to be balanced with some desire for what is being offered. One way of stating this point is that we have to sell the "sizzle with the steak." Frequently, salespeople must engage the consumer in a way that creates desire for the product. All the logic in the world alone will not make the difference, so you must incorporate the desire. Successful salespeople must also determine whether they can create an environmental setting where the consumer will have the logic and desire in some kind of balance.

- **Decision:** By the earlier definition of selling, a required ingredient calls for a choice to be made. We all have determined not to make a decision about something, and as a result, the choice was taken away from us by default because situations and circumstances changed. Learning how and when to ask for the order is part of this book. There are no decision-free sales in this industry. We call for individuals to make up their minds on a regular basis.

Advantages and Disadvantages of Selling Real Estate

A career in real estate sales can be profitable, exciting, and satisfying or expensive, frustrating, and disappointing. As a long-time teacher and practitioner of real estate, I have talked with many people about real estate sales as a career. From these conversations, some general views regarding the pros and cons of being a real estate salesperson developed (see Figure 1.4).

Figure 1.4	Positive and Negative Aspects of the Real Estate Profession

Positive Aspects	Negative Aspects
Income Opportunity	Income Uncertainty
Limited Supervision	The Work
Public Contact	Rejection
Career Growth and Flexibility	Limited Control

The positive points include the following:

- **Income Opportunity:** In most well-operated real estate brokerage offices in any city, there are a few highly successful salespeople who are well compensated for their sales abilities and consistently earn a high income. These individuals are not common, but neither are they unique. They are living proof of the income potential of this field. The key word in this positive aspect is *opportunity*. The money is available but not guaranteed. Much hard work and sacrifice are associated with success, but it *is* attainable for a salesperson.

- **Limited Supervision:** Controlling their own time and work schedule is a positive factor for many people. Being your own boss and basically in business for yourself can be a big incentive. However, being in control also implies a need for an extra degree of self-motivation and responsibility.

- **Public Contact:** In selling, regardless of the product or service, the common denominator is people. Many prospective salespersons say, "I like people." This is a helpful attitude, but it will not guarantee success in sales. Being able to *understand and work with* people is much more important. Satisfied salespeople talk about the strong feeling of accomplishment that comes when a client's complex real estate problem is solved. This sense of purpose and service can be a strong motivator. Also, the chance to meet new and different people constantly is a real attraction to some salespeople.

- **Career Growth and Flexibility:** Selling provides many career options, and there are many different career categories to consider under the umbrella of real estate. Residential selling is different from agricultural; commercial and industrial properties require an entirely different strategy than resort and recreational. Examples abound of successful salespeople who have branched out into new and different parts of real estate sales and marketing with good results. This flexibility also allows a salesperson with a good track record to find opportunities in other marketplaces with different organizations.

Many sales pros say, "Selling is selling, no matter what the product or service." You may not agree with this viewpoint, but a salesperson does have more flexibility in making career decisions than is available in some other fields. Because of this potential to enter different areas of real estate, examples from several aspects of real estate are included in this book. Just because the example used is a ranch rather than a residence, or a strip center or a resort project, don't forget that many of the basic selling points still apply. Clearly there are differences in some areas of real estate, but not many.

The negative points include the following:

- **Income Uncertainty:** Many newcomers to real estate sales are accustomed to earning constant and regular income. They often experience economic shock during the transition from salary to commission. Even after this adjustment period is over, you'll still need careful budgeting to account for an uneven income flow. You may have three or four sales closings within a short period of time, and then have to wait several months for the next one. Handling fluctuating income can be difficult.
- **The Work:** Some potential real estate salespeople think that all they need to do is sit around the office and wait for prospective customers to call, but it doesn't work that way. Selling is *hard work.* To be effective, an individual must be willing to do many activities that are not exciting or enjoyable. Being available to your clients for long and varied hours (even during weekends and in the evening) is just one part of the sacrifice required for long-term success in selling real estate.
- **Rejection:** Sales professionals in any field encounter people who react negatively to them. Veterans in selling realize they cannot help or please everyone with the product or services offered. In real estate, an owner attempting to sell property might respond rudely to your offer of help. A frustrated buyer may blame the salesperson for the high cost of housing. Such rejections are very hard for many salespeople to accept.

    Rejection is unpleasant, but the experienced salesperson realizes that such behavior seldom is meant personally. Even if an occasional rejection is personal, the salesperson should not become discouraged. Part of the cost of excelling in sales is being able to handle such behavior from people and not allowing it to have a negative effect on motivation and efforts.
- **Limited Control:** There are many circumstances in selling that the salesperson cannot control. An increase in interest rates may prevent your buyer from qualifying for a loan. The same increase may cause mortgage money to disappear completely from your area. A seller suddenly may want to cancel the listing on which you have worked so hard because his job transfer was cancelled. An industry may close in your area and severely damage the real estate market. These situations are not the fault of the salesperson, but the impact on the market is still significant.

Many people have trouble dealing with these kinds of problems and maintaining the high level of motivation necessary for sales success. There are many other advantages and disadvantages of selling real estate, and you may have some of your own to add to the list. Like your selling style, your reasons for entering or leaving the field may be personal. Each individual must analyze realistically the positives and the negatives before deciding to enter the profession.

Professionalism

Selling real estate is becoming increasingly complex. Experienced salespeople remember when most transactions were simple in comparison. Because the industry is changing so rapidly in response to economic conditions, with competition continually on the rise, being successful demands that salespeople never offer mediocrity and adopt service as the focal point of their careers. This never-ending drive to "be the best you can be" in spirit, character, and behavior is known as professionalism.

Professionalism has been the concern of real estate leaders since the formation in 1908 of the National Association of REALTORS®, originally the National Association of Real Estate Boards, organized to educate the public about the real estate profession while assisting real estate people in improving their ability and service. Today, it is the world's largest business trade association and the parent organization of most local real estate boards. The professional activities of members of these local boards are governed by the association's Code of Ethics.

A real estate business is only as good as its reputation, and the importance of practicing ethical business standards cannot be overemphasized. The *Code of Ethics and Standards of Practice* of the National Association of REALTORS® is a statement of good business practices that everyone in the business should follow carefully. The preamble explains that land is our basic asset and that survival and growth of our civilization depends on wise use and wide allocation of ownership. The REALTOR® is responsible for dealing with the use and ownership of the land, and the resulting grave social responsibility demands that agents continually improve their ability and standards. Nothing can justify departure from this. The Golden Rule should always be the REALTOR®'s guide in dealing with other people.

Following the preamble are 24 articles that outline the standards of professional conduct for REALTORS®. The complete *Code of Ethics and Standards* appears in Figure 1.5 for your careful review. You should investigate and take advantage of the information, training, and support available through your local Board of REALTORS®.

Trends & ISSUES

Effective January 1st, 2001, The National Association of REALTORS® requires its membership to test over the *Code of Ethics* every four years. Members are required to attend a $2\frac{1}{2}$-hour ethics training class to maintain status in the association. Today, members can complete this course online from http://www.realtor.org or from their local member association.

Members of the association are also privileged to a wealth of information on the *Code of Ethics* at http://www.realtor.org and can download and print the entire *Code of Ethics* and other professional standards information.

Code of Ethics and Standards of Practice of the National Association of Realtors®

Figure 1.5

Effective January 1, 2006

Where the word REALTORS® is used in this Code and Preamble, it shall be deemed to include REALTOR-ASSOCIATE®s.

While the Code of Ethics establishes obligations that may be higher than those mandated by law, in any instance where the Code of Ethics and the law conflict, the obligations of the law must take precedence.

Preamble

Under all is the land. Upon its wise utilization and widely allocated ownership depend the survival and growth of free institutions and of our civilization. REALTORS® should recognize that the interests of the nation and its citizens require the highest and best use of the land and the widest distribution of land ownership. They require the creation of adequate housing, the building of functioning cities, the development of productive industries and farms, and the preservation of a healthful environment.

Such interests impose obligations beyond those of ordinary commerce. They impose grave social responsibility and a patriotic duty to which REALTORS® should dedicate themselves, and for which they should be diligent in preparing themselves. REALTORS®, therefore, are zealous to maintain and improve the standards of their calling and share with their fellow REALTORS® a common responsibility for its integrity and honor.

In recognition and appreciation of their obligations to clients, customers, the public, and each other, REALTORS® continuously strive to become and remain informed on issues affecting real estate and, as knowledgeable professionals, they willingly share the fruit of their experience and study with others. They identify and take steps, through enforcement of this Code of Ethics and by assisting appropriate regulatory bodies, to eliminate practices which may damage the public or which might discredit or bring dishonor to the real estate profession. REALTORS® having direct personal knowledge of conduct that may violate the Code of Ethics involving misappropriation of client or customer funds or property, willful discrimination, or fraud resulting in substantial economic harm, bring such matters to the attention of the appropriate Board or Association of REALTORS®. (Amended 1/00)

Realizing that cooperation with other real estate professionals promotes the best interests of those who utilize their services, REALTORS® urge exclusive representation of clients; do not attempt to gain any unfair advantage over their competitors; and they refrain from making unsolicited comments about other practitioners. In instances where their opinion is sought, or where REALTORS® believe that comment is necessary, their opinion is offered in an objective, professional manner, uninfluenced by any personal motivation or potential advantage or gain.

The term REALTOR® has come to connote competency, fairness, and high integrity resulting from adherence to a lofty ideal of moral conduct in business relations. No inducement of profit and no instruction from clients ever can justify departure from this ideal.

In the interpretation of this obligation, REALTORS® can take no safer guide than that which has been handed down through the centuries, embodied in the Golden Rule, "Whatsoever ye would that others should do to you, do ye even so to them."

Accepting this standard as their own, REALTORS® pledge to observe its spirit in all of their activities and to conduct their business in accordance with the tenets set forth below.

Duties to Clients and Customers

ARTICLE 1

When representing a buyer, seller, landlord, tenant, or other client as an agent, REALTORS® pledge themselves to protect and promote the interests of their client. This obligation to the client is primary, but it does not relieve REALTORS® of their obligation to treat all parties honestly. When serving a buyer, seller, landlord, tenant or other party in a non-agency capacity, REALTORS® remain obligated to treat all parties honestly. (Amended 1/01)

- **Standard of Practice 1-1**
  REALTORS®, when acting as principals in a real estate transaction, remain obligated by the duties imposed by the Code of Ethics. (Amended 1/93)

- **Standard of Practice 1-2**
  The duties the Code of Ethics imposes are applicable whether REALTORS® are acting as agents or in legally recognized non-agency capacities except that any duty imposed exclusively on agents by law or regulation shall not be imposed by this Code of Ethics on REALTORS® acting in non-agency capacities.

  As used in this Code of Ethics, "client" means the person(s) or entity(ies) with whom a REALTOR® or a REALTOR®'s firm has an agency or legally recognized non-agency relationship; "customer" means a party to a real estate transaction who receives information, services, or benefits but has no contractual relationship with the REALTOR® or the REALTOR®'s firm; "prospect" means a purchaser, seller, tenant, or landlord who is not subject to a representation relationship with the REALTOR® or REALTOR®'s firm; "agent" means a real estate licensee (including brokers and sales ASSOCIATES) acting in an agency relationship as defined by state law or regulation; and "broker" means a real estate licensee (including brokers and sales ASSOCIATES) acting as an agent or in a legally recognized non-agency capacity. (Adopted 1/95, Amended 1/04)

- **Standard of Practice 1-3**
  REALTORS®, in attempting to secure a listing, shall not deliberately mislead the owner as to market value.

- **Standard of Practice 1-4**
  REALTORS®, when seeking to become a buyer/tenant representative, shall not mislead buyers or tenants as to savings or other benefits that might be realized through use of the REALTOR®'s services. (Amended 1/93)

- **Standard of Practice 1-5**
  REALTORS® may represent the seller/landlord and buyer/tenant in the same transaction only after full disclosure to and with informed consent of both parties. (Adopted 1/93)

- **Standard of Practice 1-6**
  REALTORS® shall submit offers and counter-offers objectively and as quickly as possible. (Adopted 1/93, Amended 1/95)

- **Standard of Practice 1-7**
  When acting as listing brokers, REALTORS® shall continue to submit to the seller/landlord all offers and counter-offers until closing or execution of a lease unless the

Continued

Figure 1.5 / Continued

seller/landlord has waived this obligation in writing. REALTORS® shall not be obligated to continue to market the property after an offer has been accepted by the seller/landlord. REALTORS® shall recommend that sellers/landlords obtain the advice of legal counsel prior to acceptance of a subsequent offer except where the acceptance is contingent on the termination of the pre-existing purchase contract or lease. (Amended 1/93)

• **Standard of Practice 1-8**
REALTORS®, acting as agents or brokers of buyers/tenants, shall submit to buyers/tenants all offers and counter-offers until acceptance but have no obligation to continue to show properties to their clients after an offer has been accepted unless otherwise agreed in writing. REALTORS®, acting as agents or brokers of buyers/tenants, shall recommend that buyers/tenants obtain the advice of legal counsel if there is a question as to whether a pre-existing contract has been terminated. (Adopted 1/93, Amended 1/99)

• **Standard of Practice 1-9**
The obligation of REALTORS® to preserve confidential information (as defined by state law) provided by their clients in the course of any agency relationship or non-agency relationship recognized by law continues after termination of agency relationships or any non-agency relationships recognized by law. REALTORS® shall not knowingly, during or following the termination of professional relationships with their clients:

1) reveal confidential information of clients; or
2) use confidential information of clients to the disadvantage of clients; or
3) use confidential information of clients for the REALTOR®'s advantage or the advantage of third parties unless:

   a) clients consent after full disclosure; or
   b) REALTORS® are required by court order; or
   c) it is the intention of a client to commit a crime and the information is necessary to prevent the crime; or
   d) it is necessary to defend a REALTOR® or the REALTOR®'s employees or ASSOCIATES against an accusation of wrongful conduct.

Information concerning latent material defects is not considered confidential information under this Code of Ethics. (Adopted 1/93, Amended 1/01)

• **Standard of Practice 1-10**
REALTORS® shall, consistent with the terms and conditions of their real estate licensure and their property management agreement, competently manage the property of clients with due regard for the rights, safety and health of tenants and others lawfully on the premises. (Adopted 1/95, Amended 1/00)

• **Standard of Practice 1-11**
REALTORS® who are employed to maintain or manage a client's property shall exercise due diligence and make reasonable efforts to protect it against reasonably foreseeable contingencies and losses. (Adopted 1/95)

• **Standard of Practice 1-12**
When entering into listing contracts, REALTORS® must advise sellers/landlords of:

1) the REALTOR®'s company policies regarding cooperation and the amount(s) of any compensation that will be offered to subagents, buyer/tenant agents, and/or brokers acting in legally recognized non-agency capacities;
2) the fact that buyer/tenant agents or brokers, even if compensated by listing brokers, or by sellers/landlords may represent the interests of buyers/tenants; and

3) any potential for listing brokers to act as disclosed dual agents, e.g., buyer/tenant agents. (Adopted 1/93, Renumbered 1/98, Amended 1/03)

• **Standard of Practice 1-13**
When entering into buyer/tenant agreements, REALTORS® must advise potential clients of:

1) the REALTOR®'s company policies regarding cooperation;
2) the amount of compensation to be paid by the client;
3) the potential for additional or offsetting compensation from other brokers, from the seller or landlord, or from other parties;
4) any potential for the buyer/tenant representative to act as a disclosed dual agent, e.g. listing broker, subagent, landlord's agent, etc.; and
5) the possibility that sellers or sellers' representatives may not treat the existence, terms, or conditions of offers as confidential unless confidentiality is required by law, regulation, or by any confidentiality agreement between the parties. (Adopted 1/93, Renumbered 1/98, Amended 1/06)

• **Standard of Practice 1-14**
Fees for preparing appraisals or other valuations shall not be contingent upon the amount of the appraisal or valuation. (Adopted 1/02)

• **Standard of Practice 1-15**
REALTORS®, in response to inquiries from buyers or cooperating brokers shall, with the sellers' approval, disclose the existence of offers on the property. Where disclosure is authorized, REALTORS® shall also disclose whether offers were obtained by the listing licensee, another licensee in the listing firm, or by a cooperating broker. (Adopted 1/03, Amended 1/06)

ARTICLE 2
REALTORS® shall avoid exaggeration, misrepresentation, or concealment of pertinent facts relating to the property or the transaction. REALTORS® shall not, however, be obligated to discover latent defects in the property, to advise on matters outside the scope of their real estate license, or to disclose facts which are confidential under the scope of agency or non-agency relationships as defined by state law. (Amended 1/00)

• **Standard of Practice 2-1**
REALTORS® shall only be obligated to discover and disclose adverse factors reasonably apparent to someone with expertise in those areas required by their real estate licensing authority. Article 2 does not impose upon the REALTOR® the obligation of expertise in other professional or technical disciplines. (Amended 1/96)

• **Standard of Practice 2-2**
(Renumbered as Standard of Practice 1-12 1/98)

• **Standard of Practice 2-3**
(Renumbered as Standard of Practice 1-13 1/98)

• **Standard of Practice 2-4**
REALTORS® shall not be parties to the naming of a false consideration in any document, unless it be the naming of an obviously nominal consideration.

• **Standard of Practice 2-5**
Factors defined as "non-material" by law or regulation or which are expressly referenced in law or regulation as not being subject to disclosure are considered not "pertinent" for purposes of Article 2. (Adopted 1/93)

ARTICLE 3
REALTORS® shall cooperate with other brokers except when cooperation is not in the client's best interest. The obligation

to cooperate does not include the obligation to share commissions, fees, or to otherwise compensate another broker. (Amended 1/95)

- **Standard of Practice 3-1**

  REALTORS®, acting as exclusive agents or brokers of sellers/ landlords, establish the terms and conditions of offers to cooperate. Unless expressly indicated in offers to cooperate, cooperating brokers may not assume that the offer of cooperation includes an offer of compensation. Terms of compensation, if any, shall be ascertained by cooperating brokers before beginning efforts to accept the offer of cooperation. (Amended 1/99)

- **Standard of Practice 3-2**

  REALTORS® shall, with respect to offers of compensation to another REALTOR®, timely communicate any change of compensation for cooperative services to the other REALTOR® prior to the time such REALTOR® produces an offer to purchase/lease the property. (Amended 1/94)

- **Standard of Practice 3-3**

  Standard of Practice 3-2 does not preclude the listing broker and cooperating broker from entering into an agreement to change cooperative compensation. (Adopted 1/94)

- **Standard of Practice 3-4**

  REALTORS®, acting as listing brokers, have an affirmative obligation to disclose the existence of dual or variable rate commission arrangements (i.e., listings where one amount of commission is payable if the listing broker's firm is the procuring cause of sale/lease and a different amount of commission is payable if the sale/lease results through the efforts of the seller/landlord or a cooperating broker). The listing broker shall, as soon as practical, disclose the existence of such arrangements to potential cooperating brokers and shall, in response to inquiries from cooperating brokers, disclose the differential that would result in a cooperative transaction or in a sale/lease that results through the efforts of the seller/landlord. If the cooperating broker is a buyer/tenant representative, the buyer/tenant representative must disclose such information to their client before the client makes an offer to purchase or lease. (Amended 1/02)

- **Standard of Practice 3-5**

  It is the obligation of subagents to promptly disclose all pertinent facts to the principal's agent prior to as well as after a purchase or lease agreement is executed. (Amended 1/93)

- **Standard of Practice 3-6**

  REALTORS® shall disclose the existence of accepted offers, including offers with unresolved contingencies, to any broker seeking cooperation. (Adopted 5/86, Amended 1/04)

- **Standard of Practice 3-7**

  When seeking information from another REALTOR® concerning property under a management or listing agreement, REALTORS® shall disclose their REALTOR® status and whether their interest is personal or on behalf of a client and, if on behalf of a client, their representational status. (Amended 1/95)

- **Standard of Practice 3-8**

  REALTORS® shall not misrepresent the availability of access to show or inspect a listed property. (Amended 11/87)

ARTICLE 4

REALTORS® shall not acquire an interest in or buy or present offers from themselves, any member of their immediate families, their firms or any member thereof, or any entities in which they have any ownership interest, any real property without making their true position known to the owner or the owner's agent or broker. In selling property they own, or in which they have any interest, REALTORS® shall reveal their ownership or interest in writing to the purchaser or the purchaser's representative. (Amended 1/00)

- **Standard of Practice 4-1**

  For the protection of all parties, the disclosures required by Article 4 shall be in writing and provided by REALTORS® prior to the signing of any contract. (Adopted 2/86)

ARTICLE 5

REALTORS® shall not undertake to provide professional services concerning a property or its value where they have a present or contemplated interest unless such interest is specifically disclosed to all affected parties.

ARTICLE 6

REALTORS® shall not accept any commission, rebate, or profit on expenditures made for their client, without the client's knowledge and consent.

When recommending real estate products or services (e.g., homeowner's insurance, warranty programs, mortgage financing, title insurance, etc.), REALTORS® shall disclose to the client or customer to whom the recommendation is made any financial benefits or fees, other than real estate referral fees, the REALTOR® or REALTOR®'s firm may receive as a direct result of such recommendation. (Amended 1/99)

- **Standard of Practice 6-1**

  REALTORS® shall not recommend or suggest to a client or a customer the use of services of another organization or business entity in which they have a direct interest without disclosing such interest at the time of the recommendation or suggestion. (Amended 5/88)

ARTICLE 7

In a transaction, REALTORS® shall not accept compensation from more than one party, even if permitted by law, without disclosure to all parties and the informed consent of the REALTOR®'s client or clients. (Amended 1/93)

ARTICLE 8

REALTORS® shall keep in a special account in an appropriate financial institution, separated from their own funds, monies coming into their possession in trust for other persons, such as escrows, trust funds, clients' monies, and other like items.

ARTICLE 9

REALTORS®, for the protection of all parties, shall assure whenever possible that all agreements related to real estate transactions including, but not limited to, listing and representation agreements, purchase contracts, and leases are in writing in clear and understandable language expressing the specific terms, conditions, obligations and commitments of the parties. A copy of each agreement shall be furnished to each party to such agreements upon their signing or initialing. (Amended 1/04)

- **Standard of Practice 9-1**

  For the protection of all parties, REALTORS® shall use reasonable care to ensure that documents pertaining to the purchase, sale, or lease of real estate are kept current through the use of written extensions or amendments. (Amended 1/93)

Duties to the Public

ARTICLE 10

REALTORS® shall not deny equal professional services to any person for reasons of race, color, religion, sex, handicap,

Continued

Figure 1.5 / Continued

familial status, or national origin. REALTORS® shall not be parties to any plan or agreement to discriminate against a person or persons on the basis of race, color, religion, sex, handicap, familial status, or national origin. (Amended 1/90)

REALTORS®, in their real estate employment practices, shall not discriminate against any person or persons on the basis of race, color, religion, sex, handicap, familial status, or national origin. (Amended 1/00)

- **Standard of Practice 10-1**
  When involved in the sale or lease of a residence, REAL-TORS® shall not volunteer information regarding the racial, religious or ethnic composition of any neighborhood nor shall they engage in any activity which may result in panic selling, however, REALTORS® may provide other demographic information. (Adopted 1/94, Amended 1/06)

- **Standard of Practice 10-2**
  When not involved in the sale or lease of a residence, Realtors® may provide demographic information related to a property, transaction or professional assignment to a party if such demographic information is (a) deemed by the REALTOR® to be needed to assist with or complete, in a manner consistent with Article 10, a real estate transaction or professional assignment and (b) is obtained or derived from a recognized, reliable, independent, and impartial source. The source of such information and any additions, deletions, modifications, interpretations, or other changes shall be disclosed in reasonable detail. (Adopted 1/05, Renumbered 1/06)

- **Standard of Practice 10-3**
  REALTORS® shall not print, display or circulate any statement or advertisement with respect to selling or renting of a property that indicates any preference, limitations or discrimination based on race, color, religion, sex, handicap, familial status, or national origin. (Adopted 1/94, Renumbered 1/05 and 1/06)

- **Standard of Practice 10-4**
  As used in Article 10 "real estate employment practices" relates to employees and independent contractors providing real estate-related services and the administrative and clerical staff directly supporting those individuals. (Adopted 1/00, Renumbered 1/05 and 1/06)

ARTICLE 11

The services which REALTORS® provide to their clients and customers shall conform to the standards of practice and competence which are reasonably expected in the specific real estate disciplines in which they engage; specifically, residential real estate brokerage, real property management, commercial and industrial real estate brokerage, real estate appraisal, real estate counseling, real estate syndication, real estate auction, and international real estate.

REALTORS® shall not undertake to provide specialized professional services concerning a type of property or service that is outside their field of competence unless they engage the assistance of one who is competent on such types of property or service, or unless the facts are fully disclosed to the client. Any persons engaged to provide such assistance shall be so identified to the client and their contribution to the assignment should be set forth. (Amended 1/95)

- **Standard of Practice 11-1**
  When REALTORS® prepare opinions of real property value or price, other than in pursuit of a listing or to assist a potential purchaser in formulating a purchase offer, such opinions shall include the following:

1) identification of the subject property
2) date prepared
3) defined value or price
4) limiting conditions, including statements of purpose(s) and intended user(s)
5) any present or contemplated interest, including the possibility of representing the seller/landlord or buyers/tenants
6) basis for the opinion, including applicable market data
7) if the opinion is not an appraisal, a statement to that effect (Amended 1/01)

- **Standard of Practice 11-2**
  The obligations of the Code of Ethics in respect of real estate disciplines other than appraisal shall be interpreted and applied in accordance with the standards of competence and practice which clients and the public reasonably require to protect their rights and interests considering the complexity of the transaction, the availability of expert assistance, and, where the REALTOR® is an agent or subagent, the obligations of a fiduciary. (Adopted 1/95)

- **Standard of Practice 11-3**
  When REALTORS® provide consultive services to clients which involve advice or counsel for a fee (not a commission), such advice shall be rendered in an objective manner and the fee shall not be contingent on the substance of the advice or counsel given. If brokerage or transaction services are to be provided in addition to consultive services, a separate compensation may be paid with prior agreement between the client and REALTOR®. (Adopted 1/96)

- **Standard of Practice 11-4**
  The competency required by Article 11 relates to services contracted for between REALTORS® and their clients or customers; the duties expressly imposed by the Code of Ethics; and the duties imposed by law or regulation. (Adopted 1/02)

ARTICLE 12

REALTORS® shall be careful at all times to present a true picture in their advertising and representations to the public. REALTORS® shall also ensure that their professional status (e.g., broker, appraiser, property manager, etc.) or status as REALTORS® is clearly identifiable in any such advertising. (Amended 1/93)

- **Standard of Practice 12-1**
  REALTORS® may use the term "free" and similar terms in their advertising and in other representations provided that all terms governing availability of the offered product or service are clearly disclosed at the same time. (Amended 1/97)

- **Standard of Practice 12-2**
  REALTORS® may represent their services as "free" or without cost even if they expect to receive compensation from a source other than their client provided that the potential for the REALTOR® to obtain a benefit from a third party is clearly disclosed at the same time. (Amended 1/97)

- **Standard of Practice 12-3**
  The offering of premiums, prizes, merchandise discounts or other inducements to list, sell, purchase, or lease is not, in itself, unethical even if receipt of the benefit is contingent on listing, selling, purchasing, or leasing through the REALTOR® making the offer. However, REALTORS® must exercise care and candor in any such advertising or other public or private representations so that any party interested in receiving or otherwise benefiting from the REALTOR®'s offer will have clear, thorough, advance understanding of all the terms and

conditions of the offer. The offering of any inducements to do business is subject to the limitations and restrictions of state law and the ethical obligations established by any applicable Standard of Practice. (Amended 1/95)

- **Standard of Practice 12-4**
  REALTORS® shall not offer for sale/lease or advertise property without authority. When acting as listing brokers or as subagents, REALTORS® shall not quote a price different from that agreed upon with the seller/landlord. (Amended 1/93)

- **Standard of Practice 12-5**
  REALTORS® shall not advertise nor permit any person employed by or affiliated with them to advertise listed property without disclosing the name of the firm. (Adopted 11/86)

- **Standard of Practice 12-6**
  REALTORS®, when advertising unlisted real property for sale/lease in which they have an ownership interest, shall disclose their status as both owners/landlords and as REALTORS® or real estate licensees. (Amended 1/93)

- **Standard of Practice 12-7**
  Only REALTORS® who participated in the transaction as the listing broker or cooperating broker (selling broker) may claim to have "sold" the property. Prior to closing, a cooperating broker may post a "sold" sign only with the consent of the listing broker. (Amended 1/96)

ARTICLE 13

REALTORS® shall not engage in activities that constitute the unauthorized practice of law and shall recommend that legal counsel be obtained when the interest of any party to the transaction requires it.

ARTICLE 14

If charged with unethical practice or asked to present evidence or to cooperate in any other way, in any professional standards proceeding or investigation, REALTORS® shall place all pertinent facts before the proper tribunals of the Member Board or affiliated institute, society, or council in which membership is held and shall take no action to disrupt or obstruct such processes. (Amended 1/99)

- **Standard of Practice 14-1**
  REALTORS® shall not be subject to disciplinary proceedings in more than one Board of REALTORS® or affiliated institute, society or council in which they hold membership with respect to alleged violations of the Code of Ethics relating to the same transaction or event. (Amended 1/95)

- **Standard of Practice 14-2**
  REALTORS® shall not make any unauthorized disclosure or dissemination of the allegations, findings, or decision developed in connection with an ethics hearing or appeal or in connection with an arbitration hearing or procedural review. (Amended 1/92)

- **Standard of Practice 14-3**
  REALTORS® shall not obstruct the Board's investigative or professional standards proceedings by instituting or threatening to institute actions for libel, slander or defamation against any party to a professional standards proceeding or their witnesses based on the filing of an arbitration request, an ethics complaint, or testimony given before any tribunal. (Adopted 11/87, Amended 1/99)

- **Standard of Practice 14-4**
  REALTORS® shall not intentionally impede the Board's investigative or disciplinary proceedings by filing multiple ethics complaints based on the same event or transaction. (Adopted 11/88)

Duties to REALTORS®

ARTICLE 15

REALTORS® shall not knowingly or recklessly make false or misleading statements about competitors, their businesses, or their business practices. (Amended 1/92)

- **Standard of Practice 15-1**
  REALTORS® shall not knowingly or recklessly file false or unfounded ethics complaints. (Adopted 1/00)

ARTICLE 16

REALTORS® shall not engage in any practice or take any action inconsistent with exclusive representation or exclusive brokerage relationship agreements that other REALTORS® have with clients. (Amended 1/04)

- **Standard of Practice 16-1**
  Article 16 is not intended to prohibit aggressive or innovative business practices which are otherwise ethical and does not prohibit disagreements with other REALTORS® involving commission, fees, compensation or other forms of payment or expenses. (Adopted 1/93, Amended 1/95)

- **Standard of Practice 16-2**
  Article 16 does not preclude REALTORS® from making general announcements to prospects describing their services and the terms of their availability even though some recipients may have entered into agency agreements or other exclusive relationships with another REALTOR®. A general telephone canvass, general mailing or distribution addressed to all prospects in a given geographical area or in a given profession, business, club, or organization, or other classification or group is deemed "general" for purposes of this standard. (Amended 1/04)

  Article 16 is intended to recognize as unethical two basic types of solicitations:

  First, telephone or personal solicitations of property owners who have been identified by a real estate sign, multiple listing compilation, or other information service as having exclusively listed their property with another REALTOR®; and

  Second, mail or other forms of written solicitations of prospects whose properties are exclusively listed with another REALTOR® when such solicitations are not part of a general mailing but are directed specifically to property owners identified through compilations of current listings, "for sale" or "for rent" signs, or other sources of information required by Article 3 and Multiple Listing Service rules to be made available to other REALTORS® under offers of subagency or cooperation. (Amended 1/04)

- **Standard of Practice 16-3**
  Article 16 does not preclude REALTORS® from contacting the client of another broker for the purpose of offering to provide, or entering into a contract to provide, a different type of real estate service unrelated to the type of service currently being provided (e.g., property management as opposed to brokerage) or from offering the same type of service for property not subject to other brokers' exclusive agreements. However, information received through a Multiple Listing Service or any other offer of cooperation may not be used to target clients of other REALTORS® to whom such offers to provide services may be made. (Amended 1/04)

- **Standard of Practice 16-4**
  REALTORS® shall not solicit a listing which is currently listed exclusively with another broker. However, if the listing
  Continued

Figure 1.5 / Continued

broker, when asked by the REALTOR®, refuses to disclose the expiration date and nature of such listing; i.e., an exclusive right to sell, an exclusive agency, open listing, or other form of contractual agreement between the listing broker and the client, the REALTOR® may contact the owner to secure such information and may discuss the terms upon which the REALTOR® might take a future listing or, alternatively, may take a listing to become effective upon expiration of any existing exclusive listing. (Amended 1/94)

- **Standard of Practice 16-5**
  REALTORS® shall not solicit buyer/tenant agreements from buyers/tenants who are subject to exclusive buyer/tenant agreements. However, if asked by a REALTOR®, the broker refuses to disclose the expiration date of the exclusive buyer/tenant agreement, the REALTOR® may contact the buyer/ tenant to secure such information and may discuss the terms upon which the REALTOR® might enter into a future buyer/ tenant agreement or, alternatively, may enter into a buyer/ tenant agreement to become effective upon the expiration of any existing exclusive buyer/tenant agreement. (Adopted 1/94, Amended 1/98)

- **Standard of Practice 16-6**
  When REALTORS® are contacted by the client of another REALTOR® regarding the creation of an exclusive relationship to provide the same type of service, and REALTORS® have not directly or indirectly initiated such discussions, they may discuss the terms upon which they might enter into a future agreement or, alternatively, may enter into an agreement which becomes effective upon expiration of any existing exclusive agreement. (Amended 1/98)

- **Standard of Practice 16-7**
  The fact that a prospect has retained a REALTOR® as an exclusive representative or exclusive broker in one or more past transactions does not preclude other REALTORS® from seeking such prospect's future business. (Amended 1/04)

- **Standard of Practice 16-8**
  The fact that an exclusive agreement has been entered into with a REALTOR® shall not preclude or inhibit any other REALTOR® from entering into a similar agreement after the expiration of the prior agreement. (Amended 1/98)

- **Standard of Practice 16-9**
  REALTORS®, prior to entering into a representation agreement, have an affirmative obligation to make reasonable efforts to determine whether the prospect is subject to a current, valid exclusive agreement to provide the same type of real estate service. (Amended 1/04)

- **Standard of Practice 16-10**
  REALTORS®, acting as buyer or tenant representatives or brokers, shall disclose that relationship to the seller/landlord's representative or broker at first contact and shall provide written confirmation of that disclosure to the seller/landlord's representative or broker not later than execution of a purchase agreement or lease. (Amended 1/04)

- **Standard of Practice 16-11**
  On unlisted property, REALTORS® acting as buyer/tenant representatives or brokers shall disclose that relationship to the seller/landlord at first contact for that buyer/tenant and shall provide written confirmation of such disclosure to the seller/landlord not later than execution of any purchase or lease agreement. (Amended 1/04)

  REALTORS® shall make any request for anticipated compensation from the seller/landlord at first contact. (Amended 1/98)

- **Standard of Practice 16-12**
  REALTORS®, acting as representatives or brokers of sellers/landlords or as subagents of listing brokers, shall disclose that relationship to buyers/tenants as soon as practicable and shall provide written confirmation of such disclosure to buyers/ tenants not later than execution of any purchase or lease agreement. (Amended 1/04)

- **Standard of Practice 16-13**
  All dealings concerning property exclusively listed, or with buyer/tenants who are subject to an exclusive agreement shall be carried on with the client's representative or broker, and not with the client, except with the consent of the client's representative or broker or except where such dealings are initiated by the client.

  Before providing substantive services (such as writing a purchase offer or presenting a CMA) to prospects, REALTORS® shall ask prospects whether they are a party to any exclusive representation agreement. REALTORS® shall not knowingly provide substantive services concerning a prospective transaction to prospects who are parties to exclusive representation agreements, except with the consent of the prospects' exclusive representatives or at the direction of prospects. (Adopted 1/93, Amended 1/04)

- **Standard of Practice 16-14**
  REALTORS® are free to enter into contractual relationships or to negotiate with sellers/landlords, buyers/tenants or others who are not subject to an exclusive agreement but shall not knowingly obligate them to pay more than one commission except with their informed consent. (Amended 1/98)

- **Standard of Practice 16-15**
  In cooperative transactions REALTORS® shall compensate cooperating REALTORS® (principal brokers) and shall not compensate nor offer to compensate, directly or indirectly, any of the sales licensees employed by or affiliated with other REALTORS® without the prior express knowledge and consent of the cooperating broker.

- **Standard of Practice 16-16**
  REALTORS®, acting as subagents or buyer/tenant representatives or brokers, shall not use the terms of an offer to purchase/lease to attempt to modify the listing broker's offer of compensation to subagents or buyer/tenant representatives or brokers nor make the submission of an executed offer to purchase/lease contingent on the listing broker's agreement to modify the offer of compensation. (Amended 1/04)

- **Standard of Practice 16-17**
  REALTORS®, acting as subagents or as buyer/tenant representatives or brokers, shall not attempt to extend a listing broker's offer of cooperation and/or compensation to other brokers without the consent of the listing broker. (Amended 1/04)

- **Standard of Practice 16-18**
  REALTORS® shall not use information obtained from listing brokers through offers to cooperate made through multiple listing services or through other offers of cooperation to refer listing brokers' clients to other brokers or to create buyer/tenant relationships with listing brokers' clients, unless such use is authorized by listing brokers. (Amended 1/02)

- **Standard of Practice 16-19**
  Signs giving notice of property for sale, rent, lease, or exchange shall not be placed on property without consent of the seller/landlord. (Amended 1/93)

- **Standard of Practice 16-20**

  REALTORS®, prior to or after terminating their relationship with their current firm, shall not induce clients of their current firm to cancel exclusive contractual agreements between the client and that firm. This does not preclude REALTORS® (principals) from establishing agreements with their ASSOCIATED licensees governing assignability of exclusive agreements. (Adopted 1/98)

ARTICLE 17

In the event of contractual disputes or specific non-contractual disputes as defined in Standard of Practice 17-4 between REALTORS® (principals) ASSOCIATED with different firms, arising out of their relationship as REALTORS®, the REALTORS® shall submit the dispute to arbitration in accordance with the regulations of their Board or Boards rather than litigate the matter.

In the event clients of REALTORS® wish to arbitrate contractual disputes arising out of real estate transactions, REALTORS® shall arbitrate those disputes in accordance with the regulations of their Board, provided the clients agree to be bound by the decision.

The obligation to participate in arbitration contemplated by this Article includes the obligation of REALTORS® (principals) to cause their firms to arbitrate and be bound by any award. (Amended 1/01)

- **Standard of Practice 17-1**

  The filing of litigation and refusal to withdraw from it by REALTORS® in an arbitrable matter constitutes a refusal to arbitrate. (Adopted 2/86)

- **Standard of Practice 17-2**

  Article 17 does not require REALTORS® to arbitrate in those circumstances when all parties to the dispute advise the Board in writing that they choose not to arbitrate before the Board. (Amended 1/93)

- **Standard of Practice 17-3**

  REALTORS®, when acting solely as principals in a real estate transaction, are not obligated to arbitrate disputes with other REALTORS® absent a specific written agreement to the contrary. (Adopted 1/96)

- **Standard of Practice 17-4**

  Specific non-contractual disputes that are subject to arbitration pursuant to Article 17 are:

  1) Where a listing broker has compensated a cooperating broker and another cooperating broker subsequently claims to be the procuring cause of the sale or lease. In such cases the complainant may name the first cooperating broker as respondent and arbitration may proceed without the listing broker being named as a respondent. Alternatively, if the complaint is brought against the listing broker, the listing broker may name the first cooperating broker as a third-party respondent. In either instance the decision of the hearing panel as to procuring cause shall be conclusive with respect to all current or subsequent claims of the parties for compensation arising out of the underlying cooperative transaction. (Adopted 1/97)

  2) Where a buyer or tenant representative is compensated by the seller or landlord, and not by the listing broker, and the listing broker, as a result, reduces the commission owed by the seller or landlord and, subsequent to such actions, another cooperating broker claims to be the procuring cause of sale or lease. In such cases the complainant may name the first cooperating broker as respondent and arbitration may proceed without the listing broker being named as a respondent. Alternatively, if the complaint is brought against the listing broker, the

listing broker may name the first cooperating broker as a third-party respondent. In either instance the decision of the hearing panel as to procuring cause shall be conclusive with respect to all current or subsequent claims of the parties for compensation arising out of the underlying cooperative transaction. (Adopted 1/97)

  3) Where a buyer or tenant representative is compensated by the buyer or tenant and, as a result, the listing broker reduces the commission owed by the seller or landlord and, subsequent to such actions, another cooperating broker claims to be the procuring cause of sale or lease. In such cases the complainant may name the first cooperating broker as respondent and arbitration may proceed without the listing broker being named as a respondent. Alternatively, if the complaint is brought against the listing broker, the listing broker may name the first cooperating broker as a third-party respondent. In either instance the decision of the hearing panel as to procuring cause shall be conclusive with respect to all current or subsequent claims of the parties for compensation arising out of the underlying cooperative transaction. (Adopted 1/97)

  4) Where two or more listing brokers claim entitlement to compensation pursuant to open listings with a seller or landlord who agrees to participate in arbitration (or who requests arbitration) and who agrees to be bound by the decision. In cases where one of the listing brokers has been compensated by the seller or landlord, the other listing broker, as complainant, may name the first listing broker as respondent and arbitration may proceed between the brokers. (Adopted 1/97)

  5) Where a buyer or tenant representative is compensated by the seller or landlord, and not by the listing broker, and the listing broker, as a result, reduces the commission owed by the seller or landlord and, subsequent to such actions, claims to be the procuring cause of sale or lease. In such cases arbitration shall be between the listing broker and the buyer or tenant representative and the amount in dispute is limited to the amount of the reduction of commission to which the listing broker agreed. (Adopted 1/05)

The Code of Ethics was adopted in 1913. Amended at the Annual Convention in 1924, 1928, 1950, 1951, 1952, 1955, 1956, 1961, 1962, 1974, 1982, 1986, 1987, 1989, 1990, 1991, 1992, 1993, 1994, 1995, 1996, 1997, 1998, 1999, 2000, 2001, 2002, 2003, 2004 and 2005.

EXPLANATORY NOTES

The reader should be aware of the following policies which have been approved by the Board of Directors of the National Association:

In filing a charge of an alleged violation of the Code of Ethics by a REALTOR®, the charge must read as an alleged violation of one or more Articles of the Code. Standards of Practice may be cited in support of the charge.

The Standards of Practice serve to clarify the ethical obligations imposed by the various Articles and supplement, and do not substitute for, the Case Interpretations in Interpretations of the Code of Ethics.

Modifications to existing Standards of Practice and additional new Standards of Practice are approved from time to time. Readers are cautioned to ensure that the most recent publications are utilized.

Form No. 166-288 (12/05)

Summary

Marketing interacts with many factors in a complex manner. Some of these include the Four Ps (product, price, promotion, and place), social influences, legal aspects, competition, economic climate, organizational aspects, and technical environment.

The *sales process* comprises several distinct stages of activity: preparation, prospecting, qualifying, selling and satisfying the client, and follow-up and referral. These stages will be discussed in detail in later chapters of the book. Successful salespeople have certain traits (CRAFT).

Selling is defined as the art of influencing other people to help them make decisions that solve problems for the benefit of all involved parties. Positive aspects of selling as a profession include opportunities for high income, limited supervision, public contact, and career growth. Negative aspects include possibilities of income uncertainty, work difficulty, rejection, and limited control.

The increasing professionalism of the real estate industry is evidenced by the membership of the National Association of REALTORS®, and the association's *Code of Ethics and Standards of Practice,* to which all members must subscribe.

Review Questions

1. What points are included in the marketing concept?

2. What is the definition of selling?

3. What are four advantages and four disadvantages of a career in real estate?

4. Is selling real estate a good career choice for everyone?

5. How would you define professionalism?

6. What do you think a salesperson has to offer consumers?

Discussion Questions

1. How would you define marketing?

2. How is marketing different from sales?

3. What is *your* definition of selling? How does it compare with the one in the text?

4. What can be added to the sales process model as presented in this chapter?

5. What do you consider to be the good and bad points of a career in real estate sales and marketing?

6. Why do some persons take a dim view of salespeople?

7. What traits do you think a successful salesperson must have?

Situation

What Would You Say?

Your best friend from high-school days is unhappy in his current job. You have been approached as a sounding board about career alternatives. One is real estate sales. Your friend asks you these three questions:

1. Do you think real estate sales is a good field to enter?

2. What does it take to succeed in real estate sales?

3. How can I find out more about the field? How would you respond?

TECHNOLOGY *IN ACTION*

For more information on mail merging, visit
http://www.easytechtips.com and click on Resources.

The Technology of Real Estate Sales and Marketing

Key Terms

- Tablet PC
- Smart phone
- GPS (Global Positioning Systems)
- Virtual tours
- PDF (Portable Document Format)
- Jump drive
- Word processing
- Database

An Overview of Technology

Today's real estate business requires a multitude of tools and tasks each real estate professional must learn. The most significant development over the past few years for the real estate industry to learn and carry out is technology. The Internet, cellular phones, and computers have all changed the face of the real estate business. A short historical perspective follows:

- In the early 1980s, the Multiple Listing Service® (MLS®) was a collection of pages printed from a local print shop with color-coded pages updated every two weeks to replace the changes. Today, a local MLS® normally resides on the Web, accessible for many real estate professionals from their handheld cellular phone.
- Desktop publishing a few years ago required a wait time for developing photographs with an enormous amount of cutting and pasting (literally) by the photocopy machine until your flyer was just right. Today, with digital cameras, color laser printers, and desktop publishing software, agents can customize brochures and flyers for consumers at an open house.
- What once required a drive across town to pick up a key for showing a home now only needs a few codes and a handheld device.

- Virtual tours, podcasts, and personalized Web sites for properties and subdivisions are changing the way real estate professionals market real estate with technology.

This chapter explains and highlights a few of the many technology tools available for use today in the real estate industry.

Developing a Technology Budget

Technology implemented efficiently requires the real estate professional to invest some fixed costs annually. Making sure that your funds are well spent and used accordingly is essential. Decisions concerning what computer you will use (desktop, laptop, or tablet PC), the cell phone or smart phone you will incorporate in your business, the type of printing (laser or ink jet) you will use, the style of Web site presence, and more must all be addressed.

The best way to develop your budget is to use a guide similar to the one found in Figure 2.1. Make a list of the technology tools you feel are important for your real estate career by placing an "x" in the proper column. Visit your local computer store or search online for available prices.

Whatever your technology choices require as a real estate professional, understanding the costs involved is important for your budgeting and business plan.

Computer Needs

As a real estate professional, much of your time will be spent outside the office. Deciding what computer needs you will have daily is important. Some real estate professionals choose to have a desktop computer at their office for all of their real estate needs with another desktop computer at home. The downside of having two computers is that information may not be as easily accessible when you're in one location versus the other. Although you can use portable hard drives to transfer this information from one computer to another, the time involved can be costly. Some real estate software vendors, such as Top Producer®, provide online systems where information can be stored and accessed from any remote computer. This can be a critical issue, however, when access is unavailable from a location (such as an open house) that does not provide an Internet connection. Note that most of these programs do not work well on a dial-up connection, so you'll likely need a high-speed Internet connection.

Real estate professionals may also choose laptop computers or tablet PCs to perform daily tasks. A mobile computer allows you to have access to your information from anywhere (including your automobile) anytime! Laptop computers are also valuable for presentations to buyers and sellers, running slide shows from open houses as well as accessing e-mail when you're on the road.

The tablet PC takes the laptop computer to a whole new level. With the **tablet PC,** you can take notes (on the computer screen), draw floor plans, and fill out sales contracts (converting the handwriting to typed text). Many real estate professionals are using their

Sample Technology Budget Worksheet   Figure 2.1

Hardware/Software Needed	Costs	Goals to Purchase

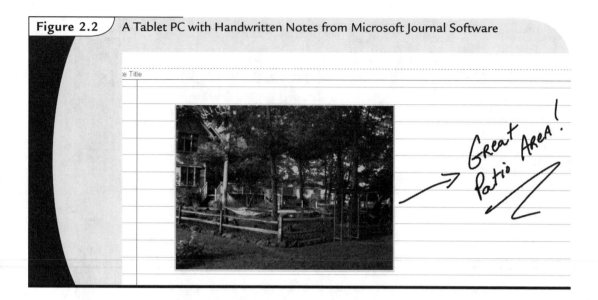

Figure 2.2   A Tablet PC with Handwritten Notes from Microsoft Journal Software

tablet PCs in the field with buyers and sellers to sign documents and then e-mailing or faxing those documents to a client or another agent across town or across the country. Tablet PCs offer extra benefits that you cannot get with a traditional laptop computer. Figure 2.2 shows an example of a photograph of a new listing with comments from the agent in Microsoft Journal. This sample illustration shows how easy it is to use your tablet PC to e-mail information to a client.

Cellular Phones/Smart Phones

Another essential part of your technology toolbox is a mobile phone. Many types of cellular phones are available, as well as the new **smart phones.** One important word of caution: real estate agents probably use their cellular phones more than most sales professionals. Understanding and abiding by all local and state laws is important! Some states are looking into banning the use of mobile phones while driving an automobile. Always make sure you use great care when using your cellular phone while driving. When possible, pull over to the side of the roadway to send and receive your phone calls or use hands-free cell phone kits that allow you to hear and speak clearly while freeing up your hands.

Smart phones are unique because they can run software programs similar to the programs found on your desktop or laptop computer. For example, although I can access my e-mail from most cellular phones, I cannot (at the time of this book's printing) open a Microsoft Word document from a traditional cellular phone. With a smart phone, you can access many programs and files, such as Microsoft PowerPoint, Excel, Top Producer data, MLS records, and more.

TECHNOLOGY *IN ACTION*

Some real estate professionals are using smart phones at a whole new level. From **GPS (Global Positioning Systems),** providing turn-by-turn directions to properties, and copying virtual tours and minidigital movies to their smart phones stored on separate media cards. agents can show clients and customers information about listings from their smart phones. Flyers, documents, and an enormous amount of information can be stored on these devices; they can also print to a mobile printer. For products and many types of mobile smart phones produced by Hewlett Packard, visit http://www.HP.com/go/realestate3.

Figure 2.3 provides a short checklist of questions you should consider when deciding whether a smart phone or a regular mobile phone is right for you.

If you answered "yes" to most of the questions in Figure 2.3, then purchasing a smart phone might be a good decision for you.

Digital Photography

Many consumers today use the Internet as a means for viewing properties in advance before making a contact with a real estate agent. Those properties that do not offer enough photos may often be overlooked or bypassed. Some consumers choose to view only those listings that have virtual tours.

Many makes and models of digital cameras are available to choose from, with various types of media cards and cables for transferring data to and from the camera and computer.

Digital photography allows you to take an unlimited number of pictures for your listings. Most MLS providers allow for an unlimited number of photos to be uploaded to their system with links to virtual tours and other virtual media. Many cameras offer wide-angle or panoramic software so agents can capture the right look for the home they are marketing.

The downside of digital photography is that if the real estate agent does not choose the right equipment and settings, the quality may not be as good as a traditional camera.

Another form of digital photography many real estate agents are using with their real estate listings is digital video. Today agents can include short digital movies complete with narration and music about their for-sale properties. These new digital

Figure 2.3	Checklist for Purchasing a Cellular Phone or a Smart Phone

Question	Yes	No
Would you like to have more than a phone number and e-mail for your clients and contacts?		
Do you need to check your e-mail on a regular basis throughout the day?		
Are you interested in tracking your income and expenses on a daily basis?		
Do you need to access the Internet or your local MLS on a frequent basis outside the office?		
Do you use Microsoft Outlook or Act as a contact manager on a daily basis?		
Do you have a busy calendar/schedule each day?		
Do you like to keep track of your to-dos and daily tasks?		
Do you get tired of carrying more than one device for your phone, contacts, and other important information?		
Would you like to show consumers and clients videos or photographs of properties you have listed while in the field?		
Do you crave 24/7 Internet connectivity?		
Are there software programs (third-party applications) such as Microsoft Word or Excel you use on a daily basis?		

commercials can also be used on a smart phone for showing consumers or uploaded to a Web site and the local MLS.

Software

Probably the most expensive technology endeavor for the real estate professional is software. Good real estate professionals will demand several types of software applications to run their businesses effectively. The following list describes a few of the various types of software programs a real estate agent may need:

> ### TECHNOLOGY *IN ACTION*
>
> **Virtual tours** are a popular way to market listings today, and several vendors provide these services. Visit http://www.ipix.com and http://www.visualtour.com to explore two vendors and their available plans and features. Virtual tour providers normally require an annual fee with an extra charge for each tour. Virtual tour costs are just a part of the new trend and cost involved for marketing real estate on the Web, which makes it also a new cost to be included with the real estate professional's annual budget.

- Contact management
- Database needs
- Scheduling calendar tasks/needs
- Desktop publishing (making flyers and brochures)
- Accounting and bookkeeping
- PDF (portable document format) (software)
- Word processing
- Presentation software
- Photo-editing software
- Specialty programs

Let's examine each of these various software needs in more detail.

Contact Management

Most real estate business revolves around a good contact management system. Being able to access records and information about your customers and clients is essential. Several programs are designed specifically for real estate agents. Top Producer is one of the most popular software programs because it does much more than contact management; in fact, Top Producer does many of the functions for real estate agents included in the earlier software list. Top Producer is easy to use because most of the work is preloaded with the program. For example, any letters, action plans, and customized flyers have already been prebuilt and loaded with the software. The real estate agent can choose to use the existing information or edit and add information as necessary. Real estate agents can access Top Producer by downloading and saving it to their hard drives or through an online monthly subscription that is best accessed with a high-speed Internet connection.

Many real estate professionals are using programs such as Microsoft Outlook. Several other contact management systems are available, such as Act and Goldmine, that also provide real estate add-ons. Using your contact management software will be the biggest portion of your workload, so having a software program you are comfortable with and can handle efficiently is essential for your real estate career.

Database Needs

Database software can normally be accomplished with a contact management software program; however, many real estate professionals who have a long tenure in the real estate industry prefer to move some records of older customers and clients into a separate database. Your database can become a gold mine for future referrals and business. Collecting information such as the interest rate one of your customers has agreed to during the loan closing can be a helpful way to contact in the future. For example, when interest rates fall you could contact your past client and explain refinancing their home mortgage, which could save thousands of dollars. It's also a good way for you to stay in touch with previous customers and clients with a birthday card, anniversary card, or the anniversary of a home purchase. Having this information available to remind you monthly will set you apart from the average real estate professional and help you create a long and prosperous real estate career.

Calendar Tasks/Needs

Most of the programs already mentioned, such as Top Producer, Microsoft Outlook, Act, and Gold Mine, all track appointments and tasks, set up reminders, and so on to keep your daily schedule running smoothly. It is critical for the real estate agent to have a game plan and a set of goals for each day. You should also have action plans for your listings, pending contracts, after the sale closing, buyers you are working with, and friends and family you are working with. The easiest way to carry out your goals and plans is to have a software program that reminds you and keeps track of those daily systems. As with the contact management software, having a program that you can comfortably use is essential, if not critical, to your success in the real estate business.

Desktop Publishing

Creating flyers for your listings is essential to showcase your product in the best possible light. Microsoft Publisher and Adobe® Photoshop are two popular desktop publishing/graphics applications. HP offers a product called the Real Estate Marketing Assistant that works with many local MLS vendors to import data from the MLS straight into the property flyer template. This feature can save the real estate agent a lot of time in creating and producing real estate publications.

Accounting and Bookkeeping

Quicken from Intuit and Money from Microsoft are two financial programs that allow real estate agents to track income and expense. Both programs are ideal for real estate

TECHNOLOGY *IN ACTION*

Map Point and Microsoft Streets and Trips are two good software programs for helping a real estate professional track mileage daily. Both programs allow the agent to draw maps, calculate mileage, and keep good records for IRS purposes.

One great way to keep track of your mileage through either one of these mapping software programs is recreate all the points or places you visited as a real estate professional. After you have listed all the addresses you can then click on Create a Map and the program calculates all the mileage for the various locations you traveled to throughout the day. Save this report or print it out and log the mileage in your record keeping book so at the end of the year, the real estate agent will have an excellent documentation of the exact mileage used.

professionals to keep track of financial items and help prepare tax information at the end of the year for a tax preparer. Both products are fairly easy to use and essential for real estate agents to incorporate in their business.

PDF (Portable Document Format) Software

The full versions of Adobe Acrobat allow real estate professionals to create **PDF files (portable document format)** that can be uploaded to the Web and/or e-mailed to real estate agents or consumers promoting a piece of property. PDFs enable all computer users to open these documents regardless of the software on their particular computers.

Word Processing

Communicating with clients and consumers plays a major role in the real estate agent's daily schedule. Having a good word processor is essential to fulfilling your correspondence needs. Many word processors allow you to produce documents and flyers for clients, mail merging through a database, and much more. Visit http://www.5-Minutes.com to view books that offer Microsoft Word document templates to use in ad writing and letters to buyers and sellers.

Presentation Software

From time to time, real estate agents might want to use a laptop or tablet PC during a buyer or seller presentation. Microsoft PowerPoint is an excellent resource for building your own presentation to use in your business. Other software sellers, such as Top Producer and Agent Online, provide presentation software templates for real estate agents too. You can visit http://www.microsoft.com/office to learn more about Microsoft PowerPoint.

Photo Editing Software

Photographs often need minor adjusting prior to publishing on the Internet or providing to local media outlets. In this case, you might need to use a special photo editing software suite. Changing sizes of the photograph, lightening, and adding overlays are all available through most photo editing software suites. Most digital cameras come equipped with a software application you can use to accomplish these tasks.

Specialty Programs

Every day, new technology products arrive on the scene. Understanding and learning about the new technology advances is an important part of the real estate agent's career. Not all new technology ideas are required for every real estate listing or agent, however. Often the price or property and the personality style of the client decide whether technology plays a role in the marketing endeavors. Some of the new technology breakthrough ideas currently include personalized interactive CD-ROM and DVD brochures for listings.

Creating e-books, podcasts, and personalized Web sites are also all important parts of many real estate agents lives today.

Many agents also use digital voice recorders to record memos, notes, daily tasks, and to-dos while on the run. Digital voice recorders have also been useful during listing

TECHNOLOGY *IN ACTION*

Many software sellers enable you to create interactive CDs and DVDs. For example, AutoPlay software (http://www.indigorose.com) can be used to create an interactive CD or DVD about a real estate listing complete with video, audio, virtual tours, floor plans, documents, and links to Web sites. AutoPlay is ideal for creating personalized technology tools for high-end listings, subdivisions, or other big marketing projects where technology is needed.

TECHNOLOGY *IN ACTION*

Thumb size removable hard drives that plug into a USB port have become popular in the past few years. These **jump drives** can hold a lot of information and are ideal for storing slide shows about properties, important documents, and other information that real estate professionals may need when working from the field or remote computer.

appointments to record extra features and information about the property for sale and then to use later at the office when compiling all the information. Some real estate professionals have used digital voice recorders at the closing to get testimonials and other voice accolades from clients and consumers to use on a Web site for promotional purposes.

Portable hard drives have also become an important tool because they allow agents to store more documents, photos, videos, and virtual tours that can be accessed from other locations. Portable hard drives are also ideal for backing up data in case of a computer crash.

Internet date cards have become popular with many real estate professionals. These PCIMA cards allow real estate agents to log on to the Internet from remote locations. A real estate agent can even log on to the Internet from an open house, a client's home, or from the front seat of your car without the need of a dial-up computer connection.

Web Sites

Another important part of the real estate professional's marketing plan is to have a personal Web site. Real estate agents are now learning the importance of having their own Web sites and not simply relying on the brokerage or office Web site. Registering your domain name and coming up with content for your Web site are issues that you'll need to take care of. Many vendors provide Web sites for agents with free reports and links to valuable information consumers can use. Many of these Web site sellers allow the agent to customize the Web site with information about their own listings, photos, virtual tours, and community information. Driving traffic to your Web site is an important part of your marketing endeavor. Be sure to include your Web site on everything! Some real estate professionals are creating customized Web sites for particular properties and subdivisions and even providing employment information for the local community. To win big with Internet technology and the Web, real estate professionals need to think outside the box about ways they can reach consumers through Internet marketing. Having plenty of information, resources, and other valuable data will keep consumers coming back to your Web site again and again.

Linking your current inventory of listings from your MLS to your Web site is essential. Most MLS vendors provide this feature for you through a simple Web link. Check with your local MLS vendor to incorporate this feature if available for your Web site.

Putting It All Together

Many real estate professionals buy technology products and tools but never find time to learn the software or hardware, and fail to make the most of their technology. To make technology successful for your real estate career, you need to devote time to learning how to use the technology you choose. You can access several online resources to learn more about technology. To make the most of your technology tools:

- Consider taking online computer classes.
- Visit bulletin boards where information is printed on how to use various software programs.
- Consider hiring a younger person who is familiar with computers and technology to train you on your new applications.
- Visit the software or hardware manufacturer's Web site and search for Frequently Asked Questions.
- See if your local community or college is offering courses on how to use computers.
- Spend a few minutes each day working with your computer and software.

Real estate professional must be sure not to get discouraged with today's technology and to take the attitude and positive approach of mastering the uses of technology tools.

As discussed, many types of software programs are available for real estate agents, including Top Producer, Act, Goldmine, Agent Online, and many more. Many free programs to create greeting cards, business cards, stationery, and more are available from companies such as Avery, HP, and Kodak. The important point for any real estate professional is to buy programs you feel comfortable with, can understand, and will use daily. This chapter only covered a small portion of the software applications available for real estate professionals. A Web search for real estate software should produce many more applications suitable for your real estate career.

TECHNOLOGY *IN ACTION*

A good Web site to visit to take online technology classes is http://www.hponlinecourses.com. This Web site offers a wide variety of classes for real estate professionals that are free!

Summary

The Internet and technology are changing the way real estate professionals do business today. Younger real estate agents entering the industry are ahead of the game in using digital applications with their businesses. It is important to take inventory of what items you will need as a real estate professional. Invest in a cell phone and computer that will work well for you. Take plenty of digital photographs and learn how to produce virtual tours for your clients. Use software that will help you keep track of appointments, send and receive e-mail, and do your word processing daily. Venture into specialty technology such as CD-ROM and DVD, digital voice recorders, and accessing the Web from remote locations. Embrace online technology by incorporating a personal Web site, linking your listing inventory from your local board of REALTORS® MLS site, providing information content, and promoting your Web site on everything and anything you do locally to drive traffic there. And remember, there will be times when technology is not suitable and doing things the old fashioned way is not a bad idea.

Review Questions

1. Describe the best way for a real estate professional to develop a budget.

2. List one technology software seller most real estate agents are using today for their real estate business.

3. How does the tablet PC differ from the conventional laptop computer?

4. Why would a real estate agent want to invest in a smart phone versus a regular cell phone?

5. List some of the advantages to digital photography.

6. List the downside of digital photography for a real estate professional.

7. What are the two companies listed in the book that provide virtual tours for real estate professionals?

8. Describe Microsoft Outlook and how a real estate agent might use it.

9. Explain why a real estate agent may want to use an interactive CD-ROM.

10. Describe how Microsoft Map Point or Microsoft Street and Trips could be helpful for a real estate professional.

Discussion Questions

1. What technology tools do you feel are essential for most real estate agents in today's business?

2. Provide a list of content you think would be fitting for a Web site in your local community.

3. Give an example of when you think technology might not be a good idea to use in the real estate business.

Defining Your Marketplace

Key Terms

. Appreciation
. Cold call
. Commercial facilities
. Competitive market
  analysis
. Government structure

. Real estate
  developments
. Market area
. Public facilities
. Public services

Selling Your Knowledge

As a real estate agent, you offer your clients time, energy, and knowledge of real estate and its related transfer. This knowledge must encompass not only the complex legal implications of interpreting listing agreements and earnest money contracts but also a thorough, accurate knowledge of the market area. Average agents know what to do, but superior real estate agents know why they are doing what they are doing. Answers to many "whys" will be examined in this chapter, including why knowing your community and defining your market area are so important.

Deciding Where to Work

Often new agents—and sometimes experienced agents—wonder in what area of real estate to begin working. That is sound logic because no one can be knowledgeable about an entire marketplace; some specialization by locale is essential for an agent to be familiar enough with an area to sell properties knowledgeably. Some agents think they shouldn't limit themselves to one specialization but instead should remain flexible. If this were true, the largest broker in a city would have only one office in the center of town, which is not the best place to have a real estate office.

Multiple-listing services often divide a city into quadrants, which represents a starting point. A quadrant is not a small enough area for an agent to know everything about

Trends **& ISSUES**

Another aspect to consider is how you might focus on a particular market niche for real estate buyers and sellers. Many real estate professionals are beginning to specialize in market niches where applicable for consumers. A senior adult specialist, first-time homebuyers agent, lakefront properties specialist, and transitional clients agent are all examples of how real estate agents are successfully concentrating in particular market niches.

Consider your market area and develop a list of possible niches that a real estate professional might consider specializing in.

If you were going to specialize in a certain niche as a real estate professional, what would it be? Why? Could your area support the niche you're interested in?

it, however, because it usually represents many little cities. At best, the salesperson should have limited understanding of several neighborhoods. Figure 3.1 is a graphic example of the need for neighborhood specialization.

From the point of view of the real estate sales professional, any major marketplace consists of many different communities. Without some predetermined selection, or **market area,** the agent can be doomed to failure. If a prospect requests service outside an agent's general market area, however, the agent may try to provide service or refer

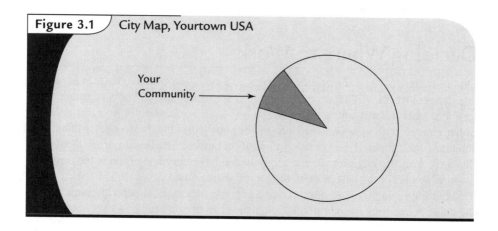

Figure 3.1   City Map, Yourtown USA

Your Community ⟶

the prospect to another office. Use any spare moment to learn your market as well as you possibly can. Good trainers recommend that new agents familiarize themselves with the neighborhood from which most of their business probably will come.

If you do this before committing to work a specific area, you will have greater confidence. One area of importance to investigate is sales activity. Other points to consider are covered in Chapter 5, but remember that individuals who learn about a community, investigate certain areas, and have answers to questions on specific characteristics of their particular market area will be ahead of the rest. Although this is extremely important, do not spend all your time trying to learn *everything* before meeting a possible buyer or seller. Spend as much time on research as you can but not to the detriment of your prospecting activities. Most successful agents will attest to this inevitable fact of life in real estate sales. There is no room for a lack of product knowledge.

Gaining Market Knowledge

What should you know about your market area? Ask yourself what questions you would have if you were moving to a new city or neighborhood. For example, you would want to know about schools, churches, public facilities in the area, public services, and so on, whether you are a consumer or a developing agent.

Always remember that in the real estate sales business, you start broad and become specific. Be sure you know your neighborhood well enough to do that and do it well. Whether a person is moving across the nation or across town, the experience can be like moving into another world. When someone says, "Tell me about a neighborhood," you have to begin with generalities and evolve to specific houses.

Everyone has experienced a salesperson who talked for about 10 seconds and then said, "I know exactly what you need. Here it is right here!" That salesperson probably didn't sell you anything. You didn't buy the product because the salesperson became too specific too fast.

Establishing Boundaries

The agent first must establish realistic boundaries, which may be natural ones, such as a river or a creek, or artificial ones, such as a major thoroughfare that divides communities. School district lines are important boundaries. Railroad tracks, shopping centers, and commercial development areas are sometimes considered boundaries as well, but whatever the boundaries may be, the agent needs to be aware of them. Map out some sort of geographic area. Be familiar with the various subdivisions or developments in your chosen neighborhoods. Before getting started in the business or in a new area, go out and become familiar with the entire layout. For example, familiarize yourself with your company's listings and then with the listings of other major companies in that area. These will give you some idea about inventory within your defined marketplace.

Schools

Information about schools is usually one of the first questions prospective buyers ask, according to market research on persons who have transferred or relocated. For example, a prospective buyer may come into town, turn north on the freeway and see an area that looks appealing. The prospect then approaches a real estate agent for more information about the area.

The agent should determine the prospect's needs, which may include finding a good neighborhood school. However, the salesperson also must be careful not to make a value judgment. Which is the best school district depends upon the particular needs of the individual's family. A good school district to people with no children may mean low property taxes, whereas a good school district to others may mean a special education program for one of their children. Another family may consider a good school district as one with an excellent reputation for athletics, music programs, or number of National Merit scholars. You need to be knowledgeable about the schools in your area and know what their strengths and weaknesses are. However, if you don't have the answer to a specific question, be honest and tell prospects you will get the information for them.

The best way to get the correct information, such as facts on enrollment trends, is to go to the administrative offices of the school district. Then visit the various schools and speak with the principals or vice principals and request a tour. Tell the principals you need to know the strengths and weaknesses of the school for your buyers. That attitude shows the school administration that you are a local real estate person who is concerned about the neighborhood and the schools and interested in getting correct data about them (which might result in some referral business from the school officials).

Whether you have children in the schools within your market area or not, get involved by sponsoring some event or participating in Career Days or some other school function. The key is that you know the schools and that the school community knows you as well! If you want to get something, give something first.

TECHNOLOGY *IN ACTION*

A great way to help consumers find out information about schools in your market area is to place a link on your Web site to vendors who provide this information. Visit http://www.theschoolreport.com for a good example of how real estate professionals can deliver statistics and figures to consumers via the Internet.

Provide a brief description of what types of information consumers can learn from http://www.theschoolreport.com.

Houses of Worship

Churches and other houses of worship are an important part of the community. For many, places of worship are as important as schools, if not more so. Knowing all the religious centers in your area is as difficult as knowing about all the schools. In fact, some schools are associated with various churches. Ask prospects the form of worship they prefer, and then make an effort to meet some of that group's officials and find out about its regular activities. These religious facilities can be resources of information or business even though you do not belong to that particular denomination. Keep in mind that being aware of a certain religious practice does not mean you must agree with it.

Public Facilities

Public facilities in your neighborhood may include swimming pools, parks, tennis courts, playgrounds, golf courses, and libraries. All the facilities that may be available to prospective buyers in this neighborhood need to be brought to their attention, whether you think they will use them or not. Even if they don't seem interested at the time, their needs may change and reliable information helps you establish yourself as the area expert. You also need to be aware of the Homeowners or Property Owners Associations and their specific regulations that new owners must be familiar with.

Public Services

Any real estate transaction entails a transfer of **public services** such as water, electricity, gas, and garbage collection services. Your prospective buyer needs to know who to contact to take care of these transfers and approximately what the fees will be. In certain cases, the agent can arrange for some of these transfers. You should have the names of people to call, their phone numbers, and the average charges for these transfers. Some subdivisions have their own utility companies or water boards, and you need to know which ones do. An introduction to officials of fire and policy protection agencies might be a good idea, particularly if the buyer has suffered a fire or burglary and is particularly concerned about incidents of this kind. Public transportation, including bus and train networks, is also important; be sure you have up-to-date information. Again, this information is significant to every area of real estate, including commercial, industrial, and residential.

Commercial Facilities

The **commercial facilities** of your neighborhood are also significant, so you need to be familiar with restaurants, stores, and banks. Next time you are able to help people who move into your neighborhood from another city, introduce them to your banker, or tell them about the particular services the bank has to offer. Suggest that if they have no previous preferences, they may visit with Mr. Banker, saying that you sent them, and have him outline what his bank can do. The buyers then can compare the bank's services to other banks, if they choose. Call the banker to say you have sent him a referral. This is another 30-second commercial on your part; you have made several people happy, and over the years, the positive feedback can add up.

The same is true for medical services. Whether people move across town or across the country, they will need new medical and dental services. Ask your customers if they want to be introduced to your doctor or dentist, and again, follow up. Most real estate agents are eager to work with doctors and dentists as prospects. This is a good way to start building an association with them. Such service will make a positive impression and help your career in the long run. Attorneys, accountants, mechanics, and other needed resources are equally valuable contacts to make and build on.

Government Structure

Many potential buyers are very interested in learning about the **government structure** of their particular neighborhood, including what form of government exists and who the officials are. People new to your city may ask you about the government structure or governing body of the city. They may ask how the city council is elected or appointed and who the chief operating officer or mayor is. Be knowledgeable in this area in advance so you'll have answers for them; however, avoid getting involved in a political debate. Provide accurate facts but be careful not to expose your own biases. If your opinion is requested, feel free to offer and briefly explain it, but be sure to state that it is only your opinion. Don't win the debate and lose the customer.

Real Estate Developments

You also need to be knowledgeable about various **real estate developments**—areas where new homes or businesses are under construction—in your community. If you work in a market where there is new development, invest at least one day a month to talk with developers and become familiar with their projects, inventories, and policies. To return the favor, comply if some builders want you to come out and introduce the prospect to an on-site salesperson.

Other builders may expect you to do the work necessary to consummate a sale. Some builders will not cooperate with an agent and you need to know this before taking buyers out to see the builder's properties.

One of our agents once approached a builder, saying that Mr. and Mrs. Buyer saw one of the builder's houses and decided it was just what they wanted. The builder responded that the company didn't cooperate with real estate agencies and had never paid a fee to any agent. Beware of the people who don't want to work with you, or you'll wind up selling those properties for practice.

If you know your neighborhood, you can provide the services your customers deserve. You may want to make a checklist to be sure you cover all these points with your prospective buyers. Printing a brief "Welcome to Our Community" brochure also might be a good investment if you work with a lot of newcomers to the neighborhood. You'll feel confident about showing houses when you have all these facts at your disposal, and your confidence will be reflected in your increased sales. Figure 3.2 illustrates the key information necessary to know about a neighborhood.

Agent Scorecard \ **Figure 3.2**

How well do you know these things about your community?

Schools: Locations, services provided, key contact.
Churches: Locations, services provided, key contact.
Public Facilities: Locations, costs.
Public Services: Costs, contact point, timetable for service.
Commercial Aspects: Contacts/referrals.
Government Structure: *Brief* explanation. *Careful* here.
Developments: Inventory, showing procedure,
cooperation policy.
History: Appreciation/fair market value. Current CMA
on hand?
Other facts about community:

Knowing Your Marketplace History

Knowing the history of your market neighborhood is a positive factor in at least two ways. First, it gives you confidence in discussing the area intelligently. Second, it projects the correct image of you as the resident expert or area professional who is capable of answering all your customers' questions about this particular area.

In choosing a market area, there are several significant factors to consider. What makes a good area for one person is not necessarily the same for another. In Chapter 5, "The Marketing Stage—Putting Your Knowledge to Work," another portion of the book, these important decisions are covered. Remember to pick an appropriate market for you and then learn as much as you can about it. One of the first and ongoing activities of a successful real estate salesperson is to become aware of and then stay abreast of activity in your area.

Keeping Up with Activity

You need to keep a continual **competitive market analysis** (CMA) about your neighborhood; a CMA is a chart of properties for sale and recently sold, as well as listings that didn't sell. Some agents keep a flow chart of what has happened in a neighborhood since they began working there. They know what is for sale and what has closed. It doesn't take much time to keep up with those details. You can certainly develop an image of being knowledgeable about the community and thereby portray more credibility by staying current. The important point to remember is that you have to update constantly. Force yourself to be informed. To keep your CMA current, monitor the activities of your neighborhood constantly to find out what's for sale, what's been sold, what has expired, not only by REALTORS® but also the for-sale-by-owner properties where no listing agents are involved.

One of the most challenging aspects of the real estate business is a **cold call** on owners or potential buyers you don't know. As a sample approach you might say, "Mr. Russell, I notice you have your place for sale. I'm not here to ask you to list your property with me, but no one knows this neighborhood better than I do. To stay informed, I'd like

Trends & ISSUES

Consider providing a "FREE REPORT" on a monthly or quarterly basis on what properties are selling for in your farm area. Placing a button on your Web site advertising consumers to sign up for the "FREE REPORT" or sending out postcards in your farm area is a good way to encourage potential buyers and sellers to "opt in" for your marketing efforts. Most consumers are curious to know what homes are selling for in their area, and this type of activity is an excellent way to get new sources of business.

to find out a little bit about your property: May I ask you a few questions?" He may refuse, but usually sellers are pleasantly surprised that you didn't immediately ask them for the opportunity to list. Either way, you need to know what is going on in the area.

Some salespeople will ask if the owner is relocating to another city. If so, the agent will offer to refer the seller to another REALTOR® in that town, thereby providing a service and possibly collecting a referral fee. It may even be a way to obtain the listing eventually, if the owner is not successful in selling.

Keeping Up with Appreciation

Appreciation—the increase in market value of a property or area based on comparable sales—of the neighborhood is probably among the most important information you will have to give both sellers and buyers in your particular area. Sellers often feel they can sell their property for more than it's worth, and their reasoning goes something like this: Neighbor Bill down the street has a For Sale by Owner sign in his yard and is asking $190,000. Bill doesn't sell the property, so eventually a local real estate agent lists it for close to the market value of $185,500. Bill finally sells it on an assumption/equity buy for $180,700. When Jack sees the Sold sign, he asks Bill how the sale went. Bill's answer is that he *got* everything he wanted. Jack now thinks Bill got his original asking price. When he compares his house to Bill's, finding it superior, Jack puts a *highly inflated* value on his own property.

A successful salesperson in the real estate business often will be called on to justify to sellers a market price for their property that is less than they originally thought it should be. The way to do this with consistent success is to be self-confident and fully informed on the neighborhood and its appreciation. To accomplish this, you must constantly monitor the changes. An accurate, up-to-date CMA, presented to the seller, will show a property's market value in a researched and definitive form. This helps you avoid an agent-versus-seller debate and decreases the chance of a conflict. Figure 3.3 shows a typical CMA form.

Figure 3.3 Competitive Market Analysis

PROPERTY ADDRESS   149 Viewridge

For Sale Now:	Bed-rms.	Baths	Den	Sq. Ft.	1st Loan	List Price	Days On Market	Terms
318 Montview	3	2	no	1569	159,500	188,000	10	Open; just redecorated
1215 Oakridge	3	2	yes	1400	123,400	187,000	25	Fireplace in Den; conventional only
181 Ridgeview	3	1½	yes	1580	–0–	167,000	40	Needs repairs on roof; no garage
166 Viewridge	4	3	yes	1800	143,000	192,000	18	Corner lot; storage shed stays

Sold Past 12 Mos.	Bed-rms.	Baths	Den	Sq. Ft.	1st Loan	List Price	Days On Market	Date Sold	Sale Price	Terms
307 Oakview	3	2	yes	1390	133,500	180,500	12	2/10	180,950	Assume
1951 Montridge	3	2	no	1600	–0–	188,000	35	2/28	184,500	Owner carry
158 Oak Circle	3	2	yes	1580	149,800	185,000	60	1/10	182,300	V.A.
1972 Lone Oak	4	1	yes	1900	148,000	192,000	45	1/1	187,000	Assume
1300 Viewridge	4	2	yes	1850	156,000	189,500	8	2/12	186,750	Conventional

Expired Past 12 Mos.	Bed-rms.	Baths	Den	Sq. Ft.	1st Loan	List Price	Days On Market	Terms
518 Viewridge	3	2	yes	1400	149,000	189,000	80	Listing withdrawn 2/20
906 Montridge	4	3	yes	1800	127,000	193,000	120	Open–Last 60 days
1129 Oak Drive	3	1	no	1250	153,250	179,900	110	Open–Last 30 days

REMARKS

Another benefit of knowing a market area comes when dealing with buyers. The market analysis will help you convince the purchasers that they are not paying over market value. Most buyers don't mind paying a fair price; they just don't want to "taken," which is understandable. You can eliminate the problem by doing your homework on the current neighborhood value. Be informed about your market area and you will become the resident pro in the eyes of your client, an important position for you to attain as a successful real estate agent.

Summary

To select a successful market area, a salesperson first should establish a set of realistic geographic boundaries within which to conduct business. The salesperson then should become familiar with this market area, investigating the area's schools, houses of worship, public facilities, public services, commercial facilities, government structures, and housing developments.

In addition, a salesperson must be knowledgeable about the market history of the area in which he or she will work. Such knowledge should include information regarding past and present sales activity and the measure of appreciation in property values that have taken place in the area.

Review Questions

1. What are the only things real estate salespeople have to offer their clients?

2. A real estate salesperson could know everything he or she needs to know about what portion of a city?

3. What natural or artificial boundaries could define a geographic area?

4. If agents know their market well, what are the seven areas in which they should be very knowledgeable?

5. What are the two advantages of knowing a market neighborhood's history?

6. What is the best way to keep up with the activity in a market area?

7. What is important about keeping up with appreciation in the area?

8. How will knowing this information build self-confidence?

Discussion Questions

1. Which segments of a market area are the most important to investigate? In what order should the rest of the areas follow?

2. How does an agent convince an owner that fair market value is 15 percent less than the sales price desired by the owner?

3. What community information do agents usually lack? How can they correct this situation?

4. What part of your community do you really know well? What part poorly?

Situation

Handling Inquiries for Unfamiliar Market Areas

An old friend from whom you have not heard for many years unexpectedly calls you with a real estate request. He and his family want to sell a piece of property they own in your city. He moved out of the state several years ago. The property is located on the opposite side of the large metropolitan city from the area in which you specialize. How do you handle his request?

Take It or Leave It

Mark and Lorene Tullos asked you to come by and explain what your company can do to help them sell their property. They have offered it for sale by themselves for four months. Your CMA tells you the property should sell in the $195,000 to $210,000 range. Mr. Tullos says he will list with you today for $240,000 but not one penny less. He has said, in effect, take it or leave it. What do you do now?

TECHNOLOGY *IN ACTION*

A good source of information for real estate professionals today is at http://www.census.gov. This site allows you to drill down to your own particular county and city for facts and figures about your local market.

Visit http://www.census.gov and go to your city on the Web site.

What's the population for your city?

Has your city experienced an increase or decrease since the 2000 census?

Personal Management

Key Terms

- BIKE approach
- Goal chart
- Goal setting
- Personal motivation
- Time management

Self-Discipline

Real estate salespeople must exercise high levels of self-discipline to be successful. A lack of personal management is the downfall of many potentially fine agents. This chapter explores three important areas of self-management: personal motivation, time management, and goal setting. Although complete books have been written on each of these topics, this chapter provides only an overview and reviews a few basic skills needed in each area.

Personal Motivaton

The real estate business can be compared with a roller coaster. When sales are climbing and commissions are rolling in, the agent experiences extreme satisfaction, and the excitement is breathtaking. When transactions fall apart through no fault of the agent, when mortgage money is unavailable, or every person canvassed "has a friend in the business," the business can be discouraging. No amount of training or good management can shield you from these possibilities. Each individual must develop a method of coping with the slow times that all agents experience periodically.

Personal motivation is the internal force that gives direction toward the accomplishment of individual goals. If you accept this definition, you place the responsibility for being motivated squarely on your own shoulders. Certainly there are activities that give agents a boost occasionally. An exciting sales meeting, a dynamic speaker, or a good motivational tape recording will provide that shot in the arm that all agents need to re-energize. Those who are successful over the long term, however, will work on building their own internal generators to recharge their energy, rather than depending solely on "jumper cable boosts" from external sources. We all need a source to turn to for encouragement and support. Why not make that source the person closest to you—you!

Top salespeople have shared their techniques for keeping motivated. Some of these follow, including my own.

Keep Setbacks in Perspective

Setbacks, one or several, should be considered only in an overall analysis of productivity and career satisfaction. An agent with no dead transactions is an agent who is not taking any risks. "I failed with the Jones' sale" is a more sensible way to feel than is "I am a failure." Everybody makes mistakes. Learn from them and make improvements to prevent their recurrence.

Expect Problems and Attempt to Minimize Them

Salespeople are problem solvers. Their jobs were created to help people solve their real estate problems, which represent large amounts of money, considerable legal complexity, and usually several—and sometimes many—people. By anticipating some problems in the transaction and working hard to resolve them, you can decrease the drain on yourself and your motivation.

Remember Victories

When some successful agents are in a down cycle, they may take a break for a while and dwell on some of their good accomplishments. A mini break to review past achievements and re-create the positive feelings that accompanied them can be a refreshing stimulant. This is not to say you should concentrate on the past, but some reflection will help you succeed in the present and future.

A good way to remember the victories is to call on past clients you were able to help. If you are new to real estate and don't have any successes yet, call a satisfied customer of the company. Reviewing the professional service provided will give you a lift, and this is also an excellent prospecting method.

Give Yourself Some Time Away

With all the demands placed on the real estate salesperson, you need to get away from work on a regular basis. Burnout is a common problem in many professions, and real estate is no exception. For a long-term, successful career, you owe it to yourself, and those you care for, to pace yourself. Leisure time with friends and family, hobbies, and outside interests all help to maintain a well-rounded attitude and preserve much-needed relationships for overall satisfaction with life. Winning the sale and losing a treasured friend or family member is *no victory*.

The BIKE Approach

At some time in our lives, most everyone has owned a bicycle. This vehicle carried you toward your destination, but only when you were willing to supply the leg power to use it. Like that bike, there is a technique you can use for personal motivation to carry you forward toward your goals, using your own power. The **BIKE approach** is an acronym for this excellent approach to personal motivation.

B stands for belief. Believe first in yourself. There are enough critics in this world; don't be one yourself. Learn to be your own cheerleader. You need to know you are competent and qualified to project self-confidence. Also believe in the service you offer. Your clients would not do nearly as well without you. The training, knowledge, and experience you bring with you provide a valuable service. Belief in your company is also necessary. The organization you represent should lend you credence and strength, and you should feel proud of your association with the firm. When you start wondering if you are with the right company, a potential problem is arising. Go ahead and resolve that question by talking it out with your manager, checking out other companies, making a move, or doing whatever you feel is best. A lack of belief in any of these areas can be like a slow-acting poison that will kill your motivation.

I stands for involvement. Staying busy is a good way of keeping motivation high. If you lose a sale or blow an opportunity, don't sit around and dwell on it. If you spend too much time on minor disappointments, they tend to grow larger and drain your motivation.

Sooner or later, all salespeople experience that first setback. Too many tend to become overly careful and hesitant afterwards. Don't "wait yourself out of business." Everyone makes mistakes; beware of being too cautious, however, as caution can decrease your motivation and performance. After all, if you don't try, you have failed by default.

K stands for knowledge. A dynamic industry such as real estate demands that you keep up-to-date to be successful. Some type of planned, consistent updating improves your confidence level and helps your motivation. Remember that school never ends for the pro.

TECHNOLOGY *IN ACTION*

An excellent opportunity for real estate professionals to further their learning today is through real estate educational courses. For a list of real estate agent course offerings, visit http://www.coursecalendar.com. Hewlett-Packard offers free online courses on how to use technology and software at http://h30187.www3.hp.com. Agents can take specific classes geared at the real estate industry and learn new ways to enhance their real estate career. You can also visit http://www.hp.com and search for online learning.

List two types of real estate courses a real estate agent can find from the http://www.coursecalendar.com Web site.

Provide one course title targeted for real estate professionals at the HP web site.

Make a commitment to yourself and your profession to invest some time in furthering your knowledge of the business. Whether you choose courses, reading, seminars, or other means of education, continued development is critical to your long-range success in the field.

Some states have continuing educational requirements. If you have fulfilled these, don't stop at the minimum. Work on a professional designation, investigate a new facet of real estate or help develop a new course or training program. The more you know, the more you realize how little you know. Years ago, one of my first prospects told me I was a nice young man but he did not want me to "practice on him." What he failed to see and what I did not yet realize was that we never stop learning, growing, evolving, and developing. Remember, there is no crime in not knowing everything. The real crime is in not trying to know as much as you can.

E stands for enthusiasm. The excitement and eagerness of a successful person is demonstrated in different ways. Some people maintain a low profile but a high degree of enthusiasm. Others are obviously interested in their work. The common element, regardless of individual style, is enthusiasm about career and self. Think about it for a minute. Aren't the successful people you know in all walks of life consistent in their enthusiasm? A person is not successful and *then* enthusiastic. The reverse is true. Enthusiasm leads to success. Next time you are low on motivation, review these ideas. They can help get you up where you should be. Your buyers and sellers expect and deserve your highest level of motivation.

Time Management

Real estate sales is a hectic way to make a living (a shock to many people who enter the business). Successful **time management** is a vital aspect of personal management. Your time is your life, and how well you use it will show how you live your life. For real estate people, time is one of two things they can offer their buyers and sellers. Knowledge is the other, which is discussed in Chapter 5. The more successful you become in real estate, the busier you will be and the more you will need to manage your time. Failure to do so can limit your growth in the business.

Guidelines to Improve Time Management

Time is an asset that you need to invest to bring the greatest possible return since you can never recover it once it has been spent. If you set up a plan to use your time better, what should you do?

Analyze Current Time Use

Before you can effectively plan for improvement, you need to examine how you currently use your time. A brutally honest evaluation of current time management (or mismanagement) is the starting point. If you analyze your schedule for one week, several common weaknesses may surface. Before addressing the five common weaknesses discussed next, remember to focus on what you are doing properly. Keep those areas of strength and proper management firmly in place, and then concentrate on the less effective areas.

Distractions. These are things that get in the way of good time management, such as television, a hobby, magazines, or some gadget that entertains you. These things are distractions when you allow them to keep you from doing what you should be doing. Remove as many as you can from your work area, and you may find your time is being used more profitably. If you cannot remove the distraction, then remove yourself from it.

People Users. Some people in your life probably get in the way of good time management. The office associate who encourages you to take long coffee breaks and tells endless jokes or war stories is a prime example. So are family members who expect you to always schedule your work world around their needs. Poorly qualified prospects also fall into this category. Be on the lookout for people who needlessly use up your time. Avoid them or tactfully explain that you need to put your time to more productive use. Don't feel guilty about this; after all, it's your time and your life. Learning to say no without guilt is a very important time management factor. Some persons in your life will, through flattery, guilt, or intimidation, try to test your resolve. Stick to your guns and become more effective in your control.

Inaccuracy. Doing just enough to get by is a common practice of poor time managers. More time is spent unsnarling the mistakes and correcting sloppy, incomplete work than it takes to do the job correctly in the first place. Remember, if it's worth doing over, it's worth doing right the first time. This is good advice for those of you who may hate to follow through with the paperwork or the less pleasant tasks necessary to complete a transaction smoothly.

Procrastination. One common time management weakness is the habit of putting things off. You can easily wait yourself right out of the real estate business. Doing the things you like to do and doing the things you should do are not always the same. A sales manager I know has a card printed with the motto *Do It Now; Don't Just Talk about It*. Whenever he hears an agent talking about putting important things off, he hands him or her the card. It sounds simple, but it can certainly alleviate a problem if you are willing to follow through with the advice.

Rationalization. This weakness goes hand in hand with procrastination. Rationalization can wreck time management plans. Once time is wasted by putting something off, you can lose more time by justifying the inactivity. These two nonactivities feed off each other, mutually weakening and tearing down a salesperson's precarious scheduling. Another helpful motto to consider when dealing with rationalization is *Substitute Action for Explanation*.

As you study how you are using your time currently, other weaknesses will become apparent. Take a good look at the problem areas you discover, take steps to rectify them, and start getting control of your time.

Decide How You Want to Use Time

For effective time management, it is critical that you establish priorities. Priorities are directly related to goal setting, which will be discussed later in this chapter. One effective method of setting priorities is to make a list of everything that needs to done, and then break the list down into three divisions: the "have to's," the "nice to's, "and the "leftovers."

The "Have To's." These items are activities that relate to appointments, deadlines that have to be met, and other obligations. They demand first priority, and every effort must be made to complete or change them. If you don't have enough time to finish the "have to's," then don't spend any time on the less important things. Keep the list flexible enough to accommodate emergencies and surprises. You may feel that you encounter surprises and emergencies every day. If that is true, your time is managing you instead of the other way around.

One harried student at a seminar I conducted on time management told me her whole life seemed to be one "brush fire" after another. My counsel to her was to get a degree in fire science and become a fire fighter! An alternative, I quickly added, was to learn to manage her schedule so that most tasks and responsibilities were attended to long before the crisis level was reached.

Some people are at their best early in the day, and others get started later and are more alert and efficient in the afternoon. Determine what time is your most productive, and attempt to schedule your "have to's" then. Respect the "have to's" and give them the attention they deserve. Remember that a daily "have to" should be time to plan for tomorrow.

The "Nice To's." This list of activities ranks second; the activities would be nice to do but they don't have to be done today. Surely some of today's "nice to's" may be tomorrow's "have to's," but your planning for tomorrow will reflect that change. Spend time on this area only when you cannot work on the "have to's" or when they have all been completed. No one else should determine consistently which activities belong in which category. If that happens, you are letting someone else set your priorities and, consequently, manage your time. Priority setting may seem difficult at first, but it's necessary if you use time management successfully. Remember to address what is best or most important versus what is easiest or fun when deciding "have to's" and "nice to's."

The "Leftovers." Don't overlook the leftovers. Does your day have bits and pieces consisting of a few spare minutes here and there? What do you do with this free time? If you put all this time together, it would be easy to work with, but that is impossible. Don't overlook its importance, though. By being aware that these brief breathers exist and using them to your advantage, you can accomplish more. You may not be able to complete a project in the spare minutes, but by the end of the day you may be able to complete one more task. The bottom line of effective time management is getting more things done in less time and working more efficiently rather than just harder.

The Peter-Paul Problem. An effective time management system must have some flexibility built into it. If not, you will find it necessary to borrow time from one project to complete another, and if this becomes the rule instead of the exception, your system will fail.

Discipline yourself to determine accurately the time needed to complete a project, and then get the job done in the time allotted. Expertise will come with experience, but it will prevent you from having to "rob Peter to pay Paul," and you will find your entire procedure working more effectively.

Have you ever heard of Parkinson's Law? It says that a task will expand to fill the time allocated. There is real merit in setting a deadline and *meeting* it even if no one else expects you to. This will eliminate the need for crisis management and taking time away from other important tasks.

Wasteful Worrying. Do you know any dedicated worriers? These people invest time and energy being concerned with a lot of "what ifs." In real estate sales, this behavior is destructive. So many things can potentially go wrong. Some concern can be constructive, but dwelling on a situation that is out of your control is a waste of time. To worry if the home will appraise out or people will qualify *after* the contract is signed serves little purpose. Spend your time on things you can do something about now. Too much fear and worry can be immobilizing and prevent you from doing the things necessary for success.

Goal Setting

Most people in real estate sales worked in other fields before entering the business and had supervisors who gave more direct guidance than is usual in real estate. This lack of control can be a real problem for some. Being left on your own is a double-edged sword. On one hand, you are free to exercise judgment and practice flexibility. But with this freedom comes added responsibility for your own actions and successes. This personal responsibility makes goal setting an important part of personal management. There are many reasons for **goal setting**, but two are prominent: (1) to help match actual progress with desired progress, and (2) to keep you informed on where you stand and how you are doing. We all have goals of one kind or another. We need to establish and use some effective guidelines when setting our goals to increase the chance of reaching the targets. Following are some guidelines.

Goals Must Be Personal

Don't allow other people to help you set your goals. This is the most important guideline. You must be committed to a goal to reach it. Family, sales managers, brokers, and other associates may have definite opinions about what is best for you, but the goals are yours. *You* must set goals for yourself to persistently and consistently attain them. Assuming the authority to set your own goals is not selfish or self-centered but rather self-respecting.

Goals Must Be in Writing

Once you know your goals, commit them to paper. This eliminates the possibility of forgetting (intentionally or unintentionally) exactly what you hope to attain. Many people write their goals on index cards and carry them as reminders and reinforcement. Others put them in a conspicuous place where they can see them often to serve as reminders. One of my psychology friends says you need to "ink it to think it."

Goals Must Be Flexible and Subject to Review

The things you hope to accomplish may not necessarily be etched in stone. Many factors that you cannot control affect your goals. If interest rates double or if your area's major industry suddenly fails, your real estate sales will reflect this downturn. This may not happen to you, but it's an example of why your goals need some give and take built into them. They also need to be reviewed for continued appropriateness. Yearly goals may need revision on a quarterly basis, and quarterly ones may need revision on a monthly basis. This review allows goals to change as soon as outside factors become evident. Change for the sake of change serves no purpose, but refusing to alter plans when you need to can be self-defeating.

Goals Must Be Measurable

When planning for the future, avoid stating your goals in broad generalities. "I'm going to work harder," "I'm going to become more successful," or "I'm going to do better for myself, my family, and my clients" all sound great, but where is the **goal chart** or yardstick to measure the accomplishment involved? In real estate selling, you can measure success by dollars earned, volume of sales, or units sold. In the example here (Figure 4.1), the four divisions are listings, listings sold, sales, and people seen. A space is provided for both the goal and the actual accomplishment.

Figure 4.1	Quarterly Goal Chart			
	Listings Taken	Listings Sold	Sales Made	People Contacted
January				
Goal	2	1	2	30
Actual	2	1	1	33
February				
Goal	2	2	3	30
Actual	1	1	2	20
March				
Goal	3	2	2	30
Actual	2	0	1	26
TOTALS				
Goal	7	5	7	90
Actual	2	1	1	33
Variance	(−2)	(−3)	(−3)	(−11)

The example is prepared on a monthly basis but could easily be broken down to a weekly basis. The first three divisions are not unique. Using a goal for the number of persons contacted will help you to include time for prospecting on a consistent basis.

The reason for the agent's failure in this example is not our concern here. Maybe the goals were poorly planned or the agent was not devoting adequate time to working toward them. Regardless, using goal charts can help agents see where they are and how their present position compares to their desired one.

Challenging Yet Realistic Goals

Correct goal setting recognizes the need for growth. Consequently, an effective goal is challenging. No purpose is served by setting goals that are sure things. Agents cannot know their real abilities until they stretch the limits. Set marks that will cause real personal satisfaction if you attain them.

Goals, however, should not be impossible. Overenthusiasm and overconfidence can cause you to incorrectly estimate what is realistic. A goal that is set too high can cause disappointment and frustration, and neither of these encourages effective personal management. A fine line exists between challenge and self-satisfaction. This is the reason for revising goals as necessary.

The single most important asset salespeople have is *themselves.* Motivation, goal setting, and time management require discipline on the part of the individual. The suggestions, techniques, and ideas presented here are not all original or complete. However, they are basic and effective. Adapt them to fit your individual needs and better personal management will be your result.

TECHNOLOGY *IN ACTION*

If you're interested in a Web-based approach to goal setting, visit http://www.goalsunlimited.com and learn how you can store, review, and post your goals online. *What types of goals should new real estate agents set for themselves during their first year in the business?*

Summary

To be successful, a salesperson must exercise a high degree of *self-discipline*. Such behavior should include personal motivation, time management, and goal setting. *Personal motivation* is the internal force that gives a person direction toward the accomplishment of goals. This can be achieved by keeping setbacks in perspective, expecting and attempting to minimize problems, remembering victories, and adhering to the BIKE approach: belief, involvement, knowledge, and enthusiasm.

A salesperson can make use of efficient *time management* by analyzing his or her use of time, deciding how time should be spent, and steering clear of tempting distractions: people users, inaccuracy, procrastination, and rationalization.

Because of the personal freedom and lack of direct supervision involved in the business, *goal setting* is of utmost importance to the real estate salesperson. Such goals must be personal, in writing, flexible, subject to review, measurable, and challenging yet realistic.

Review Questions

1. Why is the exercise of self-discipline and personal management important to real estate salespeople?

2. What is personal motivation?

3. Where does the responsibility for personal motivation lie?

4. What are four good techniques to keep yourself motivated?

5. What is the BIKE approach?

6. What are ten guidelines for better time management?

7. What are five guidelines for effective goal setting?

8. Can you describe the salesperson's single most important asset?

Discussion Questions

1. How do you go about overcoming "down" periods?

2. What are your weaknesses in managing your time? How might they be improved?

3. What are your goals? How does your goal setting compare with the guidelines in the chapter?

4. Why is procrastination such a common practice? How can you overcome this problem?

Situation

Assessing Time Management

Sarah is a moderately successful salesperson. She knows one of her major problems is lack of effective time management. Figure 4.2 shows her schedule for tomorrow. What suggestions can you make for improvement?

Sarah's Daily Schedule	Figure 4.2

Appointments	Memoranda
8:00	
8:30	
9:00	
9:30	
10:00 Sales meeting	
10:30	
11:00	
11:30 Lunch w/ Barbara Kay	Tennis Club
12:00	
12:30	
1:00	
1:30 Shopping for Groceries	Get Tom's Dry Cleaning
2:00 Meet Mrs. Jones	Check for key to new Listing
2:30 Meet Mr. Kukland	Check on his loan balance
3:00	
3:30	
4:00	
4:30 Meet Mrs. Starr	
5:00	
5:30	
6:00 Supper with Tom	menus?

TECHNOLOGY *IN ACTION*

Real estate professionals need to make sure their time management skills are used properly and efficiently on a day-to-day basis. A daily goal sheet planner is a good way to record your daily duties and to make sure your activities and work will maximize your profits for your real estate career.

Daily Schedule

Appointments	Memoranda
8:00	
8:30	
9:00	
9:30	
10:00	
10:30	
11:00	
11:30	
12:00	
12:30	
1:00	
1:30	
2:00	
2:30	
3:00	
3:30	
4:00	
4:30	
5:00	
5:30	
6:00	

PART II

THE MARKETING STAGE—PUTTING YOUR KNOWLEDGE TO WORK

Developing a Prospecting System

Key Terms

- Center of Influence (COI)
- Expired listing
- Farming
- FSBOs
- Leads
- Open houses
- Prospects
- Prospecting
- Referrals
- Suspect

Applying Your Knowledge

Earlier chapters provided you with an overview of marketing and sales. You also have some good ideas on how to prepare for the specific role of a real estate salesperson. Now it's time to apply your knowledge to the important phase of prospecting.

Two of the most important qualities any successful real estate salesperson has are a knowledge of the marketplace and a workable method of gaining exposure. This chapter will introduce you to some ideas on how to gain this exposure. You'll learn what prospecting is, why it is important, and how to use some proven prospecting techniques.

Suspect or Prospect?

Imagine that Suisan Espinoza comes to an agent and says, "I have a friend named Dr. Robert Zeigler who needs to sell his home. He is moving to another city to accept a job transfer. Bob lives near your office and wants to sell his home by the end of next month. Why don't you contact Bob and tell him I recommended you?"

Now imagine another situation. Becky Fowler comes to the agent and says, "I heard that one of the guys at work is being transferred. I'm not sure of his first name, but his last name is Zeigler. I don't know where he lives or when he needs to leave, but you might call him. And by the way, please don't use my name."

Is there a difference in the two situations? You bet there is! In the first, the agent has a reasonably clear idea of the person's needs. In the second, the agent has little, if any, accurate information. The two situations are presented here to show the difference between a prospect and a suspect. A **prospect** is someone the agent has *determined* has need of professional real estate services. A **suspect** is someone that *may* be in need of a real estate agent's services. The difference is that the agent knows something definite about Robert Zeigler in the first example and something definite about his real estate-related needs.

Just because an agent has qualified Dr. Zeigler as a prospect does not guarantee that he will become a satisfied client; the agent may be unable to help him. The chances of helping him are much greater, however, than if he were only a suspect.

How Prospecting Works

Prospecting is a planned method of gaining positive exposure to people in need of the services of a real estate professional. This definition implies certain key ideas. First, it suggests that an agent must have a well-planned method for prospecting. Prospecting is just as essential to the salesperson's success as the telephone, car, computer, or business card. Second, the definition suggests the need not only for exposure but also for the correct kind of exposure to the right people. Of course, the right people are those who need what *you* have to offer, professional real estate marketing services.

Many potential and active agents maintain that their greatest concern about real estate is the inconsistency of business. The "boom or bust" cycle of activity is a danger to the individual agent just as it is to the branch office, the company, and the profession in general. By establishing a means of continuously coming into contact with new people, the salesperson can decrease the chances of running out of prospects. Common sense tells you that it's important to prospect, but you must understand how extremely important it is. In fact, for the vast majority of getting started, as well as staying started salespeople, effective prospecting is essential to their success.

Developing a System

A common opinion regarding how to make business contact has emerged from my reading, as well as from my discussions with individual agents and entire sales forces. My personal experience as a salesperson substantiates the same finding: *For salespeople to be successful, they must develop a prospecting system.* If you reject or forget everything else in this chapter, remember this point. Never depend on anything or anyone but yourself to ensure your growth and advancement in real estate. This does not mean agents never receive help from friends, fellow salespeople, their manager or broker, and many others. Even with help, salespeople will not grow and stay in the business without initiative of their own. Therefore, an agent must not only work hard but also work effectively at developing a successful prospecting system.

The business derived from call-ins and walk-ins, and from other situations in which an agent does not really work at getting the lead, must be considered "gravy" business.

No one can build a sales career on such luck and good fortune. Don't feel guilty for the few deals that will fall into your lap. But see them for what they are. I've sold ranches to people that I did not meet until closing, and I've sold a few places I never even saw. In more than 30 years of practicing real estate, however, that's only happened a few times. Those type of sales are so atypical that they are considered "freaks" in the business.

Because you can't rely on those types of sales, you need to set up a prospecting system. We will examine some of the techniques that have proven successful.

The Satisfied Customer

As mentioned before, satisfied clients represent an excellent source of additional business. They are probably *the best* of the resources available. Many good agents work almost exclusively from **referrals**, or recommendations from clients to their friends and associates. One idea is to request letters of recommendation from clients. Another way to use this excellent source is to ask buyers and sellers for recommendations to their contacts. There is no better advertising in the world than word-of-mouth from satisfied customers. If the agent doesn't ask for it, the client may forget to recommend him or her when the opportunity arises. Also remember to reinforce the positive relationship established with customers by continuing to contact them on a regular basis.

As a getting started salesperson, this concept can still apply. Although this is the Satisfied Customers group, the people don't have to be satisfied with you in real estate to be prospects. Positive relationships built in other aspects of your life are still key contacts to jump-start your real estate sales career.

Centers of Influence

Many agents frequently hear the statement, "It's not *what* you know but *who* you know that makes you successful." Individuals who express this view have a valid point. Sometimes the remark may be used negatively to downplay the success of another person. Less successful agents may say it about the Salesperson of the Year to compensate

TECHNOLOGY *IN ACTION*

Consider using a digital audio recorder and having your clients make a quick statement about you and your firm and how pleased they were with your service. Then upload this mini-commercial to your Web site or incorporate it with a PowerPoint presentation so others can hear the positive words your satisfied customers have to say about you.

for not claiming the honor themselves. But in a positive sense, the statement means that knowing the right people definitely can help a salesperson, and positive results can come from establishing contacts in the right places. This is what the concept of Centers of Influence is all about.

A **Center of Influence** (COI) refers to a person who, over a period of time, can provide prospects for salespeople. Think about the concept for a moment. Agents cannot depend on others for all prospects, but certainly it's smart to obtain help from any source available. If a group of individuals can provide support for your sales volume and productivity, then certainly you should seek the group out.

Potential COIs

Agents often have questions about using COIs. "Who are these people?", "How can I approach them?", and "Why should they help me?" are legitimate inquiries. Many of the people agents come in contact with during the day can become COIs. Think about who you know that just might qualify. Some examples are

Medical
- Family doctor and medical office staff
- Family dentist
- Pharmacist
- Staff at local hospital
- Human resource people at local medical schools

Business
- The people at the bank, finance company, or credit union, including loan and trust officers and your favorite teller
- Insurance agents
- Personnel people at businesses in the market area
- Personnel agencies
- Moving and storage company employees
- Stockbroker; investment or estate planner

Education/Church-Related Contacts
- Faculty and administrators at all the local schools (preschools, elementary, junior high and high schools; community colleges, universities, adult programs, and community education programs)
- P.T.A. board and members
- Librarians
- Clergy and other church contacts

Merchants and Service Organizations
- Grocer
- Mechanic
- Service station operator
- Barber or hairdresser

- Department store employees
- Restaurant, hotel, and motel employees
- Airline and automobile rental and salespeople

Real Estate Related
- Title insurance company staff
- Home builders
- Remodeling contractors
- Electricians
- Plumbers
- Inspection service people
- Appraisers

This list could run to several pages with examples of contacts for salespeople. Use creativity to develop a plan to increase prospecting by using COIs.

How you approach these individuals depends somewhat on both your personality and theirs. Discussions with many successful salespeople have confirmed my feeling that what seems to work best is simply to tell any prospective COIs that you are now in real estate and you will do your best to help anyone they know who needs the service of a professional real estate salesperson. Without asking anything of the COIs, you have offered to help, which takes much of the obligation off both of you.

Some people you approach will reject your offer outright, now and forever. Others will be indifferent. But some will remember your offer to help and provide you with some **leads**, or suggestions of potential business. The lead may come in the immediate future (the exception rather than the rule), it may come next month or next year, but it will come if you continuously prospect. You cannot control how people will react to your offer to help, but if you don't ask the potential COIs for help, they probably won't volunteer it. Although agents cannot control COIs, they *can* control their own activities, and using COIs is an example of working hard *and* intelligently to expand prospecting spheres. The key is to ask consistently to be of quality service to the potential COI you meet.

Reasons COIs Offer Leads

Why would these people want to help the salesperson? There are several reasons. One reason is that the salesperson can help them. Remember that agents can easily become COIs themselves, in a modern adaptation of the barter system approach that has been effective for centuries. With all the information you know about your market area, you are in a position to refer business to someone who refers business to you, and that's a fair approach. Remember the old saying, "If you want a friend, then be a friend." You'll find it far easier to get leads from people if you are first willing to offer them something.

A second reason people will act as COIs is that it helps the people you're serving. If your grandmother's heirloom clock stopped running, you would take it to the best clock repair shop in town for repair. Naturally you want the best because it's your grandmother's treasure, not because the clock repairperson asked you for business. And it isn't necessarily because the repairperson can do anything for your business, but because it helps your grandmother. Similarly, one reason a COI will refer a third party to you is to help the third party. If you can guide the referred person through complex real estate transactions, everyone will be happy.

A third reason people will become COIs for you is simply because you asked them. You don't just walk up and say, "Would you please be my center of influence?" But by approaching key people and explaining your plan and purpose for asking, you may be pleasantly surprised at the positive response you receive. Remember, if you don't ask, they can't help. Ask regularly enough so that when they think of real estate, they think of you!

Whenever agents receive leads from COIs, it is important that they *always* follow up on the leads. Whatever the outcome, the agents must remember to thank COIs for their leads and inform them of the results. A short, handwritten note is effective, and anytime you can return the help, be sure to do so. Figures 5.1 and 5.2 are examples that can be adapted to individual situations. Keep in mind that the COI is not obligated to qualify the people for you. A lead is a lead, and we can never have too many of them in the long run.

COIs are not the only prospecting tool, but using them is definitely a proven means of increasing the agent's impact and influence to gain the exposure necessary for success.

Farming

Farming is a planned, systematic method of prospecting in a specific market area. Most of the material available on this topic is focused on sellers' listings. Keep in mind as you read this that you can also successfully farm for *buyers,* and the suggested steps are applicable to both sellers and buyers.

Choosing Your Farm

The initial step in a farming plan should be site selection. Establishing some boundaries and choosing an area are important considerations. What determines a "good" farm? One factor definitely is activity. The area must have sufficient turnover to justify the time an agent spends working there. Nearly all communities have areas that are highly popular. These are logical farm areas *if* some selling is taking place. Just the existence of

TECHNOLOGY *IN ACTION*

If you use blank postcards with your computer and printer, consider using a "handwritten" font to send your thank you notes. This adds a special touch to your correspondence. You can also use online programs such as http://www.touchpointmail.com to send cards and notes with handwritten fonts to clients and customers.

Mr and Mrs. Burnell Gates

G4 Ranch

Dear Burnell and Laura:

Thank you so much for referring Butch and Vernell Walker to me. We met last weekend and it does appear that there is a way for me to find them a property that will satisfy their needs. We will be looking at some hopefully suitable properties in the next few days. I will keep you informed of our progress. I appreciate your confidence in me and I promise to strive hard to serve the Walkers and anyone else you might send me.

Sincerely,

Johnny Cavazos, REALTOR

Figure 5.1   A Follow-Up Note

Betty Rackley, CPA

1939 Bigfoot Road

Dear Betty:

I saw the attached article on new depreciation schedules for orchards and thought immediately of you. Since several of your clients are involved in this business, I thought it might be of some help to you. I hope things are going well for you and your family and that your business continues to thrive. If there is anything I can ever do to help your or your clients with a real estate matter, please don't hesitate to call upon me.

Respectfully,

Nell Bean, Sales Associate

Ray Bean Realty

Figure 5.2   Returning a Favor

One way to track market activity in a particular area is through a program such as Map Point. This software program allows data from an MLS® to be imported and then displayed visually on a map showing where the sold activity is taking place in your locale. Data can also be tracked manually by the agent if the local MLS® does not allow importing and exporting or if the agent wants to track FSBO transactions or sold property through offices that do not belong to the MLS®. You can learn more about Map Point at http://www.microsoft.com/mappoint.

people who want to buy in the area does the agent no good unless some people owning there want to sell. Investigate the turnover to see if there is enough business to make your efforts worthwhile.

You also should pick an area that you feel positive about. Farming takes physical effort and must be consistent to be successful. Salespeople must be sold on the areas they choose, or it becomes easy to slow down or quit. To decide between two or more areas when everything else is equal, choose the one in which you would prefer to invest.

Consider only the areas in which you feel comfortable working. Not only should you be sold on the areas, but you need to be able to relax and relate well to the people living in and attracted to your farm. Most real estate agents find that they do better with certain groups of people. The people buying and selling $160,000 properties have somewhat different viewpoints than those buying and selling properties valued at $1,000,000. You will quickly learn the markets you work best in, and then you can adapt as necessary.

Years ago, I spent two sleepless nights before showing a high-dollar luxury home. The people, new to Texas from New York, wanted to discuss the symphony, catering services, and fine wine and caviar sources in our city when I felt comfortable advising about good steak or barbecue places and where the great country-western bands played. Although I probably could have sold them a nice ranch, in the above setting, I was "out of my league." The point is to find your niche and work where you feel comfortable.

Another factor in selecting a farm is competition. If an area is *really* being farmed properly by another salesperson, stop and think before entering that market. There may be another, equally good place to farm, especially if the other salesperson already has a strong reputation established. Some neighborhoods will not have such an agent, but if there is one, remember it takes time to establish an effective farm system. It will take even longer if the competition is stiff and organized. The competition referred to here is legitimate effort by another salesperson and not idle talk of what should or could be done by "armchair" agents working their mouths in the office much more than their feet in the area. Some areas supposedly will be farmed when in fact little, if any, work is being done. This is a really important point to verify; knowing who is "walking the walk and not just talking the talk" can make a big difference in the time it will take for your successful impact in the area.

The final point to consider when selecting a farm is proximity. Generally, it's not wise for an agent to select a farm area that is far away from the office or home. The agent's impact will probably diminish the farther he or she moves away from the home base. Nor is it time-effective to try to farm too far from your base of operation.

Getting Acquainted with the Residents

The next step is information gathering. Agents should become experts on their farm areas. No one should know more about the areas than the farming salesperson. Establish a method of keeping an ongoing, up-to-date journal of community activity using the concepts discussed in earlier chapters. Gather this information from other agents, the listing service, owners, builders, and similar sources. Talk with anyone who has accurate information to share. In this step and the others that follow, be sure not to violate the Do Not Call Registry laws now in effect. Make sure you and your firm are well within the parameters of what is permissible.

Only then should agents make their first contacts with the people in the farm. The goal of this step is not to generate any business—although certainly do not turn down any that is offered! The purpose behind this initial contact is introduction, to get acquainted with some of the people in the selected area. Setting any higher goal than this would be unrealistic, because an agent will be a complete stranger to many of the contacts on this first call. Be sure not to carry a lot of material on these calls, because you don't want to give the impression that you are calling cold on the people to sell them something and because all your selling tools are too heavy and burdensome to carry. Certainly have your tools readily available in your car if you need them, but introduction is the only purpose of the initial call. You'll soon tire of making these contacts if you pack around a lot of important but (at this point) unnecessary material. You will appear as less of a threat to the homeowners if you arrive empty handed.

Practice what you plan to say on this first call before you actually make it. Remember to keep your presentation short and to the point. "Good morning. I'm Becky Fowler with Massad Realtors. I plan to be specializing in your neighborhood and am stopping by today to introduce myself to the homeowners (or businesses) in the area." The conversation that develops from this point depends on the reaction you get, but you are introduced to the person. You probably will not receive many warm receptions on these first calls. Most people will be polite but reserved; they may have heard this before. Often people have experienced one-time calls from agents supposedly specializing in an area who never called on them a second time. It's no wonder that that kind of "farming" does not pay off. This prospecting method will work, but only if you have a well-planned, consistent, long-range strategy. If your visit continues past your introduction, try to gather some information about the business or homeowner with whom you are talking. Carry a supply of index cards with you and as soon as you leave, write down the information or record it in your PC or Palm Pilot. However you do it, the key is to keep a separate record for each contact that will be an addition to your previous information, and they should be revised and updated after each future call. You may refer to the examples in this chapter.

Strengthening Contacts

The next step in the farming plan is reinforcement. The first contact was for introduction; now reinforce the positive aspects of the visit. A short card mailed a couple of days after a visit accomplishes this. Review the following examples:

Dear Mr. Mackey

Thank you for letting me visit with you in your home (business, office) on Tuesday. I plan to work hard in our community and stand ready to be of service to you or anyone you may know who needs professional real estate help.

Dear Mrs. Andrews:

I appreciated the opportunity to meet you last Saturday and to introduce myself and my company's services. I plan to become an area expert in your neighborhood and will look forward to helping your family or anyone you might know who needs a professional real estate agent.

Some agents prefer to write an introductory letter before they make their first call. This is a good idea as long as you remember *you are wasting your money unless you follow up with a personal contact.* In this business, there is no substitute for personal communication. For some consumers, an e-mail may work just as effectively as a phone call or face-to-face visit. The technique may vary, but the strategy is the same. Reinforcement is the goal.

After sending a follow-up note, maintain continuing contact with members of the farm on a regular schedule. The goal for these continuing calls should be to update information and to build agent preference—to get past introductions—and reinforce to the point where when the owners think real estate, they think of you. This is accomplished only by bringing you and what you have to offer to their attention. Giving prospective clients small, useful gifts is a good strategy. Flyswatters, calendars, pens, updated street maps, and potholders are good examples. Let the technology available to you, along with your own imagination, set the standard. Agents have found that a neighborhood newsletter can be successful, especially if it includes information on the real estate climate. Whether you are sharing details on vacancy rates to commercial contacts, agricultural commodity prices to farmers and ranchers, or changes in homeowner's insurance laws to residences, the key is to have something beneficial and relevant to the contact person. One of our favorite gifts, especially for new people in our area, has been a magnet for the refrigerator or cabinet with emergency numbers such as fire, police, and other hotline numbers. How often should farmers contact people? What size should a farm be? These are relative questions. Start small and build slowly but consistently within a set period of time (weeks and months). Set a goal of contacting, say, 25 homeowners or businesses in the market area each month. As you make each call, practice and review your approach. Build your base until it is all you can adequately handle. Do not set an initial goal so high that it appears impossible to reach, or you will be tempted to scratch the whole project. Plan to contact the people in your farm at least 4 times a

Figure 5.3	Farming Checklist

A. Site Selection

1. Activity assessment—Is it economically practical to invest my efforts in this market?
2. Comfort zone—Do I feel good about working here? Am I sold on the area?
3. Proximity—Is the farm close enough to my home/office so I won't spend too much time in travel?
4. Competition—Do any other salespeople actively work this area? How effective are they?

B. Research in Area

1. Do I know enough about my farm to discuss it professionally with a potential buyer or seller?
2. Where can I get more information?

C. Introduction

1. Do I have a prepared greeting?
2. Do I have the appropriate material to carry?

D. Follow Up

1. How will I reinforce my first contact?
2. What information did I learn that should be recorded?

E. Continued Calls

1. How can I learn more about the people in my farm?
2. What plan do I have for keeping in touch on a regular basis?

year; I think more than 12 times a year is too often, as it dilutes your impact. Besides, you don't want to become a pest! A contact can be a note, a newsletter, a phone call, an e-mail, or a useful gift, as well as a visit, but at least half the contacts with any one person should be personal contacts. You may want the face-to-face contact during good weather and the others during severe weather times of the year.

There is a fine line between being persistent and being pushy. Try not to step over that line. A farm plan must be flexible enough to adapt to the individuals in the area. Refer to the farming checklist in Figure 5.3 as a beginning to your plan. You have to fine-tune according to what works for you, but remember to plan your work carefully and then diligently work your plan.

For Sale By Owners and Expired Listings

Another prospecting method centers on contacting sellers that have already demonstrated a desire to sell. This is reflected in the For Sale By Owner (**FSBOs**) signs and ads you see in most marketplaces. These property owners are clearly interested in selling. The same can be said for owners of expired listings. When you make contact, there are some things to keep in mind. Some ideas for each situation are presented next.

For Sale By Owner

There are several schools of thought on how to approach and work with a FSBO. My own preference is to contact the individual with two objectives: (1) to find out about the property, and (2) to offer some help to the owner.

The first objective has two purposes of its own: (1) If the property is in my target area, I need to know the details about the property to keep current (refer to Chapter 3, "Defining Your Marketplace," to be reminded that *all* area activity also includes sales where real estate people are not involved); and (2) knowing about the property, it's easier to determine whether the listing is worth pursuing. Some listings are best for you when they are held by your competition. These are the ones that have owners with unrealistic expectations.

The second objective goes back to the concept of professionalism. If a professional can help meet your needs and therefore meet his or her own needs, well and good, but the key is being of service. By offering the FSBO information about current values, reviewing the activities necessary to actually finalize a transaction, indicating and even offering samples of the documents to be prepared and signed, and all the other tasks that must be done, you are creating owner awareness. Some critics may feel this is giving away too much. I suggest it is exactly the opposite, because you can help the owner see how complex a sale can be and how important a role the agent can play. Some owners will use the knowledge and succeed in a sale of their own. But more will appreciate your concern for their well-being, which is the cornerstone of a good relationship with the seller. Two suggestions to consider: (1) be encouraging of the owner's efforts to sell alone, and (2) volunteer to be a resource for them and *regularly* check back until the property sells or is listed. The outcome of such a strategy is that the seller does not feel "defeated" if he or she can't sell alone; and further, there is no risk of an I-told-you-so problem. This doesn't mean you should be passive and wait. Contact sellers *immediately* after you learn of their efforts to sell, and then stay in touch, being persistent but always pleasant and positive in your contacts. Don't fall into the trap of being a continual "pro bono" professional for them, and certainly don't exceed your role by offering complex legal or tax advice. Remember, consumers have every right to sell their own property. Of course, they also can repair their own vehicles, prepare their own IRS documents, and maybe can even perform their own surgery! But most folks need help with some or all of that. Be proud of what you can do for the typical consumer, but not conceited that they *must* use your services. Offer in a professional and polite manner and then see what happens.

Expired Listings

A similar strategy works with **expired listings.** These are properties that have been listed for sale by another agent and did not sell. An important initial part of working expired listings involves verifying that the agreement between the seller and other agent is actually terminated. If another company has an exclusive listing still in effect, in most cases, you won't be able to discuss it.

If that is resolved, however, contact the seller with the same two objectives in mind as you have for the FSBO. An updated market analysis to use as a focal point in your discussion might be helpful. Also a review by the owner on handling of affairs by the first agent might provide you with some insight on the seller's perceptions and personality. For your part, avoid any criticism of the other company or salespersons involved. Remember, you don't raise yourself and your company by dragging others down.

Many factors can result in a property not selling. Usually the reasons given are poor agent effort or overpricing, but others are also important. Local supply and demand of similar real estate, general economic environment, availability of mortgages, arrangement of financial terms of sale, title or property condition issues, and general owner cooperation all can be significant to the successful sale. All expired listings are not automatically worth relisting, but you should investigate those in your area *promptly* to see if you want to pursue them further.

Open House

An effective way of prospecting can be the use of the **open house.** Potential buyers and sellers come to see what is available to purchase or evaluate possible competition for their own sales. Most companies have a defined game plan for holding an open house. Investigate and discuss those in your office. Our focus here is on the prospecting aspect. My suggestion is a combination of direct mail through flyers and face-to-face contact to promote the open house and prospect at the same time.

Direct mail, or if you prefer, hand-delivered fliers, can be used for a broad area, from the streets surrounding the property to a whole general neighborhood. Personal contact comes in the immediate area, such as the nearest 25 neighbors. A short, simple invitation stating the address and time of the open house is sufficient. Be sure to include your name plus your company's name and number on the flyer or mailer. Specific details, including list price, are not advisable. Allow the "desire to know" to bring in people. Figure 5.4 is an example of the mailer suggested. At the open house, have a registry

---

Figure 5.4 / Flyer/Mailer

YOU'RE INVITED
To an OPEN HOUSE Sunday afternoon
March 28 from 2 P.M. until 6 P.M.
Please stop by and see this very attractive home.

25 ZANE STREET
Listing agent Angelica Gutierrez will be your
hostess and will be prepared to discuss the details
regarding this fine property.

The Brad Carroll Co. REALTORS®
733-2852

where people can give you their names, addresses, phone numbers, and comments about the property so you can follow up. You may want to ask if they would like advance notice if your firm lists other properties in the area. *Follow up* within a few days to see if you can be of service if they desire it. Don't press the issue if someone does not want to offer the requested information. Make sure you are aware of any regulations regarding agency disclosure that you must follow in an open house circumstance. In my business of ranches, we also hold "open ranch previews" for the agricultural practitioners in the area. Sometimes a salesperson or broker will actually bring buyers with them to see the property. Holding a barbeque with plenty of information packets about the ranch is usually a very good way to get the exposure we desire for a new listing. Be creative and use ideas that other segments of the industry are using to gain the advantage you are seeking.

Summary

For a real estate salesperson to become successful, he or she must develop a prospecting system. *Prospecting* is a planned method whereby a salesperson gains exposure to people who are in need of his or her services. Prospects can be generated from a variety of sources, such as satisfied customers and COIs.

The key to any prospecting technique is *consistency*. Although there is no one best method, it's very important to devise a means of generating business. Too many potentially fine agents keep "waiting for something to happen" and end up out of business. Prospecting enables the agent to *make* something happen!

In addition, a salesperson may develop prospects by *farming,* a systematic method of prospecting in a specific market area. After choosing the specific area to farm, the salesperson must get acquainted with the residents of the area, gather specific information about the area, and consistently reinforce initial contacts. For Sale By Owner properties, expired listings, and open houses are additional ways of prospecting. Very few real estate people develop a successful long-term career waiting for buyers and sellers to come to them. The salesperson must be willing to make the effort to prospect.

Review Questions

1. What are two important qualities any successful real estate person needs?

2. What is the difference between a suspect and a prospect?

3. What is prospecting?

4. How important is prospecting?

5. How can you help someone who is selling his or her own property?

6. What is a Center of Influence?

7. What are some examples of people who probably would make good COIs?

8. Why would COIs want to help you?

9. Whenever you receive a lead from a COI, what two things should be done?

10. Why would someone want to hold an open house?

11. What determines a good farm?

12. What are the steps in establishing a farm?

13. What should the purpose of the initial contact with people in your prospecting be?

14. Why is it important *not* to carry a lot of material with you on these initial calls?

15. What should you do after the initial visit with people in your farm, and why?

16. If it did not sell initially, why could an expired listing still be marketable?

17. How often should you contact people as part of your prospecting efforts?

Discussion Questions

1. What will you look for in your farm area?

2. Describe some additional prospecting techniques you feel would be successful. Why would they work?

3. Prospecting has been called a never-ending activity. Do you agree?

Situation

Starting Over with Prospecting

Agent Ariel Mackey has a problem. She has recently moved to your community after living in another state. Ariel has become licensed through your company and must now begin to sell real estate in an area where she is unknown. What advice can you give her about developing a prospecting system?

The Farming Plan

Cynthia Traylor lives in a small farming community about 30 minutes outside of a major metropolitan area. There is no dominant real estate company in the area. She has found the area very closed to her prospecting efforts because she is an "outsider," having lived there "only" four years and not being involved in agriculture. Short of moving, how can Cynthia develop a farm plan for the area?

Trends & ISSUES

One effective way to prospect a farm area is by direct mail. Visit the following Web sites:

- http://www.amazingmail.com
- http://www.expresscopy.com

Compare the two postcard vendors and explain which company you would use (and why) for a direct mail program as a new real estate agent working a farm in your locale.

What types of postcard themes would be good to use in a farm area for your market area? Storyboard an example on a separate piece of paper (or card stock/postcard size) of a direct mail piece you would like to send to a farm area in your marketplace.

The Listing Presentation

Key Terms

- Fair market value
- Listing agents
- Listing presentation kit
- Rider sign
- Shopworn property
- Showing agent

Listings

The prospecting methods described in Chapter 5 are designed to show you how to offer your service. In one type of situation, the opportunity will be with a potential seller, and you will describe your services by a listing presentation. A listing presentation is made by an agent to a prospective seller to obtain a contract to place the property on the market. An effective presentation results in more listings. The experienced salesperson with a strong listing record recognizes that a well-done presentation is not an accident—much time and effort are invested to increase the chance of success. This chapter reviews the importance of listings in real estate marketing. Guidelines are presented for preparing an effective listing presentation. The final section examines what should be included when developing a listing presentation kit.

The Importance of Listings

Often a young, inexperienced real estate salesperson is taken under the wing of a veteran agent with many years of success. One of the first things the experienced agent imparts to the newcomer is that "you can't sell what you haven't got." Never forget how important listings are to the success of most people in real estate sales. Developing a method of generating a consistent inventory of listings is essential for several reasons, as described next.

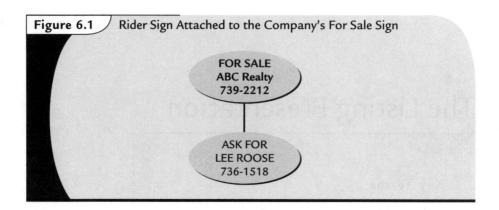

Figure 6.1 Rider Sign Attached to the Company's For Sale Sign

Exposure in a Marketplace

When an agent takes a listing and puts up a For Sale sign, the neighborhood residents will quickly know about it. Whether the property is residential, agricultural, or commercial, the point is the same: It's not uncommon to put up a sign, return to the office, and find someone has already called about it. So the listing agent must have the necessary information in the office before the sign goes up. Regardless of whether the caller is sincerely interested or merely curious, the listing salesperson has made an impression. Many a successful lister will attach a separate **rider sign**, which lists the agent's name and home phone number, to the company sign. This increases the agent's personal exposure in the area. A sample rider sign is illustrated in Figure 6.1

Generating More Business

Exposure derived from listings yields another benefit. A knowledgeable salesperson will use a new listing as a reason to call on other property owners in the area. Next-door neighbors or people down the street may know somebody interested in investing in the vicinity. Or, if a neighborhood property owner sees the listing agent's success with the first property, a new listing may result. Either way, there is a possibility of more business. Figure 6.2 gives some examples of short notes to adapt and send to property owners located near a new listing to generate additional business. Remember to inform the people in the area when the listing sells and you have proven your ability. However, avoid giving the specific details of the sale. Several more listings and sales may result from the announcement of a successful transaction.

The Stability of a Listing

Few things are certain in real estate sales. However, one stable aspect of a salesperson's business is a listing. There should, of course, be a listing contract between the seller and listing company. This legally binding contract will provide some assurance to the

Dear Mrs. Hardy:

I recently listed the Johnson home located at 734 Craigridge and felt you might know someone who would be interested in it. If I may provide you or anyone else information on the listing, please contact me.

Sincerely,

Lee Roose
ABC Realtors 739-2222

Home Phone 736-1518

Dear Homeowner:

It has been my company's privilege to list the home located at 734 Craigridge. You may know someone interested in obtaining some information on this property. If so, please have them give me a call.

Thank you,

Lee Roose
ABC Realtors 739-2222

Home Phone 736-1518

Figure 6.2   Sample Notes to Property Owners Near Listing

salesperson who is working hard to sell the property. In the legal relationship established in the listing contract, the seller becomes a client in the principal-agent concept; sometimes this is known as a fiduciary relationship.

Other People Working for the Agent

Many successful **listing agents** feel this reason is most important for methodically generating a listing inventory. Each time someone shows the listing, the potential buyer and **showing agent** are working with the listing agent to sell the property. In many cases, the lister may not even be at the showing. It is reassuring, as well as smart, for salespeople to go about their schedules knowing that several other people are working hard to help sell the property. After another salesperson actually does produce a buyer, the listing agent likely will be given credit in the area for making the sale.

Guidelines for Making a Listing Presentation

Knowing that listings are important to success is not the same as knowing how to obtain them. Each salesperson will make a unique listing presentation; however, some basic guidelines are common to most well-developed presentations. You may need to go about your listing presentation in two stages. The first is to actually inspect the property, gathering information about extensions, existing loans, seller motivations, and so on. The second stage is the actual presentation. In some cases, what you present will be based on the first visit. The circumstances will vary depending on the specific property, but don't be afraid to break these steps up into more than one contact with the seller to make the best, most professional presentation possible. Figure 6.3 is one way of seeing these tasks in a flow chart format.

Plan for the Presentation

As pointed out earlier, the successful listing agent knows that an effective presentation is not accomplished by accident. Time and effort are invested in the development of one that is truly professional. The information used in the presentation must be current. It is imperative to have up-to-date and accurate data on the area activity. A CMA will provide the necessary information.

Use the CMA
The competitive market analysis (CMA), described in Chapter 4, provides a solid negotiating tool to help the seller determine the proper listing price. An outdated, incomplete, or inaccurate analysis will result in a poorly priced listing. Prepare a correct CMA for every listing presentation you make. Careful buyers quickly learn the **fair market value**—the price a ready, willing, and able buyer would pay under normal market conditions for a given area—and will often refuse to even look at overpriced listings. Also, showing agents hesitate to waste their clients' time as well as their own showing unrealistically priced properties. After a salesperson gets a reputation among fellow agents

A Listing Presentation Flow Chart \ **Figure 6.3**

Information Gathering Stage

(1) General Information as found in your Listing Presentation Kit

(2) Specific Information

(a) CMA for subject property must be accurate, complete

(b) Physical inspection of property, to include measuring if needed

(c) Financial investigation on existing mortgages, tax valuation, loans, and so on

IF THE PROPERTY IS WORTH PURSUING AS A LISTING, THEN PROGRESS TO

Presentation Stage

(1) Compare subject property to those found in CMA.

(2) Show suggested list price in terms of actual equity at closing through seller's closing cost statements.

(3) Review your tasks and those of the seller in the joint effort to sell. (Remember to use your marketing plan similar to Figure 6.4.)

(4) Complete listing agreement forms.

IF SUCCESSFUL, THEN MOVE TO

Implementation Stage

CONGRATULATIONS, NOW GO TO WORK ON MARKETING THE PROPERTY!

for taking a listing no matter what the price, it is hard to overcome. Avoid this problem easily by using MLS central computer information, or if you don't have access to MLS, do the investigative work necessary.

Help Sellers Determine Realistic Prices

Sellers often strongly believe that their real estate is worth more than it really is. Inexperienced salespeople will feel pressured to agree with the higher asking price to get the listing. This may result in a **shopworn property**, one that remains on the market longer than comparable properties and projects the image that something is wrong with the listing. The seller becomes disgruntled and uncooperative, and the listing agent becomes frustrated. Many salespersons will simply refuse to take a listing if the price is very much above the indicated fair market value.

If a seller insists on too high a price for the listing, it may be wise to have him or her work with some other salesperson and company. After all, some sellers deserve to occupy the time of your strongest competitor! At the very least, strive to get the seller to agree, after a fairly short period at the too high (based on your research of the marketplace) price, to adjust the list price to one more in line with market values. The best plan for everyone is to start with a price that is close to a carefully researched estimate of fair market value.

Prepare Paperwork Correctly

Advance planning also means having all the necessary forms readily available for use. Items such as listing agreements, sellers' closing cost forms, and any others your company may use should be explained with clarity, conciseness, and confidence. Your ability to provide this information in the proper manner will project an image of competent and professional service to the seller and help increase confidence in you and your company.

You'll need certain information from the seller sometime during the listing presentation to perform your duties completely; the correct legal description, current tax status, loan information, and room sizes are all necessary. Be very certain to review with the seller what personal property will be included in the sale, and put it in writing on the listing agreement. Considerable time and hard feelings will be saved if both buyer and seller are clear on what does and does not go with the sale.

By determining in advance the items needed for a complete presentation, you will eliminate mistakes and delays. In addition, you will increase your chances of getting the listing and the seller's chances of selling the property.

Explain the Agent's Role

As complex as the real estate business is, it's a wonder that any sales are completed! Competence of the listing agent is an important factor in a smooth transaction. Often the seller has no idea what must occur for property to change hands. If you thoroughly explain your role in helping to sell property, the seller can better understand and value the service you will be providing for the fee.

Many firms give the service being offered a name to make it more tangible. Figure 6.4 offers an example of a professional marketing plan. You should also explain to the property owner the steps involved in selling real estate. Using something similar to the flow chart described in Chapter 1 lets the seller know and understand what happens at any point in the transaction. Review your activities at each point with the client to show your involvement in working for and with him or her. Do not be surprised to hear a seller say something like, "I didn't know you did so much to help us sell this place!" This statement is exactly what the agent wants to hear. Remember to project an image of confidence in what you are doing for the seller. No one likes to do business with salespeople who appear uncertain and unsure of themselves or the product or service being offered. If you really can help the seller, convey that message. Positive reassurance coupled with professional service is the point you want to convey.

Explain the Seller's Role

The seller of a piece of real estate also has an important role in the sale. During the listing presentation, review the seller's role and responsibilities as outlined here.

Sample Summary of Services   \ **Figure 6.4**

THE ABC REALTORS PROFESSIONAL MARKETING PLAN

This is what we can do for you:

1. Evaluate your home for the correct listing price
2. Hold your home open for both the public and other REALTORS®
3. Include the property in our extensive advertising program
4. Expose the property through our national referral system and our local multiple-listing service
5. Have well-trained sales professionals on duty at all times
6. Qualify interested prospects before showings
7. Represent you through all negotiations
8. Obtain the most favorable financing
9. Monitor all details of the transaction from beginning to end
10. Follow up after closing to offer additional help and service

If this plan interests you, contact:

Lee Roose, Sales Associate
ABC REALTORS®

739-2212 Office   736-1518 Home

Assisting, Not Selling

One thing the seller should not do is personally conduct every showing. Agents often refuse to show a listing when the seller takes over.

The showing agent will not know more about the real estate than the owner; however, the salesperson knows more about what is important to the buyer and should be left alone with the client. The owner should be willing to offer assistance and information, but only if requested. Many successful listing agents request that the seller be gone or at least out of the way when a showing occurs.

The prospective buyer needs to feel free to discuss the good and bad points about a property and cannot do so comfortably in the owner's presence.

Flexibility

Another important point to discuss in the listing presentation is the need for flexibility in scheduling the showings. All showing appointments should be scheduled with adequate notice. Unfortunately, what is best for the seller may not always be best for a potential buyer. At times, it may not be possible to give even half an hour's notice. This need for cooperation must be clearly understood and accepted by the owner or some showings will be lost. Most knowledgeable salespeople as a simple courtesy will give sellers as much lead time as they can. But sellers can be a real asset if they understand from the start the importance of being flexible in scheduling showings. By refusing to let a showing take place, the seller has taken the property off the market at least temporarily for that potential buyer.

Keeping Property Presentable

An additional key role of the seller is to make the property as presentable as possible for the showings. The chances for a successful sale are never dampened because a prospective buyer feels the property is "too nice and clean for the price." There *is* a big risk to the sale, however, when a prospect sees a property that is so dirty that he or she cannot envision paying any amount to own it. The listing agent may feel somewhat uneasy discussing this subject, not wanting to insult the seller. However, if such advice is handled constructively, it is in the best interest of the sale and the seller to point out the need for some preshowing work to make the property presentable, so don't hesitate to say so. Some of the fixing up and cleaning that must ultimately occur anyway can best be done before showing to convey a more positive image of the property.

The Listing Presentation Kit

You need to remember many things during a listing presentation. Some companies encourage their salespeople to develop a package to ensure all the necessary points are covered. This package of material is usually called a listing presentation kit and is of great value. For purposes of this text, a **listing presentation kit** is defined as a collection of carefully chosen materials that may be used in making a listing presentation. There are several key words in this definition. The kit is a collection, so time and effort must be devoted to gathering the material. The information in the kit is chosen carefully, not haphazardly thrown together. The things assembled may be used in any given situation; sometimes not all of it will be used.

Many people ask why the listing presentation kit is important. The kit is important for at least three valid reasons. First, the kit can increase an agent's chances of success. Although a carefully designed listing presentation kit does not ensure each presentation will result in a listing, it does help ensure the agent's preparedness for the presentation. Even the most experienced and successful salesperson will become rattled occasionally and forget to cover a key area. This mistake can cause a listing to be lost if that particular item is important to the seller. By having an efficient collection of pertinent information, the salesperson is more likely to make a complete and more effective presentation. Figure 6.5 is a checklist of materials that may be included in the kit.

Second, the kit can save the agent time during the presentation. Many materials needed in *any* presentation are needed in *all* of them. Having the common information that will be needed in one place in advance is an asset: The salesperson does not have to

| A Checklist of Items to Include in Your Listing Presentation Kit | Figure 6.5 |

Be sure you have the following:

1. Information on your company. Include items such as agency size, volume, any honors the company has received, and so on.

2. Information on you. Include experience, education, awards you may have won, and so on. Don't be shy. Tell the truth attractively here.

3. A list of satisfied customers. (Use only with permission of the respective customers.) Include a sufficient quantity so the prospective seller may pick several at random. This way you have not completely dictated the choices.

4. Tips on how to improve the property for showing. This may be newspaper articles, pamphlets, or your own "Ten Easy Ways to Help Your Place Sell Itself."

5. Company policy on previews, signs, ads, handing out keys, making appointments to show, and so on. Remember to explain each point in terms of how it benefits the seller: "What this means to you is. . . ."

6. Information on MLS (if applicable). For example, "Not only will ABC REALTORS® be working for you, but through us, other REALTORS® will be aware your property is for sale and will inform their clients about its availability."

7. History of the area marketplace. A complete review of present listings for sale, ones that have been sold (price and terms), and those that have expired (CMA).

8. An explanation of the money market (brief or long, depending on interest). Should include interest rates, discount points, and so on. Be sure it is current.

9. Closing cost statements showing different methods of selling and approximate net amount to seller for each alternative.

10. Listing agreement forms and *earnest money contracts*. You may leave blank copies for the seller to read at leisure. This also gives you a reason to call back if there are any questions.

11. Necessary supplies to take the listing. Include a notebook, pen, tape, rate tables, and so on. *Be prepared.*

frantically gather up all the material each and every time. The kit helps the salesperson cut down on preparation time. That time then can be devoted to concentrating on the special or unique aspects of a particular property and situation.

Third, having a kit will build confidence for the presentation. Most people have more confidence if they are well-prepared. There is security in having the listing kit and in knowing it is an effective selling aid. If the salesperson projects an image of confidence, it helps the seller relax and get involved in the presentation. In turn, seller relaxation and involvement are more likely to lead to a listing.

Contents of Kit

The most often used items in your kit should be placed in clear plastic holders to keep them clean. Arrange the material any way you feel is best. The purpose in having the listing presentation kit is to ensure you are prepared and in control of the presentation. This will greatly increase your chance of getting the listing, which is the reason you are making the presentation. Do not end without asking for the opportunity to help the owner sell his property.

The particular order, importance of each part, and additional material included in your kit will depend upon the individual sales situation, but the items described here should be a part of every agent's listing presentation kit.

Information on the Agent and the Company
Everyone likes to know something about the people and firms with whom they do business. The company's size, years in business, the training and education of the sales agent, and any professional honors should be included. Don't be shy about using your personal reputation and your company's reputation as a selling tool. Include letters of recommendation from previously satisfied customers.

Tips on How to Improve the Listing for Showing
As discussed earlier in this chapter, an unprepared property can be an obstacle to the sale. There are several sources from which to obtain well-written, inexpensive brochures on this topic that may be given to property owners. The National Association of REALTORS® is one good source for such brochures, or your company may produce its own.

The Marketing Plan
It is important to be able to go over the entire sales process with the seller. Each step should include a review of the seller's role as well as yours.

Area Activity
Have an accurate CMA to help determine a realistic listing price.

Closing Cost Information
The sales price is not as important to sellers as their net equity. Be prepared to review all the financing options and to explain closing costs; an estimate of seller's closing costs and a glossary of terms such as those shown in Figures 6.6 and 6.7 are helpful.

Figure 6.6 Estimate of Seller's Closing Costs

Seller	Property Address		Date		Prepared by	
	VA	FHA	Conventional	Cash	Assume	Owner Carry
Broker's Fee						
Title Policy						
Warranty Deed (1)	250.00*	250.00*	250.00*	250.00*	250.00*	250.00*
Note & Deed of Trust (2)	160.00	160.00**	-0-	-0-	-0-	-0-
Deed of Trust to Secure Assumption	-0-	-0-	-0-	-0-	35.00	-0-
Filling Fees Per Release	25.00	25.00	25.00	25.00	25.00	
Escrow Fees (Average)	140.00	140.00	140.00	140.00	140.00	140.00
Tax Certificates	15.00	15.00	15.00	15.00	15.00	
Termite Inspection (Average)	85.00	85.00	85.00	85.00	85.00	85.00
Appraisal (3)	350.00	350.00		***	***	-0-
Loan Discount Fee (4) VA/FHA _____ Conventional _____						
Survey (Normal Residential)	30.00	30.00	-0-	-0-	-0-	-0-
Restrictions, Amortization & Photos	47.00	47.00	-0-	-0-	-0-	-0-
Prepayment Penalty						
Fix up to Show						
Other Costs						
Total Estimated Closing Costs						

(1) *Subject to vanation.

(2) **Only if closing costs are financed.

(3) ***Normally paid by seller, but buyer can pay.

(4) Loan discount quotations are subject to change without notice.

(5) Seller should immediately notify mortgage lender of pending **FHA LOAN PAYOFF** to reduce interest and payoff charges.

(6) Insurance company should be notified when house is to be vacated.

Sales Price		
Less Loan Balance		
Gross to seller		
Less Total Estimated Closing Costs		
Estimate net to Seller**		

*Plus or Minus Prorations of Taxes and Insurance.

NOTICE: This is an estimate only and is provided as a courtesy. Costs will vary at time of closing

| Figure 6.7 | Explanation of Seller's Closing Costs |

Broker's Fee. A fee or commission paid for the marketing service rendered by the real estate company. Commission is established at the time the listing agreement is signed.

Title Policy. An owner's insurance policy against unknown liens, encumbrances, or defects in the title to the real estate being transferred. The seller generally pays this as a one-time charge for a policy value in the amount of the sales price. The policy cost is set by the State Board of Insurance and is good for as long as the buyer keeps the property. (The policy cannot be transferred to another owner.)

Warranty Deed. A deed in which the grantor fully warrants good clear title to the premises. Used in most real estate deed transfers, a warranty deed offers the greatest protection of any deed.

Note. A written agreement stating a debt and the terms of repayment.

Deed of Trust. An instrument used to create a mortgage lien on the property purchased with the money borrowed in the note.

Deed of Trust to Secure Assumption. Instrument used when a buyer is purchasing a seller's equity and assuming an existing mortgage. This instrument would, under specific conditions, allow the current seller to take up payments again in the event the buyer stopped making payments and went into default.

Filing Fees Per Release. Charges for filing and recording releases that clear the title *to* the real estate being sold.

Escrow Fees. Fees paid to an escrow agent for handling the transaction and seeing that all terms of the earnest money contract are carried out.

Tax Certificates. Statements from all concerned taxing agencies showing the current tax status on the property being sold.

Termite inspection. Statement of search and findings by a licensed exterminator as to the condition of the house regarding termites or other wood-destroying insects.

Appraisal. An estimate of fair market value by an appraiser, generally for the purpose of helping a lending institution determine how much it will loan on the property.

Loan Discount Fee. A fee (also called points) added by the lender to make the yield on the loan competitive with other investment options. One point equals 1 percent of the amount to be loaned.

Survey. An examination of the property by a licensed professional surveyor to determine exact boundary lines. Fence lines, easements, and encroachments may also be shown.

The Various Forms

Have the necessary listing forms that were described earlier in this chapter readily available and be prepared to explain each of them.

A *listing presentation* is made by a real estate salesperson to a prospective seller to induce the homeowner to list his or her property for sale with the agent's firm. When a salesperson takes a listing, the agent gains exposure in the marketplace, generates other business, and will have other people—selling agents—working on his or her behalf.

To conduct a successful listing presentation, the salesperson should plan extensively beforehand. This includes preparing a *listing presentation kit*, which is a collection of carefully chosen materials for use in the presentation. Included in the kit should be such items as information on the agent and firm, tips on how the seller can improve the property for showing to buyers, the salesperson's marketing plan, details on area real estate activity, copies of the various forms used in a real estate transaction, and any other necessary supplies.

Review Questions

1. What are the four important reasons for developing a method of generating a consistent inventory of listings?

2. Why is it important that your office get complete information about a listing before the sign goes up?

3. What are three main guidelines to follow when making a listing presentation?

4. What is the best negotiating tool to help a seller determine the proper listing price?

5. Why is it so important to explain your role in helping the owner sell the property?

6. Why is it best for the owner to stay out of the showing process?

7. Why should an agent use a listing presentation kit?

8. What are seven items that should be included in every listing presentation kit?

Discussion Questions

1. Many real estate people say, "To last in this business, you have to learn to list." Explain this statement.

2. In addition to the material mentioned in the listing presentation checklist, what would you add to your kit?

3. How do you "handle" a seller who insists on conducting a personal tour of his property each time it is shown?

4. Have you ever seen a listing presentation kit used in a sales setting? Did it help the agent?

Situation

The Wilson Listing

In preparing a listing presentation for Mr. and Mrs. Wilson, you have done a CMA of their area, as shown in Figure 6.8. Their property is similar to most of those in the neighborhood where they reside. You have thanked them for the opportunity to talk with them and have visited a few minutes in an attempt to get to know them a little better. Mr. Wilson abruptly changes the subject of the conversation with, "I am interested in getting the most money for my home in the shortest time with the least inconvenience to me and my family. What can you and your company do for me to accomplish this?" What do you do now?

The Listing Kit: To Use or Not to Use

Jo Carole Parks is well-known as a highly successful lister in your community. She has stated that no successful listing presentation can occur without advance planning and preparation. She further emphasizes all salespeople need something to keep them on track and to make all the key points in order to get the listing. What do you say to these points?

Figure 6.8   CMA for Wilson Property

PROPERTY ADDRESS   149 Viewridge

DATE   March 4

For Sale Now:	Bed-rms.	Baths	Den	Sq. Ft.	1st Loan	List Price	Days On Market	Terms
318 Montview	3	2	no	1569	159,500	188,000	10	Open; just redecorated
1215 Oakridge	3	2	yes	1400	123,400	187,000	25	Fireplace in den; conventional only
181 Ridgeview	3	$1\frac{1}{2}$	yes	1580	–0–	167,000	40	Needs repairs on roof; no garage
166 Viewridge	4	3	yes	1800	143,000	192,000	18	Corner lot; storage shed stays

Sold Past 12 Mos.	Bed-rms.	Baths	Den	Sq. Ft.	1st Loan	List Price	Days On Market	Date Sold	Sale Price	Terms
307 Oakview	3	2	yes	1390	133,500	180,500	12	2/10	180,950	Assume
1951 Montridge	3	2	no	1600	–0–	188,000	35	2/28	184,500	Owner carry
158 Oak Circle	3	2	yes	1580	149,800	185,000	60	1/10	182,300	V.A.
1972 Lone Oak	4	1	yes	1900	148,000	192,000	45	1/1	187,000	Assume
1300 Viewridge	4	2	yes	1850	156,000	189,500	8	2/12	186,750	Conventional

Expired Past 12 Mos.	Bed-rms.	Baths	Den	Sq. Ft.	1st Loan	List Price	Days On Market	Terms
518 Viewridge	3	2	yes	1400	149,000	189,000	80	Listing withdrawn 2/20
906 Montridge	4	3	yes	1800	127,000	193,000	120	Open—Last 60 days
1129 Oak Drive	3	1	no	1250	153,250	179,900	110	Open—Last 30 days

REMARKS

Advertising and the Communications Process

Key Terms

- Attitude learning
- Behavior learning
- Cognitive learning
- Distress advertising
- Instinctive learning
- Institutional advertising
- Monitoring
- Product advertising
- Reverse advertising
- Target market

Communicating with the Consumer

In the previous chapter, we discussed consumers or buyers in groups; however, usually you'll sell property one piece at a time. So understanding buyers and sellers on an individual basis also is important.

How People Learn

A potential buyer or seller who walks into your office brings knowledge and experience that shape the way he or she thinks about the world and, in particular, real estate purchases and sales. Knowing how people learn will help you communicate more effectively.

Have you ever pulled your hand away from a stove when you realized it was hot? We usually call this an instinct, but it's actually something we learned a long time ago. From early childhood, **instinctive learning** teaches us to do certain things and avoid others.

Another type of learning is **cognitive learning**, which is learning basic information. When a potential buyer is finding out basic prices and features of different properties, the buyer is practicing cognitive learning. We all go through this stage whenever we approach a new experience, particularly one that requires a decision.

Attitude learning is a bit more complicated. Throughout our lives, we gather information and make decisions, living with the consequences. Thus, we learn to react favorably or unfavorably to certain styles, brands, and kinds of products. This knowledge from our experience shapes how we react to new ideas, experiences, and products.

All these types of learning help create the fourth form, **behavior learning**. Our experience with decisions and with others influences our behavior. Similarly, reinforcement, which occurs through the repetition of experiences, leads us to feel and act in one way rather than another. Thus, all forms of learning help define how we actually behave.

Communication

Eventually we communicate with one person at a time, and that's difficult enough to do. You probably have seen one of those demonstrations in which one message is given to the first person in a long line, passed down, and the person at the end of the line repeats a completely different message than the original. The reason that person at the end of the line receives a very different message from the original one is because of "noise." Every message has a sender and a receiver, but between them is noise, that is, other things attempting to gain their attention. The receiver's own experience influences how he or she hears the message, and the sender's experience influences how he or she sends the message. Each person in that chain sends and receives a message that has slight differences, resulting from different individual feelings, values, and attitudes. This filtering effect based on personal experience has tremendous impact on personal communication.

The same is true for a mass marketing message. Although an ad or a commercial speaks to many people, it also tells the receiver that this message is speaking to that individual and to his or her specific needs. However, you as the advertiser also must contend with noise. The phone or doorbell rings, the radio is playing, or your ad is one of four on a page. All this noise distracts the receiver of your message; your message can break through those distractions in two ways. One is by the strength of the message that appeals to a broad and specific concern. Should the message emphasize safety and security, prestige, or maybe financial gain? All these messages and appeals are different. The only sure way to know which is right is to know the receiver or, as marketers say, the target market.

The second method of penetrating through the noise is by repetition. Your message might not get through the first time the receiver sees it, but it might register on the second or third time. That is why most marketers run their messages more than once or twice and why different people will respond to the second ad or mailing than those who answer the first one.

All this eventually affects the individual when you meet a person face to face. Although most of this book deals with personal selling, the important point to remember is that knowing your buyer or seller in the broader sense will help you on the personal level. You'll recognize signs that indicate the buyer's readiness to buy, his or her concerns (both stated and unstated ones), and how to appeal to those concerns most effectively.

Communication Barriers

The communication process is not without obstacles. What people *say* and what they *mean* are sometimes very different. Likewise, what is *meant* and what is *heard* differs radically at times. We all have experience with breakdowns in the communication process. This is especially true in real estate sales. Veteran salespeople talk about sales that have fallen apart because of this problem. The person who gets blamed when this occurs is—that's right—the salesperson!

The following are four common barriers to communication that the salesperson must be aware of and try to eliminate. There can be, and frequently are, more than these four, but they represent a sample of what to look for in the sales setting.

1. **Prejudice**—Presented here, this does not relate to race, religion, and so forth, but rather to "false knowledge." A seller who believes her $185,000 property is worth $225,000 is operating under a strong prejudice. The consumer who is convinced all REALTORS® are crooks out to take advantage also is operating out of prejudice. Sometimes this obstacle cannot be overcome, but usually, through the use of logical, consistently fair explanations, it is possible to eliminate prejudice. If the person insists on remaining inaccurately informed, respect his or her right and move on to another opportunity.

2. **Distractions**—As mentioned before, distractions or noise can severely hinder communication. Some distractions are controllable, but others are not. For some potential buyers, the presence of the seller may represent a significant distraction while touring a property. The astute salesperson, sensing this distraction, will make every effort to show property when the seller is not present. Tired, bored children can be another common distraction in real estate sales settings. This may be resolved by leaving the children with friends, family, or at a day-care center. I've personally spent money at day-care centers numerous times so that qualified, out-of-town purchasers can make a purchase decision without their children present. Remember, every distraction you can eliminate will increase your chances for success.

3. **Inattention**—Have you ever had a class on "Learning to Listen"? Listening is hard work and most of us are not good at it. Customers are sometimes inattentive. Not always, but usually, you can solve this problem by enthusiastically involving the person in the communication process. Give the person a real "equity" in the conversation. Remember, people generally will support what they help to create. Ask your buyer or seller for his or her ideas, opinions, and feelings and then listen to understand. The selling process does not have to be one of constant chatter by the salesperson. At times, silence is perfect for giving the customer time to think something through. Remember the difference in talking *to* someone and talking *with* someone.

4. **Perception**—This refers to a personal interpretation of the happenings around us. If you don't believe perceptions differ, ask six eyewitnesses to an accident for details and see how many different stories you get. What is reality to me is exactly that: reality . . . to me. For example, read the next phrase carefully:

FINISHED FILES ARE A RESULT OF YEARS OF SCIENTIFIC STUDY
COMBINED WITH THE EXPERIENCE OF MANY YEARS.

Now read it again, concentrating on the meaning of the words. Go back and count the number of Fs in the phrase. How many did you get? Three? Maybe four or five? There are actually six Fs, but through the years I have seen hundreds of people (including myself, the first time) notice only three to five of them. Some people have adamantly bet lunches, drinks, even commissions and grades on their faulty perceptions of the phrase. The next time you confront a perception obstacle, remember the Fs test. What is a nice neighborhood, good value, or adequate return will differ from one person to the next. Do your best to get a reading on how a particular buyer or seller perceives situations and then work from that understanding. The results that more effective communications make in increased sales productivity will surprise you.

Advertising

An important aspect of communications with potential buyers and sellers involves advertising and promotion. Certainly promotion on a broad scale involves many facets: publicity, public relations, specialty advertising items, and many more. Those are important, but the largest segment of real estate marketing promotion is *advertising*.

Advertising to Attract Sellers and Buyers

The success of any promotional plan will be judged on how much new business it generates. Attracting new prospects is the most important reason for investing in advertising. Notice the word *prospects* is used rather than *buyers*. Prospective buyers will probably read ads in the classified real estate section of the papers. However, keep in mind that potential sellers also read these same ads. Property owners who are considering listing with a company often read a company's ads for a few days. If a seller is not impressed or cannot relate to the ads your company runs, the listing will end up with another company. Consider the reactions of an owner of a lower-priced home who only sees your ads for executive-priced listings, or the seller of a commercial property who believes that your company only sells residential real estate because that is the only type of ad your company has run. These examples point out the advantage of considering both the potential buyer and seller when you develop ad copy.

Enhancing Your Agency's Image

Another reason for advertising is to create the desired image. If a real estate agent's owner wants to project a certain image to the public, a carefully planned ad campaign can help. Politicians have used this strategy for years. All business organizations are in a particular stage of their life cycles. A company concentrating on growth may decide to project itself as an up-and-coming force in the marketplace. A well-established firm might prefer to project its stability and long-standing reputation. Either way, advertising can help.

Exposure in the Marketplace

Every business wants to inform the public about its product or service. Exposure in the marketplace is an important reason for advertising. Most consumers do not need professional real estate help often, and there is a tendency for past customers to forget a salesperson or company after time elapses following a transaction. Unless reminded on a regular basis, a satisfied customer may go elsewhere for help the next time. This illustrates a need for salespeople to keep their names and the name of their companies before the public. A newcomer to the community may not even know who is available to provide help. Consistent advertising can prevent this problem.

Educating the Public

The complexity of the real estate field today is staggering. For many practitioners, the opportunity to educate the public is a good reason for advertising and ties in directly with other purposes. If potential buyers and sellers recognize the need for professional help, they will seek it. The real estate company that has been providing information through a well-planned advertising campaign will be more likely to be the company a consumer thinks of for this help.

The education also extends to additional areas. An impressive display of your company's previous advertising and an explanation of how your overall advertising program works to benefit sellers can make a consumer decide to list with your company rather than another real estate firm. Education of a buyer also can be extended through advertising. Buyers rarely buy a property they first see, which is discussed further in Chapter 8, "Telephone Techniques." Educating buyers means working with them to determine which properties are most suitable for their particular needs.

Satisfying the Seller

A seller expects and deserves professional service in the marketing of his or her property. The advertising exposure that a listing receives is an important aspect of this service because it is tangible evidence of effort—a valid reason to advertise.

Types of Advertising

There are two distinct types of advertising. **Institutional advertising** is designed to promote the overall company. Figure 7.1 illustrates how real estate firms use institutional advertising. Other examples may range from sponsoring a free homebuyer's seminar to supporting a Little League team. Some classified advertising even may be designed primarily to reinforce the company's image and reputation: The effectiveness of goodwill advertising is difficult to measure and must be viewed as a long-term investment toward the betterment of the company.

The other type is called **product advertising**, advertising that helps to sell a particular listing. The classified ads found in newspapers or trade publications are the most

Figure 7.1	Institutional Advertising to Promote the Overall Company

MAY WE HELP YOU?

Our real estate firm is dedicated to serving our clients in a friendly, professional manner. For 17 years, it has been our privilege to help people in this town with their real estate needs. Call on us today. We promise to answer the phone with the question, "May we help you?

V. WALKER,
REALTORS 733-2852
or contact us at VWALKER@FREDTX.com

THE PROFESSIONALS

At Chris Pursch Realty, we are proud of our community. As professionals in the field of real estate, it is our responsibility to take an active part in improving the area where we work and live. We hope you share our attitude. For professional real estate help, you can call on us.

Chris Pursch Realty
218 N. Ash 344-3535
or Toll Free 1-866-555-1951

common examples, but any advertising that attempts to inform the public about the company's products and services falls into this category. The astute salesperson and broker quickly recognizes the needs to focus on the **target market,** the group of likely candidates for the product or service being offered. The target market approach helps to eliminate wasted money spent reaching the wrong group. Whether you are dealing with a personal or company Web site, or have invested in a television show, the investment made in real estate advertising is staggering, and every effort must be made to ensure that each ad does its job well. This begins by understanding the parts of an ad. Clearly, this information will differ somewhat based upon the medium being used, but there is some common ground to consider.

Advertising is *not* the place to work all on your own. Seek professional help and work within well-defined goals. Modern technology is wonderful, but it isn't a replacement for hard work and professional service of the highest quality. Don't expect the fanciest promotional efforts to overcome poor performance.

Classified Advertising

Classified advertisements in the local newspaper are the most common form of advertising used by real estate companies. A well-written ad is an effective sales tool that can attract both prospective buyers and sellers.

The ad writer should keep in mind that the classified ad has a number of parts, each with a specific goal to accomplish. Each part must complement the whole.

Headings Attract Readers

The first part of an ad is the heading. The objective of the heading is to attract attention. No matter how well the rest of the copy is written, if no one chooses to read it, the ad is wasted effort. The effective heading will grab the reader's attention and hold it. This is important; consider that one full page of classified real estate advertising can contain more than 200 ads that compete for the reader's interest. Remember also that the only people who read *all* the ads are the real estate salespeople.

The Body Gives the Facts

The body of the ad must provide meaningful information to the reader. A balance must exist between telling too much and too little. If not enough information is given, the reader will skip to another ad. If too much is presented, there may be no need to call the salesperson! According to veteran real estate writers, prospective purchasers want to find out about the property's location, price, and physical characteristics.

Location

One approach successfully used by some firms is to list the general area rather than a specific address. See Figure 7.2 for a sample ad of this type. "Near Jones High" will give the reader a sufficient clue to location.

Some property owners do not want their street addresses to be printed in an ad. This may be for security or other personal reasons, but be sure to ask the seller's preference before printing the address.

An exception to this approach, of course, is when you advertise an open house. In that case, include the address and any other helpful directions to find the property.

Price

Listing the price is another consideration. Many readers might assume the property is priced too high if the price is not included. My personal experience *is* that more people call about a property if the general price range is included.

Be sure to follow the guidelines established by Regulation Z when stating price, down payment, interest rates, or other relevant information. Regulation Z is the Truth-in-Lending Act that outlines specific guides on making disclosures about credit terms. The Federal Trade Commission enforces the guides, which must be followed by a real

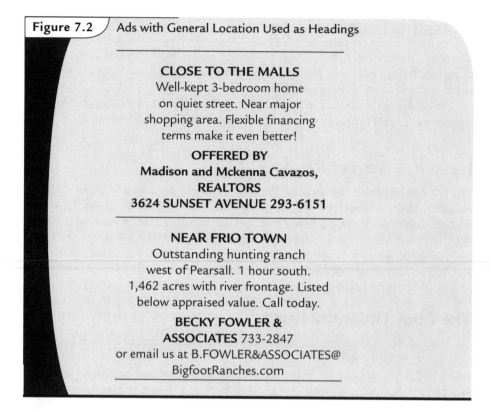

Figure 7.2 Ads with General Location Used as Headings

CLOSE TO THE MALLS
Well-kept 3-bedroom home
on quiet street. Near major
shopping area. Flexible financing
terms make it even better!
OFFERED BY
Madison and Mckenna Cavazos,
REALTORS
3624 SUNSET AVENUE 293-6151

NEAR FRIO TOWN
Outstanding hunting ranch
west of Pearsall. 1 hour south.
1,462 acres with river frontage. Listed
below appraised value. Call today.
BECKY FOWLER &
ASSOCIATES 733-2847
or email us at B.FOWLER&ASSOCIATES@
BigfootRanches.com

estate licensee who is advertising information on annual percentage rate, down payments, monthly payment amounts, and length of payout period.

Physical Characteristics

When using the ad body to describe the physical characteristics, exercise caution in how many details you include. Each time you add a feature, the chances increase that the reader will not want that particular feature and will eliminate the listing from consideration. A well-written ad will state only one or two special features about a property. Also, remember that one feature in the listing can attract different buying groups. A cul-de-sac location with low traffic flow might be attractive to a young couple with small children and to an older couple with no resident children who seek peace and quiet. A property with limited maintenance requirements might attract someone physically unable to do repairs, as well as the person who does not enjoy working outdoors.

The Conclusion Brings Action

After a listing is described sufficiently in the body, the conclusion should generate action from the reader. Potential purchasers should not only be attracted to the ad and interested enough to read it, but should turn passive interest into positive action, or the ad copy has not accomplished its real goal. The true test of any product advertising is whether or not it brings results. The truly effective ad will result in a buyer contact.

Effective Ad Techniques

When you are reading real estate ads from your firm or from a competitor, try to determine if all the parts work together to form an effective sales tool. Consider the following to determine the effectiveness of your ads.

Monitoring Ad Results

Well-managed real estate marketing firms use **monitoring**, a technique that involves recording the number of calls received from the placed ads to determine advertising effectiveness. Through monitoring, an organization can determine more accurately the best times and places to invest its advertising dollars. For example, it might be ineffective to spend money only for weekend advertising in the community's largest paper. The weekend paper may be the most expensive, but it may not be the most cost-effective. Successful real estate ad writers tell me that some of their best responses are generated from neighborhood papers that are published once a week. After reviewing the total calls received over a period of time, you can improve your timing and effectiveness in ad placement.

Ad Location

The placement of an ad in relation to others on the page is a hotly debated topic. Proponents for the upper-left corner point out that this spot is where we are taught to begin reading. Other marketing experts defend the center of the page. Based on observations and discussions with veteran ad writers, location is secondary to content. A well-written ad will receive more inquiries than a poorly written one, regardless of where it is placed.

Judge for yourself. Select three or four full pages of classified real estate ads and choose the five ads per page that you rate as best. Compare ad locations. In most instances, there will be no order that indicates that one spot is superior to another. An exception to this might be a block ad in which a company will block out a large area, as in Figure 7.3, and include descriptions of several properties in a box. This approach sometimes attracts more attention than a single-property ad.

Concise Wording

The use of appropriate wording is important in writing effective ads. Although there is no secret list of words that guarantees multiple calls, certain general rules hold true. Short phrases of three to five words are more readable than lengthy passages. Reader interest tends to drop if the sentences and paragraphs are excessively long.

Figure 7.3	A Block Ad with Prices Serving as Headings

$198,000
A neat 2-bedroom condo; a pool and covered parking plus outside maintenance are only part of the benefits.

$200,000
This charmer is great for a young family! Near the elementary school, it has 3 bedrooms and a storage building that stays!

$220,000
A corner lot with big shade trees comes with this well-maintained older home located near downtown.

$259,000
Large. custom-built 4-bedroom brick in prestigious neighborhood. Well-maintained, one-owner home.

**CALL ANY OF OUR
AGENTS REGARDING
THESE FINE HOMES**

**MACKEY & ASSOCIATES,
REALTORS** 349-4279
Lovell H. Mackey, Broker 928-3703
or email at LHM@SAK.net
Christi Mills 257-1311
or email at ChristiM@Southgate.net
Jean Kutz 498-1585
or email at Jkutz@Marion.com
Jon Kelly 281-5511
or email at JKCOC@PST.net

Brevity, however, can be carried to extremes with the use of abbreviations. An ad such as the one in Figure 7.4 will confuse most readers. Salespeople know the ad is for a three-bedroom, two-bath home with a two-car garage and a single living area floor plan that has a fireplace. It is important, however, to write for buyers, not real estate people.

Conveying the Right Image

The well-written ad also attempts to create a visual image of the property being described. This image may be positive or negative. In an ad headed "Price Reduced," the

Poorly Written Ads with Too Many Abbreviations	Figure 7.4

WHAT IT SAYS:	**WHAT IT MEANS:**
FSBO 3BR 2Ba SLA w/FP DBL.GAR	3 Bedrooms 2 Baths Single Living Area with a Fireplace and a Double Car Garage
200 ACS. S. TEX. 70 mi. S. of S.A. G. htng. wi 1/2 min. No O or G leases now.	200 Acres South Texas 70 miles south of San Antonio Good hunting. Buyer receives 1/2 of the mineral estate. The property has no current oil or gas leases on the property.

wording might cause a reader to wonder why or what defects the property has. Sometimes a heading will read "Owner Transferred" or "Must Sell." These examples are called **distress advertising** because they create the impression of a problem with the property. This ad *will* generate calls, but in this situation, callers probably are looking for a bargain and will be more interested in taking advantage of a seller in a tight spot than they will be in paying fair market value.

Before using distress advertising, the ad writer should decide if this is the kind of caller he or she wants to attract. Figure 7.5 is an example of distress advertising.

Reverse Advertising

Every office occasionally has a listing that is difficult to sell. These properties are called many uncomplimentary names. Listing agents, brokers, and sellers may not be able to devise a method to promote the listing effectively. One idea that may help is the use of *reverse advertising.* This term is probably not found in any advertising textbook, but the idea can be converted into an effective strategy.

In critically reviewing property, agents may uncover a major deterrent to a sale. For example, a problem may be that the property is in an isolated or hard-to-reach location. Or it could be that the property is in poor physical condition and needs a great deal of repair work. Whatever the obstacle, **reverse advertising** attempts to focus on a property's problem to turn it into an asset for promotion purposes. For example, the isolated location may attract a person seeking solitude and seclusion. The home in poor condition might be an ideal house for someone with an interest in and talent for remodeling. Figure 7.6 shows two such ads. By viewing the listing through the eyes of a prospective owner, agents can multiply advertising opportunities. Capitalize on this, and problem listings suddenly might generate response.

Figure 7.5 / Distress Ads That Generate Bargain Hunter Calls

PRICE REDUCED

Must sell lovely 4-2-2. Good
condition, flexible terms. Call 972-
0101.

Betty Anderson Realty

OWNER ANXIOUS

Forced sale due to transfer. Must
sell before end of month. Nice 3
bedroom house in northwest. Call
owner collect at 733-0089.

DIVORCE SALE

Court ordered sale of 2.6 acres.
Zoned commercial. At corner of
Massad and Pulliam. Low price for
quick sale.

L.G. Bailey Realty
342-4628

Figure 7.6 / Reverse Advertising for Homes in Need of Repairs

REMODELER'S DREAM

Older home in popular area. Needs
repairs. Sound investment for the
"fix it up" person. Call 349-3131.

M&M GRAF REALTORS®
733-3136

NEEDS WORK

But your efforts will be worth it.
Small 3-bedroom, 1 bath cottage
near downtown. Would make
excellent rental unit once repaired.

SPLITROCK REALTY

466-5515

or visit us at our website
www.splitrockrealty.net

General Guidelines for Ad Writing

Writing a real estate company's ads takes time. Effective ad writing is challenging work and should be treated as an important responsibility. For most people, creativity is not automatic. The following suggestions are designed to make the task easier.

To develop effective ads that will generate interest, most writers need some quiet time to think. Attempting to write between activities and interruptions will lead to dissatisfaction and ineffective ads. The writer must habitually "block out" some regularly scheduled time to work on ads.

Some "ad help" books are available that give suggested samples of successful ads. Building on these ideas may be effective for some writers.

Nearly all successful real estate ad writers believe it is important to *preview the property* personally *before* attempting to describe it. This exposure helps them to get a better feel for the listing and the type of prospective purchasers that will most likely be attracted to it.

Seek help from many sources when attempting to develop improved ad-writing skills. *Sellers* will tell you what attracted them to their property when they bought it. They can also tell you of other important features that they have learned about their property. With this information, you can generate a good description of the positive aspects. Involving sellers in ad writing also assures them that you are doing something to help sell the property. If sellers feel part of the marketing team, they usually become less critical and more cooperative.

People in the office may be good resources as well. Ask for their opinion on what should be featured in the ad. One successful brokerage operation holds ad-writing contests to see which agent can write the best ad on new listings. Some excellent ads come out of this weekly event, resulting in faster sales.

Prospective buyers who inspect the new property can also be helpful. A prospect once mentioned disliking a home's large breakfast area. This was my signal that the breakfast area was an unusual characteristic of the house. Knowing that another buyer would see the breakfast area as an asset, I featured the extra space when advertising, and the home sold immediately. A large breakfast area was exactly what that new owner wanted.

Employees in the *classified advertising department* of your company's newspaper probably have some experience they are willing to share. Remember to pay attention to the ads being run by your competitors. Are they using any special techniques or strategies that attract your attention? If so, maybe your style needs some revision. Many ad writers subscribe to one or two out-of-town papers to see what is being used in other areas.

Keep in mind that an *advertising course* offered by a local community college or continuing education program also might be a worthwhile investment. Or employ *professional advertising people* to improve advertising. This might be worthwhile on a trial basis and may prove cost-effective.

Advertising represents a sizable expenditure for most businesses involved in marketing real estate. No matter who is responsible for creating the ad or who pays for its creation, everyone benefits from improvement in the overall program. A good place to start is by gaining a better understanding of the role each ad plays in the company's overall plan. Review the purpose of advertising and the objectives of each part of an ad on a regular basis. Monitor the response to each classified ad. This helps you in the development and placement of future ads.

Other Media

The emphasis in this chapter focuses on newspaper-type, printed media, but other forms of advertising are available. Television, for example, is a medium used by some larger independent companies and many franchise groups. At certain times of the viewing day, you may achieve quite an impact by using this medium. Nevertheless, the high costs and brevity (15 to 60 seconds) of broadcast advertising are negatives. Other forms of advertising include radio, billboards, direct mail, and magazines. Each approach has its own advantages and disadvantages. Frequently, these advertising media will be restricted to institutional advertising uses.

Radio enjoys wide popularity and usage, yet is somewhat selective because of varying program formats. An advertiser can customize for different target markets with somewhat greater accuracy. On the negative side, only audio messages can be presented, which prohibits demonstration or any other visual support. Also, because of the fragmented audience, unless substantial investments are made, only small parts of the overall market will be reached. For example, the country and western music listener rarely knows what is promoted on the classical music station.

Outdoor advertising offers repeated exposure, as people frequently travel by the same routes. On the other hand, some cities do not allow signs to be placed within their boundaries, and there has been federal pressure for their removal from major interstate highways. The fleeting time frame of exposure limits the message to just a few words. Multiple distractions, including safe driving and traffic conditions, weaken the effective use of outdoor advertising. Remember, however, that outdoor advertising can be more than just billboards, including bench signs and even transit advertising on buses or subways.

Magazine advertising has its own set of unique strengths and weaknesses. One of the merits is very high selectivity, based on geographics (regional publications are very common) or various demographics. Such factors as personal and professional interests, age groupings, and income ranges can be more readily differentiated with magazines. However, magazines do have some weaknesses, including rising postage, production, and paper costs. There also is the proliferation of special interest magazines, which slices the target markets, as well as the general decline of readership as television, computers, and videos gain more of the public's attention.

Internet and Web marketing is now making a fast approach in overtaking print media as a dominant source in how consumers find real estate for sale. Today, consumers can easily find listings in their desired area of preference, view virtual tours and or photo galleries of the homes for sale, and do most of their home viewing in advance by computer. Tech savvy real estate agents have gained an edge over the traditional real estate professional by developing Web sites that incorporate many options for consumers. Today, pricing of real estate Web sites for agents and offices have become so reasonable that Internet advertising is open for all agents to use and compete. Benefits of Internet advertising and an easy to navigate Web site will bring consumers back time and time again to view and search for real estate for sale. Providing free reports on home ownership and selling information is also essential to gain traffic to your Web site. The key to a successful Web presence in your market is to promote your Web site address on "everything!" Many real estate agents believe that you need to have your Web site linked to as many search engines available to gain maximum exposure on the Web. True, being a top placement on search engines such as Google®and Yahoo!® provides great exposure for Web surfers searching for real estate in a particular community, but making sure your community knows your Web address is also important.

Generally, these types of media are conducive to institutional advertising. Some limited product advertising occurs, but very little is dedicated to specific property. *Direct mail,* however, can offer a nice balance of specific product and overall company promotion. Some firms use direct mailings as an important part of their overall advertising plan. Certain advantages are clearly available with this medium. For example, you can control the timing of the mailing. You are contacting specific people at their addresses. Decisions on format considerations such as size, color, and spacing also can be better controlled. Of course, there are limitations. Keeping an accurate mailing list is difficult when the mailing includes a large number of people. There is also the problem of readership, as many receivers may consider your contact "junk mail." And, there is some difficulty in obtaining the creative skill needed to make readership high and loyal.

Decide on what combination of these various approaches works well for you and your company. Because advertising costs can be very high, it's important to monitor the investments made to determine the highest effectiveness and return.

Summary

Knowing, understanding, and communicating with the consumer are keys to success in real estate sales and marketing. Too often, salespeople don't really think about the buyer or seller until he or she walks in the door. Many times that mistake leads to disaster, and even when it doesn't, it's the hard way to present real estate. Good marketing preparation—understanding your customer's needs, motivations, and aspirations—can be critical to getting more listings and selling more homes.

The largest segment of real estate marketing promotion is *advertising*. Advertising enhances the image of a firm, gains exposure for it in the marketplace and educates consumers to the services the firm can offer.

Generally, there are two types of advertising: *institutional ads* designed to promote a company's image, and *product ads* designed to promote a specific commodity or service.

When writing a real estate ad, a salesperson should create a heading that will attract attention, construct the body of the ad to provide the reader with pertinent information about the property, and write the conclusion to generate reader action. Further effective advertising techniques include consideration of page location, concise wording that conveys a visual image of the property being described, and reverse advertising—promoting a property's drawbacks as assets in certain instances to help sell it.

Ideas for writing ads can come from a variety of sources, including sellers, prospects, other people in the office, newspaper classified advertising departments, advertising courses, and advertising professionals.

Other media sources include television, radio, outdoor signs, magazines, and direct mail advertising. Each has its own strengths and weaknesses to consider before using.

Review Questions

1. What are the communication barriers?

2. What are the major reasons for investing in advertising?

3. What are the two distinct types of advertising?

4. What purpose does each of the three parts of an ad serve?

5. What three points are real estate ad readers most interested in?

6. What is the true test of effective product advertising?

7. According to veteran writers, is ad location or content more important?

8. Why is it wise to monitor all calls received from ads?

9. How should ads be worded for effective reading?

10. What is the strategy of reverse advertising for hard-to-sell property?

11. Why is previewing property before writing an ad for it important?

12. What are five good resources to help you write effective ads?

13. Besides classified advertising, what are some additional media sources available?

Discussion Questions

1. What are some additional barriers to effective communication not mentioned in the chapter?

2. How can a real estate company accurately evaluate the effectiveness of its advertising program?

3. In addition to the ones mentioned in this chapter, what are other reasons a firm might advertise?

4. Whose responsibility should it be to write the classified ad copy for a real-estate brokerage organization?

5. What other media alternatives not discussed here are you aware of in the real estate industry?

Situation

Effective Ad Writing

You have just listed a very fine home located in a popular area of your community on a pleasant cul-de-sac. The property has three bedrooms, two baths, a two-car garage, a covered patio, and a privacy fence. It is well cared for and beautifully decorated. Your task is to write an effective ad on the listing. How do you tell prospective buyers about it?

The Only Way?

Susan Gilbert has been a respected real estate broker in your community for a number of years. She has stated numerous times in her sales meetings that the only place to spend advertising dollars is in the newspaper on specific properties. Is that really the only way to advertise?

TECHNOLOGY *IN ACTION*

For more information on Web site marketing for real estate professionals, visit http://www.realtor.org/ and search for *Web* or *Internet marketing*. You'll find a long list of information and articles to help you learn the essentials of building the perfect real estate Web site.

Telephone Techniques

Key Terms

- Call-in sheet
- Floor duty
- Open-ended questions
- See-saw techniques
- Switch sheet
- Telephone image

People Contact

After the presentation has been made and the listing obtained, telling other people about the property becomes important. Often first contact with an important individual is over the telephone. Certainly we don't want to limit the various other communication tools such as Web sites, e-mails, and all the other innovative creations at our disposal; however, the old tried and true standby, the telephone, still has a very important role in our profession.

The telephone is an effective sales tool for successful real estate agents because it puts them in contact with many persons they need to talk with. Suspects, prospects, satisfied clients, other agents, lenders, attorneys, title companies, and other individuals and firms are readily accessible. Proper use of the telephone saves a tremendous amount of time.

Unfortunately, the telephone can also work against the agent. Potential hazards are the time lost to giving and receiving incorrect information, wrong numbers, busy signals, and being placed on hold. There is also the inherent danger of using the current technology of mobile phones in its variety of forms while driving or doing something else at the same time.

This chapter reviews some basic telephone techniques. These techniques are ideas and suggestions, not hard and fast rules. The immediate circumstances, your particular approach, and the style of the individual caller all will influence the telephone style you choose. The material is divided into three parts: receiving calls, placing calls, and general telephone techniques.

Receiving Incoming Calls

Floor duty, floor opportunity, up-time, and many other terms are used to define time during which an agent handles the call-ins. Some suggestions for effective handling of floor duty follow.

Prepare for the Calls Beforehand

Nothing is more frustrating than to talk with salespeople—in person or on the phone—if they know nothing about their product or service. After callers receive several answers such as "I'll check on that," or "Let me find out," they perceive a lack of knowledge and preparation on the part of the salesperson. Effective agents have key information in front of them when the phone rings.

What information should agents always have at their fingertips? Specific details on homes listed are foremost. There is no substitute for firsthand exposure to the property, and all new company listings should be previewed as soon as they come on the market.

Having copies of *all* the ads the company is running also is essential. It hurts the image of the agent, the company, and real estate people in general when you cannot effectively discuss your own inventory. You also need to prepare a list of other properties comparable to specific listings. An old but effective idea is the **switch sheet**, as shown in Figure 8.1. This list of alternative properties allows the agent to continue discussing other properties with a caller if the specific one asked about does not meet his or her needs. And the experience of most agents will bear this next point out. The odds of a particular property meeting the caller's needs are not good. So having other properties ready is to your advantage.

Another aspect of being prepared is having a pen and paper ready to jot down the information you obtain from the caller. Many firms will use a **call-in sheet**, a visual aid to remind the salesperson of what information should be obtained about the caller. Figure 8.2 is an example of a call-in sheet.

Figure 8.1	Switch Sheet

ABC REALTY

Newspaper	Heading	Address	Alternate Property
Horizon	Cool Comfort	507 Stamo Ave.	1300 San Pedro
Current	Large Living	1500 Sara Place	1950 Bobby Dee Lane
Globe	Sunny Acres	Rt. 2 Box 82	NONE!!!
Express	Country Palace	6391 Tullos Circle	1998 Jenkins Place
Sunday only			
New	Easy to Like	1502 N. Electra	218 N. Ash

ABC Realty Call-in List \ Figure 8.2

REMEMBER: Project the desired image and get the appointment!

Date: _____ Time: _____

Name: _____ Tel. No.:_____

Ad Call? _____ Sign Call? _____

Which Newspaper? _____ Which Ad? _____

_____

_____

_____

_____

Price Range: _____

Now Owns _____ Now Rent _____

Date & Time of Appointment: _____

Other Information: _____

_____

_____

Follow-up: _____

_____

Agent: _____

Be Aware of Telephone Image

On the telephone, you should sound knowledgeable, enthusiastic, interested, eager to help—or in a single word, professional. To achieve this, as you are talking, you might ask yourself, "What kind of image am I projecting to the caller?" Don't allow the

TECHNOLOGY *IN ACTION*

Most local MLS® and software programs such as http://www. lucero.com/ allow the real estate agent to search for information by address or listing number. Some software programs allow the user to click a button to bring up similar properties in the same price range or general area. It's important to become familiar with your local MLS® or other software programs your company chooses to use for handling property calls.

question to paralyze you, but let it challenge you to work toward improvement. Occasionally have your broker or sales manager monitor and evaluate your calls. Practice with your fellow agents. Some firms tape record calls for playback and analysis as part of their telephone training. The idea behind the various methods is to improve the image the agent projects.

Following are specific suggestions for a positive **telephone image**.

Answer Promptly

Answer the telephone promptly; do not be concerned about appearing too eager. You do not want to risk having the caller hang up. Some agents feel that if prospects hang up quickly, they must not be good prospects. But it makes more sense to make that decision after you have talked with them, instead of judging their sincerity on the basis of persistence.

Identify Company and Ask to Be of Assistance

Answer the telephone with a phrase similar to, "ABC Realty. May I help you?" Consider the reasoning behind this suggestion. First, company identification tells callers immediately what firm they have reached. If the caller has dialed incorrectly, the mistake should be called to his or her attention as early in the conversation as possible.

Offering your assistance serves two key purposes. First. salespeople should sound eager to please and not as if they have been interrupted. Projecting a helpful attitude will accomplish this. The other purpose concerns the single most important point in this chapter: *The person asking the questions is the person controlling the call.* By asking an immediate question you have—at least momentarily—obtained control of the direction of the conversation. You may lose control later in the call, but you have increased your chance of retaining it by asking the first question.

Identify Yourself and Obtain Caller's Identity

Some salespeople begin the conversation with their name, but it works more effectively as a separate step in the conversation. If you introduce yourself in your opening statement, often it is wasted or lost. The caller has something to say or a question to ask, and at this point is primarily interested in getting a turn to talk. Keep your opening short and refrain from offering your name immediately. Although some schools of thought disagree with this approach, the best advice is to choose the procedure that works best for you.

If the caller offers his or her name as an introduction, return that courtesy by giving your name, and at this point, it will be heard and maybe even remembered. Many times callers will not identify themselves. A technique to consider when a caller's name is not volunteered is to wait until the caller asks for something (usually following your offer of service). A cordial. positive response to this request is a good procedure. "I will be happy to give you that information" sets a warm, friendly tone for the remainder of the conversation. The caller will be pleased to find such cooperation. After this initial exchange, request the prospect's name by volunteering your own. An appropriate approach would be, "By the way, my name is Andy Agent, may I please ask yours?" You have offered before asking and this softens the request.

Relax with the Caller

Books and articles on telephone techniques suggest that you establish rapport with the caller. This is good advice. Many new agents (and some experienced ones) tense up with a caller. Their entire personality changes the instant a call comes in. Work on sounding relaxed and confident. The caller may be ready to do battle with a high-pressure salesperson, and will be sensitive to your approach. Why not surprise callers with warm, pleasant conversation? They will let down their defenses. Remember, a first impression is important, and your goal is conversation, not interrogation.

Discipline, Speed, and Volume

Experienced, successful agents verify that discipline on the telephone is important. The previous suggestion describes disciplining yourself to have a relaxed tone. Discipline also is necessary in the speed and volume of your conversation. We have all felt the need to get a hearing aid or crawl into the receiver to better hear the quiet, timid talker. We have also wished occasionally that our arms were longer to keep the loud talker from damaging our eardrums. There's also the chatterbox who talks so fast our ears cannot keep pace, and the drawler we want to prod to complete the conversation. These problems irritate people with whom we talk just as much as they irritate us. Anticipate such possible situations with your callers, patiently handle them, and do not let them interfere with your effectiveness on the telephone.

Use the See-Saw Technique

Playing on a see-saw as a child, you learned the importance of balance. If both participants in the game did not mutually give and take, the game did not progress. Balance is equally important in effective telephone selling. Be careful not to become an information booth. If you only answer the caller's questions, the conversation is not in balance. In contrast, if you ask all the questions, there is no longer pleasant, positive conversation but a good possibility of losing the caller.

"What is the price of the property?" is a common question from callers. How do you answer? If you answer and say nothing else, what happens? Callers either thank you and hang up or ask another question. It is far better for them to ask another question than to hang up, but every time they ask something, you run the risk of your answer not being what they want to hear. If you answer the question with another question, you have not given them the answer and they may feel manipulated.

Consider using the combination of both or **see-saw technique**. This is an attempt to provide a balance between the caller and the agent, as both parties give and receive information. An agent answers a caller's question and *immediately* returns a question. Answering, "There are four bedrooms in this home; how many bedrooms do you need?" would be appropriate use of the see-saw or give-and-take telephone technique. It may be altered to fit your style and the individual caller, but the key is balance. Both parties are giving and receiving information on a fair trade arrangement.

Ask Questions

For the see-saw approach to work, you *must* ask questions. Some callers will volunteer needed information, but as discussed previously, the person asking questions controls the calls. In Chapter 9, "The Qualifying Process," you'll learn methods for determining a person's needs. The questions you ask are vital if you hope to help the caller. A good telephone qualifying explanation is to point out the reason for the questions and obtain callers' permission for you to ask them. Answers to your questions should convey all the information possible about the callers' needs. Word questions so that some explanation is required as an answer and not just "yes" or "no." Such questions, called **open-ended questions**, force you to really listen to the caller. An example of an open-ended question might be: "What items are essential for your new ranch?" or "What area of town do you think your family prefers?" It's harder to give short, cryptic answers to those questions, and you can learn more about the caller and his or her needs. Remember that what people say (or don't say) and how they say it are both important.

Watch Your Words

Often you will be requested to describe a property over the telephone. Select your words cautiously: Meanings are not in the words we use but in how the other person interprets them. We may tell a caller a home has a "nice, big yard." For a person living in a downtown high-rise apartment complex in a major metropolitan area, *any* yard is a big one. When people who have lived nearly all their lives in a country home several miles from any major thoroughfare and then move to the city, *no* yard is big enough to isolate them from traffic noise.

Be careful about painting a picture of the property. Words such as "nice," "big," or "good" are interpreted differently by different people. Definitions should be dependent upon the individuality of each person with whom you work and talk. You can always tell the caller that based upon your personal exposure to a good many properties, the one in question by your standards is . . . whatever you think it is. But hasten to add that you have learned not to evaluate a property for others without knowing what their views are.

Don't Argue

Sometimes agents get into a heated discussion with callers and end up winning the debate and losing the sale. Being diplomatic and patient with some callers is difficult. When a caller wants a price or an address to a property and you do not have the authority to give it, you must stand by your company's policy. If you have authority to release such information when you feel it's appropriate (as in most companies) but you are not sure about the caller, remember your fiduciary responsibility to the seller before deciding.

Regardless of what you decide, make every effort to maintain a professional approach. One successful technique is to use objections or differences as a reason to get together with the caller for further discussion. Remember that your first objective is to arrange for face-to-face personal contact with the qualified call-in prospect. Your efforts should center around accomplishing this.

Minimize Hold Time

In some situations, you need to place the caller on hold. When you do this, think of yourself as placing the person "on hang." If you let people hang too long, they die. The same is true for call-ins. Caller enthusiasm, interest, and positive attitude toward you and the subject of the call diminish in direct relationship to time spent holding. Do everything you can to minimize this threat to the sales process. If hold time begins to become excessive, inform callers how long you estimate they will remain on hold. How long is too long to keep callers holding is a question without an answer. You need to get back to callers before they become angry with you, and that length of time varies with the individual. Ingrain this in your thinking: Minimize hold time.

If it is going to take some time to gather the information, volunteer that fact quickly. Then volunteer to call the person back or set a time for them to call you back. This is not the best situation, but it is better than having the caller hang up on you after suffering on hold too long.

Be Enthusiastic

Every salesperson has experienced some unpleasant situations with call-ins. Perhaps the caller was rude, the agent was unprepared, or for other reasons the call went sour, and the prospect was lost. As you work on your telephone image, remember the telephone as a sales tool is a percentage game. In this aspect of sales (as in all selling), if you don't lose some, you're not trying enough. The key is not to get discouraged or anticipate problems with each caller. Keep your enthusiasm working for you, and it will improve your success in dealing with the call-in prospect.

To review the points made here, keep a checklist, such as the one in Figure 8.3, as a visual reminder. Keeping it by the phone may be a worthy idea.

| **Figure 8.3** | Checklist for Receiving Calls |

1. Prepare beforehand: Current ad sheet
   Call list
   Preview
2. Answer promptly with a positive greeting.
3. Identify company and ask to be of service.
4. Remember to maintain a professional image.
5. Ask callers to identify themselves: By the way, my name is. . . . May I ask yours?
6. Relax! Watch speed and volume of your voice.
7. Use the see-saw technique.
8. Ask for the caller's telephone number.
9. Ask if the caller has an e-mail address.
10. End the conversation by making an appointment.

This checklist should be placed near each telephone in the office as a quick reminder that it will pay off. Even jotting down a few notes on key points to present will help you clarify your thinking and increase your effectiveness.

| **Figure 8.4** | Checklist for Placing Calls |

1. Plan calls in advance to get the most out of calls. Gather necessary material first.
2. Offer to identify name and company; ensure person has time to talk: "Have you got time to talk with me? If not, I'll call back at a more appropriate time."
3. State purpose of call. Avoid sidetracking!
4. Keep hold time to a minimum.
5. Establish a return call timetable.
6. Be sensitive to National Do Not Call Registry issues and the policies in your office.

Placing Calls

When you are making calls, your telephone strategy will differ from the one you use with call-ins. Following are specific recommendations for your strategy with outgoing calls. See Figure 8.4 to review effective techniques for placing calls.

Plan Calls in Advance

You defeat your purpose if you make a call, get the proper person, and then are not prepared to talk. Have the information you need for your calls readily available. Spend a

TECHNOLOGY *IN ACTION*

Many new services are offered by companies and online for scheduling and tracking property showings. Visit http://www. showingsolutions.com to learn about one such company that will perform all the tasks necessary to set up a showing on a real estate listing along with following up with the showing agent after the appointment and notifying all the parties involved as to the results of the showing.

few minutes before the call reviewing the points to be discussed. This preparation can also include making sure there is an adequate signal on your cell phone. In many of the larger communities and certainly out in the country and around smaller communities, there will be "dead spots" where your phone will not work. I drive through one in my usual daily route and try to plan my calls so the signal, and consequently the phone conversation, is not lost.

Identify Yourself and Clear Time to Talk

You have read about the strategies of not offering your name immediately when prospects call. However, when you place a call, it is appropriate for you to give your name and your firm's name immediately. "This is John Smith with Jones Realty" gives the receiver essential information about whom they are talking to and the nature of the call.

Clearing time to talk is a strategy many agents learn the hard way. There will be occasions when you call people at the wrong time; no matter how good the news or how effective your technique, your timing will be bad. Asking a simple question such as, "Do you have a few minutes to talk?" will increase the chances of getting your message through. If people you call say they really don't have time to talk, ask if you may call back and do just that. Don't waste what you have to say by delivering it at an inappropriate time. This small consideration will go a long way toward helping set the tone for the conversation.

State Purpose of Call

Have you ever called someone, finished the conversation, and hung up, only to remember you did not cover the main purpose of the call? Without sounding rude or abrupt, state the purpose of your call as early as possible. This decreases the chance of getting sidetracked from the real reason you called. It also helps you get to the correct party if you are not sure to whom you should talk.

Don't Waste Time on Hold

Excessive time on hold diminishes your effectiveness and time management when calling as well as when receiving calls. When you are to be placed on hold, ask yourself if it would be easier to call back or leave a message. Either choice may be more productive than hanging on hold.

Give a Timetable for Return Calls

If you cannot talk to the desired person when you place your call, don't leave your name and number without stipulating a timetable for the return call. This may increase the chance of your call being first when there are several calls for an individual to return. This idea also conveys that you are not sitting around waiting for calls and helps improve your time management.

General Telephone Techniques

The following suggestions are less specific; however, their applicability and usefulness are important in an overall view of telephone techniques.

Keep in Touch

The successful agent does not spend excessive time waiting for the telephone to ring, but outside activity should not keep the salesperson from being in contact to receive messages. Make it a practice to check in regularly. Pagers and mobile phones are an asset, but the responsibility rests with the agent, regardless of his or her equipment.

TECHNOLOGY *IN ACTION*

Many successful real estate agents are using what is referred to as a "drip marketing campaign." This allows the real estate professional to set up saved searches through the local MLS® system. This system allows you to set up the desired features a buyer requests in a home and then the MLS® system monitors any new listings that become available matching these criteria. When a match is found, the information is e-mailed directly to the customer and the real estate agent. Through the use of certain programs, you can also have regular e-mails delivered to your clients and customers at regular intervals.

Handle Messages with Care

An agent often takes messages for another agent. The agent passing on information to someone else should do so accurately. He or she should commit the message to writing and see that the associate gets it. The other agent should keep in touch with the office to ensure that messages are picked up promptly, but the person taking the message should make every effort to obtain the correct facts. The message taker is not responsible for deciding what is important and what is not regarding messages, but the person is responsible for recording an accurate message. If you are not concerned for your colleagues and do not record messages well, your fellow agents may respond in the same manner when handling your messages.

Return Calls

You probably have reached the end of the work day only to wearily review the many calls you should return. The temptation is strong to forget all or some of them until tomorrow. A good alternative is to take a few minutes and relax. After this short rest, make those calls. Whether or not you reach each caller, at least you've tried. A While You Were Out message is a debt. If you value the callers or feel you might value them, fulfill your obligation by attempting to make contact. This is basic telephone courtesy, and after all, don't you expect it from people whom you ask to call you?

Don't Tie Up the Lines

A real estate office is a place of business. The investment in making the telephone ring is substantial. Be courteous of your broker or owner by avoiding long, pointless conversations. At least one line into the office should be open at all times. Keep your personal calls short, and if there is a need for lengthy explanations to buyers or sellers, consider talking face-to-face with them to increase your effectiveness.

National Do Not Call Registry

No presentation today regarding telephone techniques can be complete without referencing the National Do Not Call Registry. Congress has decided that consumers should have some control over unsolicited phone calls. There is now a legal method to, in effect, give telemarketers and others using the phone for promotion purposes a "Do Not Trespass" signal. Without going into excessive detail, real estate companies, like nearly all other businesses, need to become familiar with the law. A resource for this is found at http://www.donotcall.gov/. The industries using the telephone as a prospecting tool may want to also look at http://www.tellemarketing.donotcall.gov/ to review the rules and regulations. Wise firms will have policies regarding this law and should make sure the salespeople in the organization are well trained and respectful of the correct process to follow. No matter what your personal beliefs are about this point, keep in mind this is national legislation and salespeople are expected to honor the law. Failure to do so is not only potentially costly, it can go a long way in hurting the reputation of an individual and a company.

Practice, Practice, Practice

One of the most challenging aspects of using the telephone as a sales tool is that no two calls are the same. You need to strive continually to improve your telephone skills to increase your sales. It takes practice and discipline to realize the full potential of this valuable asset. Seek qualified assistance and you will improve. Adapt the suggestions in this chapter to fit your individual style and situation, and you'll be on your way to more effective telephone techniques.

Summary

When managed properly, the telephone can be an effective sales tool for the successful real estate salesperson.

The salesperson on floor duty and *receiving incoming calls* should prepare for the calls beforehand, be aware of his or her telephone image, answer promptly, identify the firm, ask to be of assistance, identify himself or herself, and obtain the caller's identity. Further, the salesperson should be relaxed with the caller, discipline the speed and volume of his or her speaking voice, use the so-called see-saw method of give and take, ask the caller questions, watch the words used, refrain from arguing with the caller, minimize hold time, and be enthusiastic.

When *placing calls,* the salesperson should plan the call in advance, identify himself or herself, state the purpose of the call, minimize hold time, and, if the person being called is not readily available, give a timetable for the person to return the call.

Other telephone techniques include keeping in touch with the office regarding incoming calls, handling messages with care, promptly returning calls, and keeping phone lines clear whenever possible.

Review Questions

1. What suggestions described in this chapter can make receiving telephone calls more effective?

2. What information should floor duty agents have at their fingertips?

3. What are some ways to determine what kind of image you are projecting to callers?

4. How soon should the telephone be answered after it starts ringing, and why?

5. Why is it wise to identify your firm when answering?

6. Why should you offer your assistance in the form of a question after you identify your firm?

7. Should you immediately offer your name when receiving calls? Why? Why not?

8. What is a good technique to obtain callers' names if they do not identify themselves?

9. Why is a warm, pleasant tone so important?

10. What is the see-saw technique?

11. What are some advantages of using the see-saw technique?

12. What is a good two-step telephone qualifying explanation?

13. Why does the agent need to be especially careful about word choice?

14. Why is it poor practice to argue with a caller?

15. What is the danger involved in placing a caller on hold?

16. What are five guidelines for effectively placing calls?

17. Why is planning the call important?

18. Why is clearing time to talk important?

19. Why is stating the purpose of your call effective?

20. What are two reasons for using a timetable for having calls returned?

21. What is the best way to improve your telephone technique?

22. Explain why a drip marketing software program would be good for a real estate professional to set up.

Discussion Questions

1. What are some weak telephone techniques you have experienced as a caller?

2. How should a salesperson handle a demanding, domineering caller?

3. Explain the importance of being a good message taker for other salespeople in your firm.

4. What are the laws in your community regarding talking on cell phones while driving? Do you agree or disagree with the laws?

Situation

How Not to Handle a Call

    Agent: Hello
    Caller: Is this Varsity Realty?
    Agent: Yes it is.
    Caller: I'm calling about a home you have for sale.
    Agent: Okay.
    Caller: What I want to know is how many bedrooms the home at 418 Low Oak Street has.
    Agent: Two.
    Caller: Thank you; goodbye.

How might *you* have handled this situation?

Stuck in the Office

Scene: Floor duty on a cold, wet, Sunday afternoon. You are the agent on duty with no backup agent to call on.

Agent: ABC Realty, may I help you?

Caller: The house you advertised today under the heading "Country Living," where is it?

Agent: Sir, it is south of town about 15 minutes outside the city limits. Are you familiar with that area?

Caller: Not really, but this is what I want to do. Just give me directions to the place, and if I like it after driving by, I'll call you back.

What do you do now?

The Qualifying Process

Key Terms

- Afford amount
- Buying motives
- Explain-and-request method
- Qualify amount
- Qualifying

What Is Qualifying?

In this chapter, we will look at how qualifying fits into the sales process by answering four main questions:

- What is qualifying?
- Why do you qualify?
- When do you qualify?
- How do you qualify?

In the overview of the sales process, we learned that a salesperson does not have a prospect until *after* qualifying. Before people are qualified, they are only suspects. **Qualifying** is determining a person's real estate needs to try to fulfill those needs. The key words are *determining needs*. Salespeople must sift through all the wants that suspects express and zero in on their real needs. Salespeople also need the ability to satisfy those real needs if they are to have a successful relationship with the consumers they are trying to serve. Start with the basics. Salespeople must help the people they are working with to set priorities. If a person comes to an agent with a list of 142 requirements for one piece of real estate, the agent's best bet might be to refer that person to the strongest competitor! These are the kinds of people with whom agents want their rivals to spend time. There is a bumper sticker that says "I Want It All." Maybe that is possible for a few folks, but most of us have to "settle" in one or more areas of our lives, including our real estate expectations.

From a psychological point of view, a salesperson is wise to work with suspects and establish priorities early. Many people want more than they can afford.

If agents can start with the suspect's needs and then add some of the wants, it will be better than having to take away some of the extras that a buyer has seen but cannot afford. Remember to start simple and add features rather than starting fancy and sacrificing features. Concentrate on helping the suspect get down to basic needs. This may take some time and require some patience on the agent's part, but it is well worth the effort. Keep this motto in mind: If I qualify better, I will show less but sell more. Don't ever underestimate the logic of being a solid qualifier.

Why Does an Agent Qualify?

There are four reasons a salesperson should qualify prospective buyers. These are outlined in the following sections.

Time Savings

The first reason is that a qualified buyer saves everyone's time. Qualifying saves the agent from wasting time (and money) showing real estate that is inappropriate for the potential purchaser. Inexperienced agents sometimes question the value of sitting down and getting to know their suspects; they would prefer to immediately start "selling." It generally is advantageous to visit with the people for a while, giving everyone a chance to relax and learn a little about each other. Keep this always in mind. Success is not about showing more properties; it's about showing the right properties.

Qualifying also saves the suspect's time. There is no point in showing property that does not meet the needs of the potential buyer. Too many alternatives will only confuse a buyer, especially those properties that do not fit the bill. And remember that qualifying is more, a lot more, than just money issues, as you'll see a bit later.

Seller time also is saved. Remember that sellers have agreed to let you, your company, or a cooperating company list their property because they were most likely promised that anyone coming to look at it has been qualified first. An agent can help keep that promise by first qualifying any prospective buyers. An important fiduciary duty is involved here as well. Exposing a client's property to someone who is not qualified to purchase it endangers that duty, and we have to take care of our clients.

Qualifying also saves time for many other parties involved in a real estate transaction. Suppose an agent shows property to a couple without qualifying them; they really like it and decide to buy. The agent draws up a contract, and the buyers and seller sign it. Terrific! How does the agent feel when the loan application procedure shows that the buyers will not be able to pay for the mortgage? All the work done by important allies in the salesperson's life, such as the title company, lender, property inspector, and so on, can be wasted. This is not the way to form the lasting alliances that we all need in this business, and it surely does not build a positive professional image.

Client Relations

Qualifying also saves the agent buyers. The couple who really wanted the property could not afford it. Although it isn't the agent's fault that they did not have enough for a down payment, unhappy buyers often hold their agents partly, if not totally, responsible for their failure to get the desired real estate. This transfer of blame may not demonstrate much logic, but the result is the same: The people are no longer "sold on you."

The sellers are also disappointed because they feel they have to start all over again. Any time a sale falls through, the agent-client relationship is strained. The necessary trust and confidence may be restored in some cases, but if the salesperson does not do the job well by failing to qualify prospects, the chance is slimmer of getting back on the right track with the buyer or seller.

Buyer-Property Match

The third reason you qualify is to match buyers with property. Without a thorough qualifying job, a salesperson will have trouble determining which properties to show. When suspects tell you they are looking for a three-bedroom, two-bath, with a two-car garage in a nice part of town, how many properties for sale fit that description? Maybe hundreds. You could grow old in a hurry working with such sketchy information. Qualify your suspects so that you have a good idea what to show them. A later section of this chapter discusses some specific areas to investigate. Well-qualified prospects will be easier to work with in the long run because you will have a sense of direction and standards to use when showing them properties later on. I've never had good luck when people tell me "they will know what they are looking for when the see it." At the very least, effective qualifying will help you know what *not* to show.

Increasing Confidence

The fourth reason to qualify is to build everyone's confidence. If agents sit down with their suspects and get to know them, everyone will feel more confident. Agents will have some solid information about what suspects need and want, which will increase the agents' chances of helping them and should do wonders for the agents' confidence level. The suspects will see that their agents are truly interested in them and are professional enough to form a plan for helping them. After this becomes evident to the suspects, they will relax and have more trust and confidence in their agents and their ability to help find them real estate. At this point, the suspect becomes a true prospect, someone you have a real sense of being able to help. And all agents really want that!

When Does an Agent Qualify?

Qualifying is an important part of the sales process, and for some salespeople, it is a difficult task. Agents use many ideas and techniques concerning *how* to qualify, but they are in agreement about *when* to qualify. Successful salespeople start to qualify *as soon as possible*. They need to gather basic information during the first contact with people to start helping them immediately. When do you stop qualifying? After the contract is signed? After closing? As long as you are in the real estate business and your buyer or seller is in your market area, you should never stop qualifying. The concept of the sales process and the use of follow-up and referral were presented in Chapter 1.

How Does an Agent Qualify?

Is there any one approach to qualifying that works better than the rest? Probably not. As in all parts of the selling process, the salesperson must work in a manner comfortable for both the agent and the buyer or seller.

Avoid Insulting Suspects

One qualifying approach definitely is *not* recommended. A new agent in real estate received an ad call about a nice townhouse in a prestigious neighborhood. After asking and answering a few questions, the agent set up a time to get together with the caller and discuss the property further. They arranged to meet at the real estate office. At the appropriate time, a well-dressed, middle-aged couple arrived and introduced themselves as the callers. The agent reviewed the highlights of the listing. The young salesman nervously had asked his sales manager to sit in on the qualifying session to evaluate his approach. It quickly became obvious to the manager that money would not be a factor in the couple's decision about the property. The agent was inexperienced and nearly blew the whole transaction when he abruptly asked the couple, "About the money necessary to buy this place, have you got the bread?" Only some frantic work by the manager saved the buyer. Money *is* a factor is qualifying but not the *only* factor and may not be the first issue to bring up. Remember, we can have three different buyers, all with the same monetary qualifications, that are looking for three entirely different types of properties. This is true because of requirements they need satisfied that are of a noneconomic nature.

Explain-and-Request Method

One of the better basic techniques to use in qualifying is the **explain-and-request method**. Sometimes this is known as the justify-and-request method as well. As mentioned earlier in this chapter, most experienced salespeople like to sit down and get to know the people they are going to work with. This get-acquainted session reveals something about the personalities of the people and also gives them a chance to learn something about you. Remember, all salespeople have to sell *themselves* before they sell anything else. After you have relaxed and visited a little, use the explain-and-request method, which entails explaining to the people the need to ask qualifying-type questions and then requesting permission to ask the questions. Most people will not react negatively to the questioning if you explain in advance the reason you are asking.

An example is, "Mr. and Mrs. Jones, in order for me to do the best job I can for your family, there is some information I need to obtain from you."

The second part of the explain-and-request method is also important. In the step of explaining, you justify the reason for asking the qualifying information. In the request step, you ask for permission to begin the qualifying. Mr. and Mrs. Jones can understand it may be important for you to ask questions, but they may not be ready to answer them. It is just good business to get the suspect's okay before you start. If there is some doubt or hesitation on their part, you need to know, *before* you get in trouble by asking necessary, although personal, questions.

The problem may be that they are not sold on you. If you feel this is the case, remain relaxed and ask more general questions for a while. The problem could be that they are still not sure why you want to ask these questions. If you sense this, then go back to the explanation step again. The words you use are not as important as how you go about it. Remember to explain and then request.

If you are uncomfortable in asking some of these questions, it may be appropriate to acknowledge your discomfort. Some people grow up with a background that emphasizes that it is impolite to question a person about his or her successes or failures in business or on a personal level. This conditioning can carry over to your role in real estate. I have found it best to admit frankly that asking some of the qualifying-type questions can make me nervous. But it is essential to know, not *everything,* but *some* things if I am to properly serve them.

Areas of Investigation

The list of qualifying information you would *like* to have about any given suspect can vary depending on the situation; however, there are some basic things you *need* to have for all your suspects.

Qualifying Issues Checklist

Note that the following qualifying list starts with general questions and then becomes more specific to reduce the risk of getting too personal too quickly. There is no specific order, but you would be wise to start with the general and gradually become more specific.

Name
Get the people's names early and correctly. Be sure you know how to pronounce and spell them properly. Determine if first names are legal names or nicknames.

Family Size
If appropriate, find out the number of people who will be living in the home and the sex and approximate ages of adults, teenagers, or young children. (Remembering the names of the children indicates real interest in the family.)

Local Residents or Out of Towners

If the people are from your city, they may know as much (or more) about the area as you do. If they are from out of town, you may want to give them your "Welcome to Our Town" overview and then narrow down the scope as the sales process continues. With either approach, the level of knowledge of the suspect will necessitate altering your selling pattern accordingly.

Current Real Estate Situation

If the people own property that needs to be sold before they move, this presents a different selling situation than if they are able to act immediately. You need to have this information.

Urgency of Purchase

Investigating this area will give you some projection of a time frame for the entire transaction. If they have been looking for a while and would buy "if we found the right one," your approach needs to be different than for the legendary "we need a place by sundown" suspect.

Special Requirements

There may be one or more absolutely mandatory things a property must have to meet a particular set of needs. Some examples are a positive cash flow before taxes, certain zoning, a particular neighborhood, or large master bedroom. If there really are some must haves—or must not haves—you need to know right away.

Lifestyle

This concern is in line with special requirements. Many salespeople meet with possible buyers in their environment. This is done to find out something about how the people use their property. For example, to many families, home is a stopping place to eat, sleep, and occasionally spend some time. For others, home is the center of family activities. It is important for you to get a feel for how each family perceives the role of their home or home-to-be. Spending time at the present location of potential buyers can help you "feel" what they want or don't want in their next home. This area of qualifying is less specific than other areas, but it is equally necessary.

Decision-Making Ability

Salespeople often discover that after finding what they think is the correct property, the prospect cannot decide to purchase. Often this hesitation stems from lack of self-confidence. To help deal with this potential snag, one successful technique is to say

---

One of the mistakes often made is to get too specific (that is, particular property focus) too fast. If the prospects have some current and local knowledge (two different things, remember), give them credit for it. If they do not have that information, it's best to present a broad-scale picture first. Refer to Chapter 4 about knowing your community for examples of areas to highlight.

something like, "Buying or selling real estate is a big decision. If you want to bring in some additional help to make this important decision, it is understandable and often done." Bringing this up during the initial qualifying may save you problems later.

This outside help might be a parent of one of the suspects who is putting up the money, or it could be a friend with more experience than your buyer. It may be an accountant or an attorney. Regardless of who it is, you need to know early in the process that another party exists and possibly may be involved. What do you then do with this "expert"? You accept him or her and respect the helping role in the sales process in this particular transaction. If you alienate a trusted ally or begrudge his or her involvement, the helper can ruin your relationship with your prospects. The only reason that person is involved is to help the buyers, and after all, this is why you are involved too.

Financial Situation

When many agents hear the term qualifying, they immediately think of money. Certainly income and financing are an important part of the qualifying process, but they comprise only one part. As stated before, we are conditioned in our society to feel that a person's finances are really no one else's business. But salespeople must have some guidelines to work with to be able to help the suspects become real prospects. Many agents have had some problems in working up the courage to broach this subject. However, there are ways to get the necessary information about people's finances without getting too personal. Remember, your goal is to be knowledgeable, not nosy.

Many prospective buyers will need a review of the various financing options available. The agent should be able to discuss accurately the advantages and disadvantages of the more common ones. Some of the basics include equity purchases, conventional mortgages with 5 to 25 percent down, VA, FHA, buy downs, graduated mortgages, variable rate mortgages, owner carry, and second liens. Of course, there are other approaches to consider, and to do so requires a current working knowledge of the money market in the area. An agent can save (or lose) his or her buyers and sellers thousands of dollars by being informed (or uninformed) about the various choices available.

Many agents like to use a discussion about these options as an introduction to financial qualifying. Qualifying financially is broken down into two parts: the initial down payment and the ongoing payments. Establish some general amounts for each. Few people feel comfortable asking or answering blunt questions such as, "How much money do you make?" or "How much money do you have in savings?"

Fortunately, there are other, more subtle, ways to get this information. One approach to consider is, "Mr. Buyer, have you discussed approximately how much of your savings (or proceeds from the sale of your other real estate) you plan to invest as a down payment on your new property?"

The next question would be, "Have you determined approximately how much of your income you plan to invest in ongoing payments?" These may be monthly or annual or anywhere in between, depending on the situation. After you have some general dollar amounts, you can see if the numbers correspond with the rest of the qualifying information.

A dollar only buys so much real estate. You do not set market value, and it's not your fault if prices are different than your prospects believe them to be. If there is some

> **TECHNOLOGY** *IN ACTION*
>
> One excellent way to qualify buyers today is by using online loan calculators. Web sites such as http://www.fanniemae.com and http://www.bankrate.com provide several good online loan calculators for borrowers.

perception problem about the true cost of real estate, this needs to be brought to light early and resolved, or all your other attempts to help the people will serve no purpose.

Each market has different qualifying guidelines. Figures 9.1, 9.2, 9.3, and 9.4 are some examples of check sheets. Your company should already have some of these printed and should revise them as required. **Check with several lenders periodically to make sure you are using current guidelines**. These check sheets will help you get the correct information in a systematic manner so that you don't miss anything important. Using the sheets also will show your professional approach to getting and recording necessary information about personal situations so you can provide better service. In some cases, it may be best to have a loan officer prequalify prospective buyers. This will help eliminate the questions about financial abilities before a contract is tendered on any property.

> **TECHNOLOGY** *IN ACTION*
>
> Consider using a software program such as Excel to build a spreadsheet that will automatically do the mathematical calculations for you during your qualifying consultations with customers. You can also upload these spreadsheets to your Web site so consumers can use them to discover whether they qualify for a home loan. Make sure that you have a loan officer or two verify your calculations and always place a disclaimer on your Web site that this information and the qualifying ratios can change without your knowledge. For more information on building Excel spreadsheets, visit http://www.microsoft.com.

ABC Realty Prospect Information Form   Figure 9.1

REMEMBER: The information you obtain from prospects will enable you to better help buyers with their real estate needs. Explain this to prospects *before* you begin the questioning and obtain their permission before you ask the questions.

Name: _____ Telephone: _____

Address: _____

How Contacted?   Walk In ☐ Ad C8J1 ☐ Prospecting/Referral ☐
Other ☐

Number of Childrens _____ Ages _____ Other relatives _____

Area Preference: _____

Special Features Needed (Help the prospects concentrate on "have to's"):

_____

_____

_____

Urgency: Sell First _____ Renting _____

Desired Move-in Date: _____

Financing (Refer to New-Loan Qualifying Form): _____

_____

Approximate Initial Investment/Down Payment: _____

Approximate Monthly Payments: _____

If property is found today that meets prospects' needs, can they make a decision on it? Yes (   )   No (   )

Must someone else see the property before they can decide on it?
Yes (   )   No (   )   If yes, who? _____

Date: _____ Agent: _____

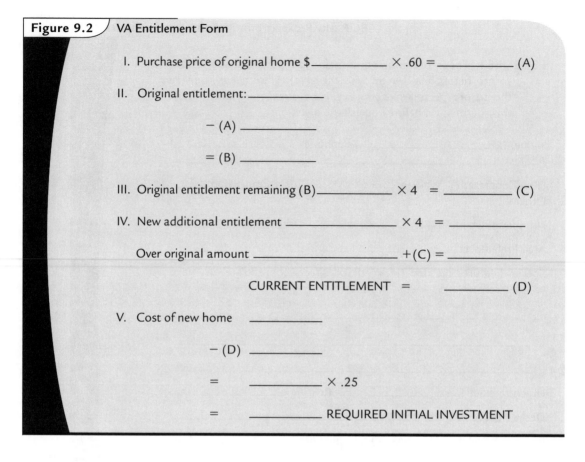

Figure 9.2 VA Entitlement Form

I. Purchase price of original home $_____ × .60 = _____ (A)

II. Original entitlement: _____

   − (A) _____

   = (B) _____

III. Original entitlement remaining (B) _____ × 4 = _____ (C)

IV. New additional entitlement _____ × 4 = _____

   Over original amount _____ + (C) = _____

   CURRENT ENTITLEMENT = _____ (D)

V. Cost of new home _____

   − (D) _____

   = _____ × .25

   = _____ REQUIRED INITIAL INVESTMENT

Qualify versus Afford

Sometimes there is a difference between what people feel they can invest in real estate and what they actually qualify to invest. It is the agent's responsibility to know the difference. **Qualify amount** is what people should invest in real estate based on averages for a particular market area. This is the amount an analysis shows they should spend. The **afford amount** is what the person feels comfortable investing. This is not a statistical average but the individual's own comfort level for investment. Let's look at three examples.

A middle-aged, two-career couple are looking for a new house. Their children are grown and on their own; the couple has few debts, adequate savings, and an excellent credit rating. On paper, this couple might qualify for a monthly payment that is double what they feel they can afford comfortably.

One buyer in a similar situation said, "I'm thinking ahead to slowing down and retiring. I couldn't sleep nights thinking about a monthly obligation of that size for the next 20 or 30 years." Under these circumstances, the successful real estate agent should respect the afford amount the buyers feel comfortable with.

Formula for VA Qualifying   Figure 9.3

Applicants' gross monthly income _____

If weekly × 52 ÷ 12 = average monthly   Remember: Not only
If 2 weeks × 26 ÷ 12 = average monthly   pay but retirement,
If annually ÷ 12 = monthly   Social Security, child
                                             support or alimony,
                                             rental incomes,
                                             commission, and
                                             bonuses will be
                                             considered for income.

Total the Following Obligations:

  1. Income tax (taxable income only)   _____   (see chart)

  2. Social Security or retirement   _____   .0765 × gross
                                                         monthly income
                                                         up to $250
                                                         per worker

  3. Monthly payments (6 mos. or more) _____   (loans and retail
                                                         accounts)

  4. Life and medical insurance premiums _____

  5. Child care and/or support   _____

  6. VA family factor   _____   (see below)

  7. Projected new home maintenance   ($140 per
     and utilities   _____   1,000 sq. ft.)

  8. TOTAL   _____

                                                         VA FAMILY
                                                         FACTORS

GROSS MONTHLY INCOME   _____   1 person—$400
                                           2 people—$660

MINUS TOTAL OBLIGATIONS _____   3 people—$835
                                           4 people—$960
                                           5 people—$1060

MAXIMUM MONEY   Add $90 per
FOR HOUSE PAYMENT   _____   person thereafter

Figure 9.4	Formula for FHA Qualifying	
	Applicant's gross monthly income	_____
	Subtract income tax obligations (see chart)	_____
	Equals FHA income	_____
	Total the Following Obligations:	_____
	1. Social Security (.0765)	_____
	2. Monthly payments (12 mos. or more)	_____
	3. Life and medical insurance premiums	_____
	4. Child care/child support	_____
	TOTAL	_____
	Subtract obligations	_____
	ANSWER	A. _____
	FHA Income $\times$ .43	B. _____
	Pick smaller of two figures, A or B	_____
	Subtract projective maintenance and utilities ($140 per 1,000 ft. of living area)	_____
	MAXIMUM MONEY FOR HOUSE PAYMENT	_____

WARNING—Using maximum money for house payment causes your buyer to be a marginal applicant.

Another case is a young couple with a small child and plans for another baby soon, Both work and desperately want to get into a house. They want the agent to help them find a home while they can still qualify on two incomes, as the wife plans to quit working to be with the children. What this couple can afford and what they qualify for are different. The goal to provide a home for their family is a noble one, and the agent should try to help them if possible. However, no one wins if they get into a new home and can't make it on their razor thin income. What happens? Forced sale? Marital problems? Are these people likely to ask the agent for help again? Part of the agent's responsibility in qualifying sometimes is to help "tone down" aspirations. Remember that the qualify amount and afford amount have entirely different meanings.

Buying Motives

Another part of qualifying is trying to establish **buying motives**—why people are looking for real estate. What difference does it make as long as they are buying? It makes an enormous difference! The way you present the property will depend on the prospective purchaser's reason for buying. You are not being encouraged to alter facts: you do not have to lie to sell, but you can present information in various ways. And it is an important part of qualifying suspects to discuss why they are purchasing. People have many reasons for purchasing; some predominant buying motives follow:

- **Size change**—More or fewer people in the family or company.
- **Financial reasons**—*Taxes,* appreciation, return on investment.
- **Pride of ownership**—Knowing that it belongs to them.
- **Prestige/social reasons**—Stepping up or stepping down; keeping up with family and friends.
- **Convenience**—Location and labor-saving devices.
- **Career changes**—Whether across the city, state, or nation, this is one of the most common motives.
- **Technology change**—Workplace is out of date or obsolete.
- **Desire for change**—A common but difficult motive to pinpoint. People get tired of the same car, clothes, food, and real estate. Change for change's sake may not seem as acceptable a reason as some others, but watch for it in your prospects.

This list is just a starting point; there are many other motives. Some are stronger than others for individual prospects, but remember, it's necessary to find out why the people are buying or selling. Sometimes prospects will not reveal their motives directly, so the agent must look for clues that give insight into this important area of qualifying.

Summary

A salesperson develops suspects into bona fide prospects through qualifying. *Qualifying* is a salesperson's determination of a person's real estate wants and needs in order to fulfill those wants and needs. This process saves the agent time and money and builds good relations by showing potential buyers only properties they might want or can afford.

A proven technique used to qualify potential buyers is the *explain-and-request method,* wherein the salesperson both asks and justifies the reasons for asking a customer for qualifying information. Such qualifying information should include the prospect's name, family size, whether he or she is a local resident or from out-of-town, current living situation, urgency of purchase, special requirements, lifestyle, decision-making abilities, and financial situation.

An integral part of the qualifying process is determining the prospect's *buying motives;* such motives might include family change, pride of ownership, desire for added prestige, convenience, career changes, or a general desire for change.

Review Questions

1. What is qualifying?

2. What are four reasons a salesperson should qualify?

3. When should the salesperson start to qualify?

4. When should the salesperson stop qualifying?

5. What is the explain-and-request method of qualifying?

6. When qualifying, why should you start with general questions and then become more specific?

7. What are some qualifying areas you need to investigate?

8. When asking questions about family size, what is one excellent strategy to convey a genuine interest in the family?

9. If a suspect seems to be having difficulty making a decision, what is a good strategy to use?

10. What are the two parts of financial qualifying with which you must deal?

11. What is the difference between what buyers can qualify for and what they can afford?

12. What are some predominant buying motives?

13. Visit http://www.bankrate.com and list the various types of loan calculators available for the consumer who is considering a home mortgage loan.

Discussion Questions

1. Do you believe a salesperson should qualify all potential buyers? Why or why not?

2. How would you begin asking the qualifying questions that are so important to the sales process?

3. In addition to the qualifying areas mentioned in the chapter, what else would you want to know about your prospects?

Situation

Successful Qualifying Technique

You are the agent on floor duty one afternoon when a well-dressed couple enters your office. They are interested in learning about several new homes your company has listed in a nearby development. After the introductions are completed, you begin to ask qualifying questions. The gentleman responds to the first one with a very general answer and responds to the second one by saying, "We can talk about all that later. Let's go *look* at the properties right now!" What happens next?

None of Your Business

Suppose in the preceding situation the suspect (at best for now) simply refuses to answer any qualifying questions and flatly states, "That is all personal and absolutely none of your business." Now what happens?

Presenting the Property

Key Terms

- Mini-decision approach
- Previewing
- Stair-step

Role of Showing in the Sales Process

This chapter examines ideas for showing property, including some techniques a salesperson should know to present the property effectively and efficiently. The role of showing in selling also is discussed, as are some showing guidelines.

In any sales presentation, regardless of the product or service, the actual demonstration is critical. This may be a little harder for the salesperson offering a service, such as in a listing presentation. It is unrealistic to think a prospect (remember the qualifying stage just occurred in the previous chapter) will purchase without interaction with the product. In nearly every case, potential owners try on clothes, test drive cars, and ride horses before deciding to purchase. Assuredly people look at property, sometimes more than once, before seriously considering it. The effective real estate salesperson has a firm grasp on how critical a good showing plan is. The purpose of this chapter is to point out the role showing has in selling. Another purpose is to list some significant guidelines for showing to help increase your sales success.

Why Showing Is Necessary

As stated before, the average and below average salesperson knows *what* to do. It is the superior person that knows *why* he or she is doing a particular task or activity. There are at least four major reasons for showing (see Figure 10.1): to sell, to create excitement, to point out features and benefits, and to further qualify.

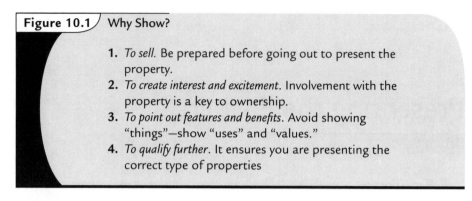

Figure 10.1 / Why Show?

1. *To sell.* Be prepared before going out to present the property.
2. *To create interest and excitement.* Involvement with the property is a key to ownership.
3. *To point out features and benefits.* Avoid showing "things"—show "uses" and "values."
4. *To qualify further.* It ensures you are presenting the correct type of properties

To Sell

An agent should not present a property without competence *and* confidence to carry out the rest of the sale. For many salespeople, the need for preparation becomes very significant. The well-trained person will still be nervous and excited when the time to show comes, but at least he or she will be able to represent the property, its owners, and the agent's company in an adequate manner. Don't be like I was when my first prospect said to me, "This is a fine house, I'll take it." All I could do was gulp and stammer, "Are you sure?" Talk about *unselling!* Frankly, I did not yet feel comfortable enough in the role of a salesperson to carry out my task. The prospect was ready; I wasn't. Don't make that mistake. Go out and show as soon as you feel ready, don't delay. But avoid rushing out ill-prepared. This step is not for practice—it's for real and you want to do it right.

For Involvement

Showing is an action process, and one reason for the activity is so the prospect can get involved. Up to this point, the salesperson and possible buyer have been passive while

TECHNOLOGY *IN ACTION*

As noted in previous chapters, photos, virtual tours, and many other types of media formats have provided consumers opportunities to view properties in advance. This new practice of home viewing helps buyers narrow the number of properties to look at before meeting with the real estate agent. Savvy real estate professionals understand the need to keep good photos and virtual tours on the Web to streamline the home-buying course of action.

together. Sitting around and talking about properties is different from actually getting out and seeing them. Part of the *why* in showing is so the prospect can determine how the property "fits" or "feels." The astute salesperson is sensitive to this and allows time for it to occur. No matter what phase of real estate you practice, this point is the same: Give the person some time to interact with the place.

To Point Out Features and Benefits

To accomplish the desired involvement, sometimes the agent must call certain facets to the person's attention. One important role of showing is to allow the agent to point out the features and benefits of a particular property and the area in which it is located. Notice that the foregoing sentence reads "features and benefits" rather than "things," because the first concern in matching people with properties is *how* the prospective buyers are going to use the property. What is their lifestyle? You should learn how buyers plan to use the property or their particular means of incorporating the real estate into their pattern of living.

You need to present the property showing how buyers can best use it, based on the ways they live. For example, a dishwasher cleans the dishes, but it can be presented to a buyer in terms of the ease and convenience that appliance offers his or her family and the time it will save performing a chore. Similarly, consider how delighted most people are to find a fireplace. It is a masterpiece of masonry that certainly complements a room, but we present it to the buyer as hours of relaxation amid the comfortable atmosphere the fireplace can create for the family on a cold night. Remember that it's not *what we* think is important or *how we* would use a property that counts—it is the prospect's interpretations we need to support. This approach definitely requires "features and benefits," not "things," to be presented. Keep this in mind when conducting showings.

Further Qualifying

A prime role of showing is to qualify prospects further. Buyers may have visited with the agent in the office and verbally assured the agent that they know exactly what they want, without question. So the agent finds the perfect offering to meet all the buyers' stated requirements, sets the appointment, and believes the sale will be closed easily. Then the agent is surprised to learn that the buyers just don't like the property at all—maybe even hate it. Is this a negative being injected into the agent's perfect plan? Not at this point. The reason is that the agent has further qualified the buyer and therefore has accomplished something. When people say no in the showing process, it isn't a negative; it's a definite positive because the salesperson has eliminated one thing that stood in the way of making the sale. If too many things stand in the way of making a sale, the agent probably won't make it. But at least he or she knows the buyer's opinion about that particular piece of property and a general idea of what the buyer doesn't like. When this happens, what should the agent do? Simply shift gears and start over. It is not uncommon for buyers who insist initially that they know exactly what they want eventually to buy something almost entirely opposite. The only way the agent can discover this is by showing them some properties. From their reactions, the salesperson can get a much better feel for what they really want, as well as accomplish one of the roles of showing—to qualify the buyers further.

Some Showing Guidelines

What are some guidelines to remember when showing? Suppose you have a cash-in-pocket prospect, Mr. Haskill, and you are ready to take him out to present some properties. You have qualified him, you have determined his financial ability, you have determined his wants and needs, you think you know all you need to know about him, and now you're getting ready to formulate your game plan. What are some features you want to cover while you're showing? Let's talk about some guidelines and establish a checklist for showing. At least 11 points should be included. Be sure you don't leave out any step. They are all of equal importance, and they are all necessary for a really good showing presentation.

Preview the Property

Suppose a salesperson is going out to show the house at 456 Peachtree Street, and the buyer asks a question about it. It would be unwise to answer, "Please don't ask me any questions about it, Mr. Buyer; let's just go and become informed together!" One of the most important steps on the checklist should be **previewing the property**, examining it before showing it to potential buyers.

On the way to the property with a potential buyer in the car, a salesperson needs to talk about something. Most good real estate agents agree they usually get better results if they talk about business rather than sports, the stock market, or other unrelated topics. How can the salesperson talk about the property they are going to see if he or she hasn't seen it? There are emergency situations when it is necessary to show a piece of property without previewing, but rarely does anything positive come out of these "cold showings." Most of the time, the surprises agents get showing property in this manner are negative ones. If there are going to be negative surprises for people, it is to the agent's advantage if the folks are warned before they get there. Try to let your prospects find some of the positive surprises themselves. But if there is anything negative that you know is going to turn up, it is best to bring it up beforehand.

Maybe the house meets every need the people stated to you, except they wanted a big back yard, and this house has everything but a big back yard. If you say, "Joe and Jennifer, I would really appreciate your looking at this piece of property—everything you *asked* for is there, except that the back yard is small." They immediately think the yard is postage stamp size! The buyers like the front and the inside of the house, and then you get to the back yard. After what you said, it really doesn't look so bads after all! They're excited about the rest of house, and so they go ahead with it. But if your prospects walk out there thinking the house has everything they asked for because you haven't said anything to the contrary, and they are excited with the front yard and the inside, only the smaller yard hit them unprepared—right there you run the risk of your sale. If you make it a rule never to show without previewing (except in isolated situations), you have better control of the situation. If you are new or getting started in the real estate business, stop a minute and think about who comes to your open houses. Often the top agents in town come alone because they are checking out properties for future buyers. These agents have found that *pays* because in the long run you cannot sell what you have not seen.

Plan the Showing

Before taking any other steps, an agent must plan the showing. Three key aspects of showing that require planning are the appointment, the route to the property, and determining the audience.

Making Appointments

One of the first steps in good planning is setting up an appointment. Set up appointments you can keep. Avoid situations such as these:

> You call up XYZ Real Estate, and agent Jack Jones answers the phone. You say, "Jack, I'd like to show your house at 123 Main Avenue at 1:30." He says, "Fine, I'll see that it's open for you." He's there at 1:15; he's still there at 2:00. If you aren't prompt, he's going to be one mad salesperson when you get there.

> Or suppose a buyer says, "I'll have a couple of hours. We'll get together at 1:30, but I need to be home at 3:30." At 4:15 when you take her home—she is frustrated and angry.

Both situations describe an agent who was not conscientious about appointments. Set appointments early in your plan, and then be sure to keep them. Plan your time, do it realistically, and be reliable. Customers and colleagues will appreciate it if you follow this crucial first step of the planning process. It is always best to be a little flexible on setting appointments. To tell Mr. Jones you will be at Main Avenue around 1:15 to 1:30 but will call if you can't be there by 1:45 is a wise strategy. Also, to determine *in advance* how many appointments can be established comfortably is a good plan.

Choosing the Route

The route you drive to approach the property is also an important part of your planning. Nearly all property is accessible through routes less desirable than others. You need to emphasize the positive and take the most advantageous route to show the highlights of the neighborhood.

Be careful, however, if you drive through a $250,000 neighborhood on your way to show a $150,000 house. How are the less expensive houses going to look after the lovely trip? A route that is too attractive or too expensive can work against you, but by putting a little planning and effort into selecting the route, you can choose the most advantageous one to approach your property. Your goal is to present the property as attractively, yet still honestly, as possible.

Knowing Your Audience

Another important part of planning is to determine your audience. This makes a significant difference. Previously we discussed the decision maker and the importance of finding out as early as possible who the decision maker is in the group. If that person is

TECHNOLOGY *IN ACTION*

A good DVD/video to use with buyers in advance of showing properties is *8 Steps to Buying a Home* by David Knox Productions. This video helps buyers learn more about the home-buying process and can help the real estate agent as a good introductory tool in building trust and a relationship with the future homebuyer.

someone other than Mr. and Mrs. Prospect, a vital part of your planning is to arrange for this person to be present for the showing. Having him or her on board early can save you time and headaches down the road.

Figure 10.2 illustrates how to prepare a showing plan.

Keep the Sellers Away

Another important point for our showing checklist is moving the seller out of the picture. Recently I presented a ranch with which I was impressed. The sellers said they would be in the back of the place in case we needed them; obviously, the listing agent had briefed them well. This is the most advantageous kind of situation, rather than the sellers asking prospects what they would like to know about the property. Arrange to keep the seller out of the picture as much as possible. Sometimes you can't control the situation, and this can make the difference in whether you make a sale.

A few years ago, I listed a beautiful house sitting on a hill with a glass wall overlooking the skyline of the city. There was only one time to show it to its best advantage—at sundown, when the view of the city from the patio as city lights started to twinkle was absolutely breathtaking!

The people loved it! I had one prospect on the patio at sunset inhaling the clean country air and that gorgeous view, when the seller popped out the back door and screeched, "You forgot to tell these people we've got 128 square feet of kitchen cabinet space!" Wham! The buyer's enthusiasm for this house was gone because he didn't care a bit about the cabinet space. I had him sold completely on the patio and the great outdoors that came free with it, but he bought another house. If only the sellers had been out of the way! This is also true in other phases of real estate. The retiring farmer/rancher telling the possible "city slicker" owner all about how to run the tractor at the first showing is making a mistake. So is the developer who insists on justifying building design to the group of investors first previewing the property. Those things are important, but not now. If the seller has (and he or she frequently does) some significant points to share about the property, you can obtain that information when you preview. In fact, it makes good sense to spend some time with the seller and learn as much as you

June 25 @ 1:00 P.M. Meet at sales office. Confirmed
6-24 @ 6:00 P.M. Client: Jane L. Garner. No one
else will be going along.

1:30   9327 Brimer (Confirmed with seller, Mrs. Fredrick).
Take Rosewood Street off expressway. Turn left on
Kirks Street. Point out landscaping and proximity to
middle school.

2:15   3450 Farmerland (Take key). House vacant.
Mention it may be hot and stuffy. Get on
University Oaks (north) when leaving. Turn right
on Foster Road.

3:15   18304 Foster Road (Larry Neal or Mike Wilson
to open. 681-7770) Point out neat neighborhood lawns. Seller
will repaint bedrooms per listing agent.

Approx. 3:45 Talk about properties over coffee. Remember!
Ms. Garner wants to be home by 5:00 P.M. at the least.

Figure 10.2   Tentative Showing Plan

can about the property. But it's best to do this without your prospect and before your showing.

Again, if at all possible, keep the sellers out of the picture. This is partially the job of the listing agent, but don't be afraid to check that this part of the job has been done. If he or she has not done a good job, report back to the listing agent.

Maintain Control

The aim of keeping the sellers out of the picture is to help the agent maintain control of the showing situation. Maintaining control is a key showing guideline. This can be complicated, because the salesperson certainly never wants to appear pushy, but *agents* need to run the show. Don't let the sellers—or another agent—run it.

An example of no control can be observed when opening a house for another agent. The agent and prospects arrive first, and as you are unlocking the door, the agent says to the people, "You know, I haven't seen this house yet. Since I'm not the one planning to live here, why don't you just go on and take a look at it." This is certainly not the way to show property. The agent seems to be offering to hang around in case the prospects decide to buy! This is not the way to be a success in the real estate business. Be sure you call the shots; but do so in a relaxed, discreet manner.

To maintain control, just be firm and assertive with the prospects and be careful never to be rude or aggressive. When you get together with the people, you simply have to say, "Mr. and Mrs. Prospect, I'm going to present some properties to you today, and this is how we're going to do it." Go on to explain your plans; set the pace, and if the people stray from the plan, tactfully bring them back to it. Regardless of how much time and effort you have put into planning and being ready to show, you can't do it effectively if your buyers go off on tangents. Controlling is something you develop with experience; you will find the more you show, the more proficient you will become. Make a concentrated effort to maintain control, and it will show in increased sales.

Take Enough Time

Another guideline for showing is to let people take their time—don't rush them through a showing. Remember, if you've done a good job of qualifying, the property you show should be close to meeting the people's needs; so don't rush. Give the buyers time to inspect the property. If you are off base in your selection, you will know it. These people say, "This is fine, looks good, let's go someplace else." A lot of real estate agents seem to think, "If I can show them enough places, one is bound to stick." Agents and prospects can learn a great deal from showing, but to do it properly, it must be done thoroughly.

Also remember that you continue to qualify your buyers with each presentation, and their reactions are your cues. Sometimes when people first enter a property, they have a negative reaction. It will either be overcome after a time, or it may stick. They may say, "I don't want to see any more places like this." It takes time to show, so give yourself time to do a good job. Early in your showing with the prospects, they may need to learn current prices or the local styles, and these things take time. The people may be shocked at prices if they haven't looked in 20 years, so they may need time to catch their breath. Don't confuse them further by taking them through a myriad of choices all at once.

Limit the Choices

Some agents come in at the end of the day thoroughly exhausted, complaining that they have shown their buyers 19 houses, but they can't make up their minds. Is it any wonder? Many agents get confused after just 4 or 5 properties, so certainly prospects can do the same thing! Another guideline to incorporate into the showing checklist is to limit the choices.

This doesn't mean that an agent should say, "Look, Mr. Gray, in the last two weeks I've shown you four places, and my training director said I'm supposed to limit your choices, so that's all I'm going to show you! Take it or leave it!" He'll certainly leave it. Limiting choices as advocated here refers to showing not too many alternatives at one time. Show a maximum of three or four at a time. Then sit down and talk a while. Discuss the pluses and minuses and evaluate the buyer's reactions—work through those three or four. If there are too many, the details start running together.

Psychologists tell us the human mind can handle only a maximum of six or seven choices before it begins to become confused. This is especially important if people are new to an area. How many new listings do agents usually see on preview? Can anyone keep them all straight? Sometimes properties just don't make an impression. Or four or five will have one or two outstanding features, and soon the salesperson can't remember which one had which feature. The buyers say, "Hey, we want to see the one that had the green master bedroom, the paneled family room, and the beautiful rock fireplace again. It was a terrific house." You really hate to break the news to them, but those features were in three different houses!

If you are showing more complex properties, such as a highly improved agricultural unit or a commercial project, there will be myriad details to present and discuss. One property could take the entire time allocated for showing. The same principle applies here. It is wrong to "sell one while showing another." While presenting a product, concentrate on that one, then move on to another.

Ask for Comparison

To involve the people with the property, ask them questions. Remember, during each showing, you're continually pointing out features and benefits, and it is important to ask your buyers to compare.

Some agents think it is a good idea after a couple of showings to say something like, "Mr. Rodriguez, how does this choice compare to the last one?" Do you use this question? It is *not* a good idea. Take each feature individually, because if the salesperson throws out too many comparisons at once, the buyer can't deal with them. Go over the property one step at a time. Reword this question to something like, "Mr. Rodriguez, how does the living room of this house compare with the living room of the house we saw before?"

If agents have properly qualified the buyers, agents know their needs. If a particular feature is important to them, they can focus on the important features. For example, you might ask, "How do the family rooms of these houses compare? Is this one more adaptable to your needs?" Remember to ask the people to compare.

Don't Defend the Property

When you ask questions about pluses and minuses of the property, you may get a negative reaction. "Ms. Rose, how does the layout of this retail center compare to the last one we saw?" She may reply, "I don't like it!" How are you going to respond to that? "Well, you ought to like it! It's better!" It may be better for you, but that doesn't mean it is better for them. So don't defend the property.

One reason sellers have problems when they try to market their own property is that they are too close to it. They are involved emotionally and thus too sensitive about little problems and negative comments regarding it. As an agent, be sure that you don't project this same defensiveness when the property is criticized. If Mrs. Jones says, "Gosh, this paneling is a strange white color," you might reply, "You're right. Is there some way we could eliminate that problem? Maybe changing the drapes would make it look different. Could the room be decorated differently to draw attention away from the color?" If she says, "No, it's just no," this is okay, too. The buyer has told you something you need to know. The is not always right but is always deserving of respect.

By asking the prospects what they think about something and then heeding their tempers and feelings, you can present property in a manner that is appropriate for them. After all, it's *your* job to be flexible and bend to meet their requirements, not the other way around. Remember, *they* are investing in the property, not you.

Watch People's Reactions

Why are you showing this property? What do you want to know about how they match the property? You want to know their reactions to it, and you must watch for these reactions.

You can learn a lot by watching other agents work. When you open a listing that your company has for another company's agent, try to blend into the wallpaper for a while and learn from his or her mistakes. I've watched agents ask: "Mr. Jones, this is a nice fireplace isn't it?" Mr. Jones replies, "Yes, I guess it's okay." Okay? Why he's absolutely transfixed by it! He loves it! But he's not going to say so! Then the agent says, "Why don't you come out and look at the pantry?" This is a bad move for that agent. Mr. Jones couldn't care less about the pantry. He's interested in the fireplace, and the agent could lose the sale by neglecting to key in on this obvious reaction. Jones might buy that fireplace and just happen to get the rest of the house with it!

For example, I might present a ranch with tremendous hunting potential. Now I'm a big hunter (mainly with a camera anymore) and excited about how to manage the game. But the potential buyer likes the place because of its isolation, peace, and quiet. The effective showing will focus on the silence and tranquility because that is what the buyer wants.

Key your presentation to your prospect's reactions. If they point something out, express an interest in some feature, or if you notice one thing that is important to them, emphasize it and tell them everything you know about it and how much enjoyment it can afford.

But if you say, "What do you think about the kitchen?" and Jones replies, "It's okay" without showing any nonverbal interest as he wanders off to another part of the house, should you talk about the kitchen anymore? No, this lack of interest is a signal to go on to something else. The only way you can check the barometer measuring changes in your prospects' attitudes is through not only listening to what they say, but through checking their reactions. Your cues come from your buyers. Anything that is important to them should become *very* important to you. Remember, you have previewed the property and know in advance what to try to emphasize and what to minimize, and now you have the added cue of the people's reactions. Many times, little cues will fall into place and begin to fit together.

Prepare the Prospective Buyers to Make a Decision

When you show properties and ask your prospects to make comparisons, you hope they will make a decision. Should you gamble the whole sale and make them come up with one big decision by asking, "Do you want it?" A good salesperson will not run the risk of losing buyers by forcing them to make one big decision. Instead, you should prepare them by asking them to make smaller decisions.

A new agent came in at the end of the day, discouraged despite having left quite excited that morning with his first buyer. Together we reviewed his day to analyze the reason for his discouragement. He had done most things right; he had attempted to follow most of the showing guidelines presented here, except one. I asked the question, "Why did you stop showing? What was your termination point?"

He said, "Well, I'd shown them eight places and I felt it was time to ask them some questions." This was too late. You need to set the pace as you go. Have the prospective buyers compare the first with the second. Ask them to make little decisions during the showing process because you want the last decision, the buying decision, to be simple. Understand that effectively closing a sale is not a trumpet-blowing affair with banners flying. It should be a simple, easy conclusion to the selling process, and the way you get there is a little at a time. This is a **stair-step** or **mini-decision approach:** Little decisions lead to a big one; prepare for the big one by having the buyer make small decisions. If you ask, "Sam, what do you think about the tenant-mix in this office building compared with that in the previous one we saw?" this question can be answered comfortably. Go to the next one. You also can scare him out of a decision-making mood by saying, "Well, you've seen four now; which one do you want?" Having easily made a number of small decisions enables prospects to make the buying decision more easily.

Give the People Time Alone

When people react positively to a certain property, they often want to talk to each other about it. You need to allow your buyers some private conversation time for this while you tour the home. "Mr. and Mrs. Buyer, we've gone over the property together. There now may be points of interest you might like to see again and discuss with each other." This is important. Give them time alone if they seem to need it.

Most co-decision-makers will need to have what I call a "board of directors' meeting." This is simply a time to clarify individual views and crystallize their expectations into a

TECHNOLOGY *IN ACTION*

As noted earlier in the chapter, David Knox Productions (http://www.DavidKnox.com) provides DVDs and videos for buyers and sellers to help make the home buying and selling process a little easier. Other good videos from David's Web site are *Pricing Your Home to Sell* and *Preparing Your Home to Sell*.

It's also important to keep the sellers informed of the feedback from any and all showings. http://www.showingsolutions.com is a new concept that is allowing real estate agents to use virtual assistants in coordinating and providing feedback on real estate showings.

joint decision. Acknowledging this need and allowing for it to occur while showing is a sound strategy. You may, for security reasons, want to give them this time alone in your vehicle or outside so there can be no doubt that the seller's property and interests have been protected.

Doing your homework pays; there is no substitute for good planning. Set the tone of the showing easily and create the kind of environment in which you work best. The importance of showing properly cannot be overemphasized. At this point, you are dealing not only with the prospects but with the property, and how well your first showing or two goes with the prospective buyers can be critical in determining whether or not you maintain your relationship with them. If you are off base and don't realize it, you're in trouble. Some buyers may bear with you tactfully until the end of the day, but they will never return. From the standpoint of the buyer, this is where you start earning your money, so it is critical to know exactly how to go about correctly presenting property. Figure 10.3 is included as a reference sheet of the guidelines for showing presented in this chapter.

Showing Checklist   Figure 10.3

1. Preview the property. You can't sell what you haven't seen. Mention negatives in advance.
2. Plan ahead. Choose the proper route and allow adequate time between showings.
3. Minimize seller contact. Can they be absent?
4. Maintain control of the showing. Don't let the sellers or buyers run the show.
5. Don't rush. Let the people set the pace.
6. Limit the showings. Remember the difference between comparison and confusion. Show a few, and then talk.
7. Ask for comparisons between properties. Review the good and bad points of each property.
8. Do not defend the property.
9. Watch the buyers. Their reactions can be your guide.
10. Ask buyers to decide about features they prefer in properties. Your goal is to get decisions leading toward the final close.
11. Allow for "talk time." Give buyers some time alone to compare their feelings.

Summary

In the real estate sales process, *showing* is the means by which a salesperson presents his or her inventory to prospects who can select the property that meets their needs.

The first role of showing is to further qualify and more precisely determine wants and needs. Another important function of showing is to point out the features and benefits of a particular property and the neighborhood in which it is located. Showing can create interest and excitement in a property and can act as a barometer of changing buyer interests.

Effective showing techniques include previewing the property beforehand, planning the showing in advance, choosing the best route to the property, determining who among the prospects is the decision maker, keeping sellers out of the way, and maintaining control at all times. Other techniques include taking enough time to show the property, limiting the number of showings to buyers in one day, asking buyers to compare properties, refraining from defending a property, paying attention to buyer reactions, preparing buyers to make decisions and giving buyers time alone to inspect the property.

Review Questions

1. What is the overall purpose of showing in the sales process?

2. Within this overall purpose, what are four functions of showing?

3. How can showing further qualify a buyer?

4. What is one big concern when matching people with property?

5. How can a salesperson use showing to create interest or desire on the part of the prospective buyer?

6. How can showing act as a barometer?

7. What are the 11 guidelines in the showing checklist?

8. What are four important parts of planning a showing?

9. Why is it important to keep the seller away when showing?

10. Who should "run the show" during a showing?

11. How are you going to accomplish this?

12. Why should a salesperson preview property before showing it?

13. What are two reasons for showing property slowly?

14. How many houses should a salesperson show at one time?

15. What is a good way to get the people involved with the property?

16. When a prospective buyer criticizes a property, what should you do?

17. Why is it important to watch for reactions?

18. How can a salesperson prepare the buyer to make the decision to buy?

19. Why should salespeople remember to allow for clients some time alone?

Discussion Questions

1. What other techniques would you add to the showing guidelines presented in this chapter?

2. What are some methods a salesperson can use to keep in control of showings?

3. How many properties should you attempt to show before taking a break?

4. What should *you* as a salesperson do during the break?

Situation

The Fewer the Better?

Fred Johnson is a highly successful salesperson in your area. He is conducting a showing seminar at the local Board of REALTORS®, and you are a participant. Fred offered the opinion that effective salespeople usually show fewer properties per sale than less successful salespeople. What does he mean?

What about Children?

Tracy Schmidt is the top selling agent in your office. She frequently has said that children, especially the young ones, should be locked inside the trunk of the car during showings. They are such distractions for the parents and often hard to control while viewing the property, so Tracy does not encourage their participation. What do you think of this approach?

PART III

THE CLOSING STAGE: MAKING THE SALE AND KEEPING IT TOGETHER

Handling Objections and Closing

Key Terms

- Action close
- Advisory close
- Alternative close
- Assumptive close
- Ben Franklin close
- Buying signal
- Close
- Machine-gun approach
- Stair-step close
- Urgency close

Why People Object

Different people can present an unlimited number of objections in the course of a sale. Note we are talking about objections that *can* be raised. Sometimes there are few, but a trouble-free sale is definitely the exception rather than the rule. We are talking about an objection versus a passing comment. The objection requires considerable attention while the comment might require only respect and acknowledgement. A successful salesperson should anticipate having to deal with objections and have a well-planned technique available for immediate use. The first part of this chapter discusses reasons why people object and suggests a method to help you deal with objections.

One of the most difficult aspects of selling for many people is closing. The second part of this chapter will examine several closing techniques and some buying signals that will help you know when to close. The second part also reviews some guidelines for closing.

Before a salesperson designs a plan or method of handling objections, he or she must understand why people are objecting. Possibly there are many reasons; in this chapter, we will look at five common ones.

Slowing Things Down

Have you ever felt that you were in a situation that was moving too fast? What was your reaction? To put on the brakes! Salespeople often want to "get on with the selling" and attempt to proceed to the next step at their own pace. If this is an uncomfortable speed to prospects, they may resist. Psychologically, some people may feel pulled along and will object to maintain a speed at which they are comfortable. A salesperson needs to be sensitive to this and attempt to adjust the progression of the sales process accordingly. Prospects will relax and be more cooperative if they do not feel threatened.

Gaining or Maintaining Control

Another reason people object is associated closely with the first one. Many prospects want to feel they are in control of the situation. Your own experience may confirm this point. Some people greatly resist when they feel manipulated or steered. Remember to maintain control but not in an overbearing manner. There is a definite difference between guiding people and driving them. You should not display rigid or aggressive behavior, but should appear relaxed and agreeable. This attitude will make your buyers and sellers more comfortable. They will be more willing to listen to you and to follow your suggestions. Successful real estate agents are judged not by the number of prospects they can "put in their places," but by their ability to help people find the right properties. Don't win the battle for control and lose the prospect for sale purposes.

Misunderstanding

You may present questions to prospects regarding their preference for one alternative over another. "How do you like the first area compared to the last one we saw, Mrs. Jones?" "Mr. Jackson, do you feel this ranch has a better layout than the first one we saw?" These are reasonable questions to ask, but what if prospects *don't know* how they feel? They might experience mild internal panic.

Buying and selling real estate is a complicated affair with many considerations. In addition to the questions you pose, prospects must answer ones they ask themselves. Am I doing the right thing? Should I wait a while longer? Am I buying (selling) for too much (too little)? All these represent potential problems and hazards for prospects.

Salespeople have to look for objections that stem from the prospect's lack of understanding. The agent should attempt to help the prospect obtain the needed information and assurance. A major objection can come from lack of self-confidence. At one time or another, most of us have doubted our own ability to make the correct decision. Often a salesperson will sense that objections have been raised to postpone or delay a decision. Remember, the people you work with must decide positively about you first. If you fail to "read" the objections as possibly a lack of confidence in you and force prospects to make choices, they may decide against you. Then you are really in trouble!

Hiding the Real Reason

Have you ever been invited out to lunch and to avoid going, saying, "Thanks so much but I have another commitment." This "little white lie" technique also is pretty common among real estate prospects. A person may say to you that the price per square foot for the office building is too high when there is doubt in his or her mind that a lender will loan the money because of marginal qualifying abilities. You have to give each stated objection the respect and attention it deserves, but remember that the stated problem may not be the *real* concern.

Valid Objections

There are some objections to which there are no acceptable answers. Agents need to recognize this fact and help prospects recognize it also. The fair market value for an area may be too much for the buyers. There may be no available places for sale with a particular zoning or exterior design. You need to remember that there will be prospects you cannot help and objections you cannot solve. The salesperson who never lost a prospect and who never failed to find an acceptable solution to an objection is rare—and more likely does not exist.

If there is a legitimate problem area, deal with it openly. There is no sense in denying the problem exists, because it will resurface later in the sales process. Admit to the buyer or seller that you are stumped, and ask if you can put your heads together and come up with a solution. If not, then both of you must rethink the best way to proceed. There is no crime in not always having the answer or solution to a valid objection. It is a crime not to admit that the problem exists or not to try to find a solution.

Five Steps for Handling Objections

For years, books about selling and sales training manuals have used the term *overcoming objections*. I prefer not to imply that objections are something you have to defeat or destroy. Certainly you have to deal with them, however, so it is best to have a well-thought-out plan for handling them in advance.

The five-step approach to handling objections presented here is not original or unique. The key words or the order in which the steps are presented may be different from other sales books, but the two most important aspects of the steps are that they are simple to learn and they work! Sales techniques are much easier to accept and use if they have these traits. The five-step plan, like all guides in this text, is basic and flexible, so you may adapt it to fit your needs. Because objections are inevitable, consider this plan before you need it in your real estate practice.

Step 1: Understand the Objection

A salesperson must work hard to understand the objection voiced. If Mr. Brown says, "The asking price seems high," how should you respond? With information about appreciation in the area? With a mini-review on the merits of ownership? You probably do not know what the "correct" answer is with the sketchy information conveyed to you in that single statement; there are too many ways of interpreting Mr. Brown's objection. An answer based on a guess of the prospect's objection may miss his point and only raise new objections.

When handling objections, always remember it is not what prospects say but what they mean that is important. Ask for more information when you are not sure what the prospect's objection is. By getting prospects to elaborate, you may get a clear idea of the prospect's real concern. Another benefit is that while explaining, he may give you some insight about how to approach the problem. Let's face it, most of us need all the help we can get. We have to really understand the objection raised before we can do much about moving toward a solution.

Step 2: Respect the Objection

One of the few sales stereotypes I have is the "machine-gun-ostrich." This type of salesperson is one who, upon hearing an objection, will resort to one of two tactics. He or she may blast the objection with a multitude of answers. This **machine-gun approach** assumes that if you provide enough solutions to objections, one of them is bound to be right. Instead of taking time to find the single best answer, the agent simply throws out all the responses that come to mind.

If the objection is raised again, the salesperson pretends to be an ostrich and simply ignores the problem. After all, if the agent doesn't respond, maybe the people will forget it and the concern will just go away.

Fortunately, not many machine-gun-ostriches are left in selling, and their numbers are shrinking. The approach never works in the long run. This type of salesperson will make some sales, but many sales fail before closing. Objections are like weeds—if you don't dig down to the roots, they keep coming back.

An experienced salesperson may say that fewer and fewer objections are original. However, don't get complacent. Just because the objections are not new does not mean they are unimportant to the prospect voicing them. Show respect for all the prospect's concerns and questions. Do not alienate individuals by making light of them. Provide standardized answers if they are good answers, but make sure they sound "made to order" for this particular person. The salesperson who fails to respect prospects' objections, in effect, has failed to respect the prospects; and this is a sure way to lose them! Be interested in the doubts people have. Hear them out. This is your responsibility if you truly hope to help and to keep the prospect sold on you.

Step 3: Change the Objection into a Question

The next phase of the five-step method is to turn an objection into a question. For example, after she looked through a particular house, Mrs. Green said, "I don't like the master bedroom." Her salesperson already knows he needs to respect her objection and make sure he understands it. To change her objection statement into a question, the agent responds, "Mrs. Green, I am very interested in finding you a home with an acceptable master bedroom. Is the problem with this room its size, the way it is decorated, or the location in the home?"

Posing the problem in question form serves two purposes. First, it lets the salesperson find out if he is on the right track. Obviously his response would be one thing if Mrs. Green did not like the décor of the master bedroom and another if she disliked the location. By rephrasing the objection into a question, he will find out immediately if he has interpreted the problem incorrectly, and consequently he can adjust to find the real problem.

The second reason the salesperson should rephrase the statement into a question is so he can proceed to the next step of the process in a smooth and orderly manner.

Step 4: Provide a Solution

People ask questions to get an answer. According to the definition of selling in Chapter 1, as a salesperson, your task is to be a problem solver. If Mrs. Green has problems with the décor, her salesperson can offer ideas about modifying the color scheme in various ways. If size is the trouble spot, he may be able to offer ideas on room remodeling or on putting family members in different bedrooms. His imagination may be needed at this point to stimulate the prospect's own creativity in finding solutions. There is no assurance that the solution provided will be acceptable. If not, don't get rattled. Work patiently and diligently with your prospect's help toward finding the best possible solution.

Step 5: Try to Close

After you and your prospect have worked out a possible solution to the objection, you should attempt to close the sale. You have already been through the preparation, prospecting, qualifying, and presentation steps of the sale. You have, to the best of your ability and your prospect's ability, dealt with the objections and problems. The next step is for the prospect to make a decision, which is exactly what a **close** represents, an attempt to get a positive decision from the prospect.

Figure 11.1 is a checklist of the reasons for objections and methods for handling them that were discussed in this chapter.

Objections Checklist   **Figure 11.1**

OBJECTIONS ARE NORMAL AND NATURAL, SO PREPARE YOURSELF FOR THEM.

PEOPLE OBJECT:

1. To slow things down
2. To gain control
3. Because they don't understand something
4. To hide the real reason
5. Because they have a valid objection

HANDLING OBJECTIONS:

1. Try to understand the objection
2. Respect the client's objection and point of view
3. Change the objection into question form
4. Provide a solution
5. Try to close

Spend some time thinking about whether or not this approach to handling objections will work for you. You may want to modify it to fit your particular style or to fit the individual personalities of the prospects with whom you work. Handling objections is a necessary skill. The only way to perfect the technique is by practice.

A good way to increase your ability to handle objections is to write down all the objections that you can think of to an imaginary property. Then go back and, one at a time, answer them using the method explained in this chapter. Ask another agent or a family member to act as the buyer or seller, voicing some of the objections you wrote as you verbally answer them. Review your style and make the changes you feel necessary. Practice will improve your technique. If you are going to make mistakes in handling objections, the time and place to do it is in a practice session, not in a real sale.

There is certainly no substitute for experience, but training practice does speed up the process of acquiring the needed expertise. Work on the technique until you feel comfortable with it, and see how much it helps you in handling objections. Keep in mind that there are virtually no objection-free sales, so the successful salesperson must develop a strategy to deal with the objections that arise.

Closing

Buying Signals

The best time to close is when the prospect is ready. That sounds logical and seems simple enough. The problem for the salesperson is in recognizing *when* it's time to close. If you develop a method of determining the right time for closing, you can increase your sales effectiveness. The idea behind buying signals is to help you work with this problem.

A **buying signal** is something a prospect does or says that indicates a favorable impression has been made and a positive buying decision may occur. Be cautious with buying signals because it's easy to misinterpret them, and you can easily err about a single statement or action that a prospect makes and ruin the chances of a sale. Look for these signals as mood indicators rather than guaranteed sales. You may recall seeing these signals in other buyers and maybe even remember exhibiting some of them yourself as a buyer. The examples presented in this section represent some well-recognized buying signals, but the list is not complete or applicable to everyone. Some buying signals may apply to sellers as well. See Figure 11.2 for a summary of buying signals.

Remember to watch closely for these indicators, but do not rely overly on them. Although they are not automatically "sure things," buying signals do help you read your prospect better and increase your chances of closing at the proper time.

Reexamination of the Property
You may show prospective buyers a property that, in your opinion, best fits their needs, only to find that they seem unimpressed. Then, as they look at others, their enthusiasm begins to build for the one they viewed initially. It may take your prospects time to determine that the first property was the best. This often happens when you show your best property right away; your prospects may need to do some comparing and confirming.

Buying Singals   Figure 11.2

A buying signal is something a prospect says or does that indicates a positive buying decision may occur.

Examples include situations in which the prospect:

1. Reexamines the property: "Can we go back to. . . ."
2. Assumes mental ownership: "Bobby can have the small bedroom. The sofa would fit right here."
3. Requests specific details: "What is the monthly payment on this one?"
4. Starts negotiating for a concession: "Do you think the drapes will stay?"
5. Seeks reassurance: "This is really a nice area, isn't it?"
6. Exhibits change in behavior, either positive or negative.
7. Indicates criticism: "Would you look how. . . ."
8. Closely examines the contract: "What does this section mean?"
9. Starts to sell the other party: "Alice, you would love this design."
10. Asks about the next step: "What do we have to do now?"

Some people debate on when you should show your best alternative, assuming you have multiple choices to offer, and there is not always a correct answer to that question. Some prefer to build up to the best choice, whereas others start with the number one pick. I usually show the best first, in most situations, but that is a personal preference and not a rule. Such a tactic does insure more reexamination experiences.

Mental Ownership of the Property

Sometimes the prospects start changing and personalizing the property. Another example is when prospects verbally begin to rearrange the furniture. One of my favorite examples is when the prospects start assigning bedrooms. Whenever I hear words like "Suzie can have the corner bedroom, and then the baby will be closer to the master bedroom," I know that the house is close to having a new owner!

Another example is when improvements begin to appear in the prospect's mind. When my ranch buyers started building fences, setting up deer blinds, or planting fields, the confidence level really starts to build within me.

Requests for Specific Details

When prospects start to ask for exact information on specifics such as sales price, monthly payments, warranties, personal property that remains, and so forth, you can feel more confident of their genuine interest. They could be just curious, but often they are making up their minds to buy. A word of caution here! At this juncture in the sales process, be sure to give as accurate information as possible. This is no time to "guesstimate."

Looking for a Concession

Potential buyers look for methods to get the upper hand. The desire for control, whether real or imagined on the buyers' part, can be a good indication of their interest and involvement with a particular property. Be careful about giving in to requests for additional concessions. An effective method to handle a question like "Do you think the seller will leave _____?" is to respond by saying something similar to "If the seller were to leave the _____, would this choice fit your needs better than the others you have seen?" Another possible answer would be "We can certainly include that request as a condition of your offer to the seller." In most cases, you cannot officially speak for the seller on these added concessions, and you shouldn't. Remember your role is a negotiator, not a decider.

Seeking Reassurance

Buyers will sometimes hesitate. They may want a friend or relative to see the property first. Sometimes they will even look to you for encouragement or support for the decision. If the prospect wants Granny, Mother, Uncle Fred, the banker, the attorney, or the accountant to see the property, contact that person as soon as possible. Be careful not to resent these co-decision makers. Give them the respect they deserve. Remember, you need these people more than they need you. Also keep in mind that you can only give advice, counsel, and strategies to the people you represent/work for (a client) and not those you work with (a customer).

A Change in Behavior

As a successful salesperson, you should be sensitive to changes in your prospects' attitude or behavior. Maybe the entire relationship has been very formal. Suddenly your prospects loosen up, call you by your first name, and become very relaxed and friendly. Or the opposite can happen. The buyers may become somewhat tense and irritable. In either instance, don't interpret this change as something you may have said or done. It may be the prospects' way of coping with the pressure of making a decision. Avoid changing your style or approach in midstream because of the prospects' change. You need to be relaxed, calm, and in control at this time. No sale is "pressure free" because each sale requires decision(s). The key is not being the source of pressure.

Criticism

Often a potential buyer will criticize the property. Although this criticism is always worth respecting, don't take a negative comment as a sure-fire sign of death to the sale. Most people are sometimes critical toward things (or people) we care about. You may want to refer to the part of this chapter on objections for reinforcement. I prefer to work with a buyer who has some issues with the property being shown to a buyer that loves everything but buys nothing!

Examination of the Contract

Excessive concern with the contract itself may be a way of prospects' shifting their attention away from the real decision that has been made and is now to be committed to paper. Do not overemphasize the piece of paper itself or let it stand in the way of the buyer's decision. This is one time where effective preparation really pays off. If you are able to explain clearly what the contract means (however, avoid offering legal advice), you are better off than being nervous and inaccurate over the contract and its significance. Virtually all important decisions of the size and scope of a real estate transaction require documents. The contract is a normal part of doing business.

Prospects Selling One Another

Often, when one buyer becomes involved and excited with a property, he or she will start selling the other buyer(s). At this time the salesperson should become an astute observer. Listen to see what the prospect considers good about the property. The other prospects may not agree, and a quiet yet observant salesperson can see what objections the prospect has without personally asking. Of course, the best actual situation is when all the prospects are selling one another. This clearly gives the salesperson a buying signal.

In Chapter 10, "Presenting the Property," we mentioned a guideline on giving people some time alone. When the "selling one another" buying signal occurs, let buyers spend some time alone while still on the property to review privately their respective feelings.

Asks About the Next Step

Frequently, a potential buyer will become futuristic in focus. Without actually asking "What is next" or "Now what do we do?" the involved purchaser will be posing such questions. The astute salesperson will outline the next set of activities needed to move the sales process along. At this point, the salesperson must be able to competently and confidently go forward with the sales process.

Closing Techniques

Closing is the logical conclusion to the sales process. There are no deep, hidden secrets to effective closes. Effective sellers simply close. Effective sellers simply close when they feel their customers are ready. Buying signals help the salesperson know when to close. The untrained agent may be hesitant or lack confidence and never get to the point of closing. Or, even worse, the salesperson may overcompensate and use an overly strong sales technique. Neither approach is very effective.

In this section, you will review some proven closing techniques. First, a definition of closing may be helpful. Closing, in this sense, is an attempt to gain a favorable decision to purchase the product or service being offered. Buyers or sellers may decide that they do not want your help or the products you offer. Certainly that is a decision, but not the one you had hoped for. You have no assurance that each close will end positively. The key to remember is that you have several approaches to choose from. Eight approaches are presented in this chapter; see the summary of all eight in Figure 11.3.

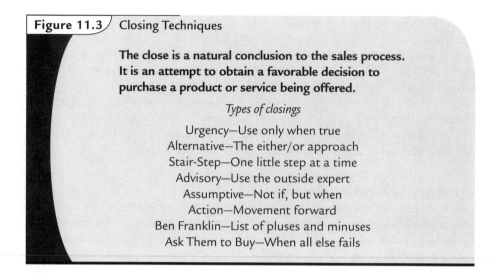

Figure 11.3 / Closing Techniques

The close is a natural conclusion to the sales process. It is an attempt to obtain a favorable decision to purchase a product or service being offered.

Types of closings

Urgency—Use only when true
Alternative—The either/or approach
Stair-Step—One little step at a time
Advisory—Use the outside expert
Assumptive—Not if, but when
Action—Movement forward
Ben Franklin—List of pluses and minuses
Ask Them to Buy—When all else fails

Sometimes an effective and powerful technique is the **urgency close**, in which the salesperson asks people to make decisions now or run the risk of regretting the delay. There is no disservice to your prospect if you use this close because it is true. The real estate business is filled with stories about lost sales and unhappy people who missed out on properties they really wanted because they failed to decide soon enough. Certainly this approach can be and has been poorly used, but it has a legitimate purpose. If you use it when appropriate, you might save a sale. Your chances for later success may decrease if your buyers miss out on a property because they may hold you partially to blame for their disappointment.

If appropriate, I will say something like "Jo-Carol, take all the time you want, as it is a big decision to make. But please don't hold it against me if someone else chooses to buy and then prevents you from the luxury of a later decision."

The **alternative close**, also called the "either/or" close, is a technique that can be used in many different ways because it scales down the buyer's decision and correspondingly scales down the pressure on the buyer to cope with many alternatives.

Certainly, few people would not turn pale at a close like this one! "Mr. Carr, don't you want to put $35,000 down, pay $5,500 closing costs, and spend more than $200,000 in interest for the next 30 years to buy this property?" Approached like that, most people would run away! The alternative close asks the person to make a relatively small decision. Examples are "Mr. Nelson, would a move-in date on the 1st or 15th be better for you?" and "Would you like me to set up a meeting with the loan officer this afternoon or tomorrow?" If the buyer can decide minor issues, you know the likelihood of buying is increasing.

Similar to the alternative close is the **stair-step close**, based on the technique introduced in the previous chapter. This approach is like driving up a mountain. Certainly it would be quicker to go straight up the side, but you encounter a great deal of gravitational resistance to that. You must make smaller gains by circling. The same holds true for the stair-step close. You would like prospects to make decisions quickly and expedite the sales process. That is hard for most people to do, so ask them to make as big a decision as they are comfortable with. Chapter 10 described asking people to compare properties they had seen. If they cannot compare entire properties at once, break the comparisons down into smaller issues—compare specific points. All the time, you are stair-stepping toward asking for their final decision on which property to buy. Obviously, you let prospects take as big a step at a time as they wish, but you are effectively breaking down the one big decision into many smaller ones.

The **advisory close**, in which prospects ask a person they trust for advice before they decide whether to buy, is an effective approach in some situations. Remember, some prospects want to show Granny because they need reassurance. You must respect Granny, the CPA, the homebuilder friend, or whomever the person chooses to serve as an adviser. Let that "outside expert" help you make a sale. Avoid resenting the adviser or trying to block him or her if the buyer wants advice, or that adviser may sabotage your sale. Sometimes you must get the adviser for them. It could be an appraiser, an inspection service, or a satisfied resident of the neighborhood. Be supportive of the adviser, but remember it is still your job to sell.

The **assumptive close** is really more a style of selling than a specific closing technique. It also could be seen as a "not if, but when" close; the idea is to assume there will be a sale at the end of the process. From your first contact with your prospects, you approach them with an expectation of successful completion of the sale. This approach also helps you qualify prospects for their sincerity and commitment to the sale. You keep people informed of the next step, always confident of working out the details and moving toward completion of the sale.

Statements like "once you give me the necessary qualifying information" or "after we find the proper location for you," sends a clear message of personal confidence. After reading this material on closing, you will have a much better grip on how important this point is. See, it works!

The **action close** assumes that the best defense is a great offense. This does not suggest excess pressure but is a little riskier than other techniques here. Action closes require some activity or task (action) on the part of the buyer or agent. The agent says, "Ms. Buyer, we will need to call and make an appointment with an officer to begin the loan application. I'll go ahead while you are right here and see when we can schedule one." If the prospect does not object or stop the agent from calling, the close worked. Another example might be when the salesperson asks the potential buyer to go ahead and see when his or her attorney can review the proposed earnest money contract offer. If the person agrees to contact the legal counselor, the closing effort was successful.

The **Ben Franklin close** also can be used effectively when trying to reach a decision. This approach involves listing on one side of a piece of paper all the advantages a property possesses. On the other side of the page are all the disadvantages. This "plus and minus" analysis causes a buyer to address the merits and weaknesses of a particular property. Such focus often can be an incentive to make a decision.

The final closing technique is simply to *ask prospects to buy.* Use this as a last recourse, when you don't know what else to do. This is a gamble because if the people say no, you have to start part of the sales process again. Some individuals, however, need that kind of incentive to make a decision, and your request may move them off dead center. In some manner, it *is important* to ask for the order.

Guidelines for Closing

The closing techniques previously mentioned are specific approaches from which to choose. Regardless of which closing strategy you use, there are some general guidelines to incorporate.

Don't Oversell

Have you ever decided to purchase something long before the salesperson stops selling? The old story about the customer who interrupts the sales presentation to say, "I'll take it," only to be told, "You can't buy it yet, I'm not finished!" has some truth to it. Unfortunately, the chances of losing the sale increase with each sales point made after the person has been sold. If you forget every other guideline, remember this one: After the customer says yes, stop selling!

After the decision to buy has been made, concentrate on the specific details of the contract. When that is completed, congratulate the buyers to reinforce their decision, inform them of what you will be doing next (presenting the offer, and so on), determine when you will get back in touch with them with needed information, and *then leave.* Do not run the risk of undoing what has been accomplished. You could accidentally say the wrong thing, and they could withdraw the offer before you leave! You have done all you can for the buyers now. Get on with the next step in the sales process.

Close with Confidence

For most people, real estate decisions are somewhat uncommon. We don't usually buy or sell properties that many times in our lives. It is normal to be apprehensive and nervous about such a major decision. A salesperson without confidence only compounds the problem. How much faith would you have in salespeople who did not seem to know what they were doing?

If you must say, "I don't know," add to that, "I'll find out right away." You have then added a positive, action approach. A relaxed, confident, successful appearance, even if you are anxious or nervous, can go a long way toward helping a wavering prospective buyer.

Stay Interested and Positive

One of the quickest ways to dampen a customer's enthusiasm is to be indifferent. Although the sales process may be somewhat routine to you, it probably is not for your prospects. You can make the close much easier for all concerned if you convey to your prospects that you are really concerned and care for their interests and needs. A good rule of thumb for the salesperson to follow is to allow your level of demonstrated interest and excitement to roughly parallel that of the prospective buyer.

Resolve the Objections Prospects Raise Before Closing

No one's purpose is served by glossing over or ignoring your prospect's objections. As stated earlier in this chapter, you should put the objections to rest before you attempt to close, or the objections inevitably will come back to haunt you. Unresolved objections cause many offers to be withdrawn and many transactions to fall apart. The objections may seem petty to you, but they are not your objections. The objections are your buyer's, and the money spent is also theirs, so solve these potential problems first if possible.

Costs may be an important part of your discussion. As mentioned before, they are a major concern for the seller. The same is true for the buyer. Figure 11.4 is an example of a buyer's closing cost statement. Figure 11.5 is an explanation of the costs mentioned on the closing statement. The professional salesperson must be prepared to go over these costs in a confident and competent manner during this part of the sale. Of course, you should make sure the costs you use are current in your marketplace.

Don't Rush the Close

Like taking too long to close, not taking long enough is a mistake. Let the customers set the pace. They should feel in control of the decision making. If prospects feel pushed or manipulated, the sale may be ruined. Most salespeople don't experience the luxury of having too many sincere buyers. Don't appear overly anxious to "hurry up and finish," or the prospects might end up believing you do not really value them. Obviously, some happy medium between this and overselling must be found.

You may be asking, "Well then, when do I close?" The clear answer is *when the prospects are ready.* Try to tune in on their level of interest and excitement. Some successful salespeople like to close while still in the property. Others use travel time back to the office to reinforce the buying decision before closing. There is no one absolute "magic moment," but clearly the best time is based upon the buyer's, and not the salesperson's, decision-making readiness.

Don't Leave Buyers in a State of Indecision

The final guideline is important. You always must attempt to leave the people you are working with in a positive, action-oriented state. To have your prospects feel confused and uncertain is dangerous to the sale. Try to create a feeling of progress during your meetings with the people. Even if you only establish another time to meet or arrange to contact them with additional material, at least something is happening. Most people can tolerate only a small amount of the unknown before rejecting the situation and moving on to a more psychologically comfortable environment. Your buyers can overreact and create major problems out of minor ones if you give them too little information. Try to reach some type of decision each time you talk.

Each one of the ideas about closing presented here can be modified to fit special requirements. Certainly, all the guidelines will not work equally well in every situation, but they can be effective in helping move everyone one step closer to the sale. No closing need be pressure packed unless the participants (salesperson *and* prospective buyer) won't or can't change it. Few salespeople want to be considered pushy. Today's

Figure 11.4 Estimate of Buyer's Closing Costs

Buyer	Property Address	Date	Prepared by

	VA	FHA	Conventional	Cash	Assume	Owner Carry
Loan Origination Fee				350.00	-0-	-0-
Appraisal (2)	350.00	350.00	350.00	350.00	-0-	-0-
Mortgagee Policy	40.00	40.00	40.00	-0-	-0-	30.00
Recording Fees	18.00	18.00	27.00	5.00	9.00	9.00
Credit Report	35	35	35			
Survey (3)	65.00 max	60.00 max.	75.00			
Escrow Fees (Average)	-0-	40.00	40.00	40.00	40.00	40.00
Photographs	-0-	7.00	10.00	-0-	-0-	-0-
Restrictions Per Set	-0-					
Note & Deed of Trust		150.00	175.00	-0-	-0-	-0-
PMI Fee ($^1/_2$ to 2%)	-0-	-0-		-0-	-0-	-0-
PMI Appraisal	-0-	-0-	20.00	-0-	-0-	-0-
Attorney Fee (If 2nd Lien)	-0-	-0-	-0-	-0-	150.00	150.00
Plus Prorations of Taxes & Insurance (1)	-0-	-0-	-0-	-0-	**	
Loan Application Fee						
Inspections Fee						
Total Closing Costs						(A)

BUYER'S ESTIMATED PREPAIDS

First Year Hazard Insurance	
One Month Hazard Insurance	
Two Month Tax Reserve	
One Month PMI Insurance	
Prepaid Interest	
Total	(B)

(c)

Sale Price $ _____

Down Payment $ _____

Loan Amount $ _____

_____ Year Loan at $ _____ %

Principal & Interest $ _____

Taxes $ _____

Hazard Insurance $ _____

PMI $ _____

Estimated Monthly Payment $ _____

A _____

B _____

C _____

Estimated Move in Costs $ _____

(1) *To be determined at time of closing

(2) **Can be paid by buyer, but is normally paid by seller.

(3) ***Survey costs may vary according to property

NOTICE: This is an estimate only and is provided as a courtesy. Costs will vary at time of closing

Loan Origination Fee—A fee charged by the lending institution for processing a loan. Generally explained in terms of points: One point equals 1 percent of the loan.

Appraisal—An estimate of fair market value, generally for the purpose of helping a lending institution determine how much it should loan on a property.

Mortgagee Policy—An insurance policy issued to the lending institution making the loan. It protects the lender in the event a bad title causes any loss. Generally it is issued in conjunction with a title insurance policy to the buyer.

Recording Fees—Fees paid for recording a transaction and making it a matter of public record (states name of new owner, any new mortgage, liens, and son on).

Credit Report—Fee paid to local credit reporting service to obtain credit history. Helps the lending institution determine a borrower's qualifications. There are additional fees if the credit history is out of town.

Survey—An examination of the property by a licensed professional surveyor to determine exact boundary lines. Fence lines, easements, and encroachments may also be shown.

Escrow Fee—Fee paid to the escrow agent for handling the transaction and seeing that all terms of the earnest money contract are carried out.

Restrictions—Copy of the building and deed restrictions placed on the property by the developer and previous owners.

Note—A written agreement stating debt and setting out the terms of repayment.

Deed of Trust—An instrument used to establish a mortgage lien on the property purchased with the money borrowed in the note.

PMI (Private Mortgage Insurance) Fee and Appraisal—Appraisal and insurance policy fees paid to a mortgage insurance company. This insurance protects the lender in case of default and allows the buyer to make less than a 20 percent down payment.

Transfer Fee (VA and FHA/Conventional)—Charge by the lender when buyer assumes existing mortgage. This changes the records held by the lender over to the buyer's name.

Attorney Fee—Fee paid if buyer's attorney will be paid from the closing proceeds.

Prorations of Taxes and Insurance—Allowances for the dividing of financial responsibility between the buyer and seller for taxes and insurance. For example, the seller usually owes current taxes that have not been billed, and the buyer would want this settled at the closing.

Loan Application Fee—Charge to a purchaser who is securing a mortgage to finance the purchase. The fee is charged by the lender (mortgage company).

Inspections Fees—Fee charged for a visible check of the premises for the presence of termites, usually performed by a licensed exterminator.

Total Closing Costs—The sum of all the preceding charges listed on this form.

consumer wants something else, and the successful salesperson adapts to consumer demands.

The ability to close successfully is critical to selling. At this step in the sales process, you begin to earn your money. Work hard at improving your closing, and you will increase your selling effectiveness.

TECHNOLOGY *IN ACTION*

The RESPA Web site provides excellent information for borrowers and closing costs related to the real estate transaction at http://www.hud.gov. It is important that real estate agents become familiar with the RESPA (Real Estate Settlement Procedures Act) laws and other information to be successful in the real estate industry.

During the sales process, a real estate salesperson should anticipate and prepare to handle *buyer objections*. Buyers generally will make objections to a particular property for a variety of reasons. They may do so to slow down the salesperson's presentation, to gain or maintain control of a situation, because they do not understand something, because they cannot make a decision regarding the property, or because they have a valid objection regarding the property.

A salesperson can handle an objection effectively by understanding the reasons for the objection, respecting it, changing it into a question, providing a solution, and attempting to close the sale.

When attempting to close, a salesperson should be aware of *buying signals,* which are a prospect's actions or words that indicate a favorable impression has been made and a positive buying decision may occur. Such signals might include a buyer's reexamination of the property; expressions of mental ownership of the property; request for specific details, concessions, or reassurance; changes in behavior; questioning; closer examination of the contract; and selling other prospects.

Successful closing techniques include the urgency close, minor point close, stair-step close, advisory close, assumptive close, action close, and asking the customer outright to buy the property.

Among the general guidelines for closing a sale are refrain from overselling, close with confidence, stay interested and positive, resolve objections before the close, refrain from rushing, and refrain from leaving the prospects in a state of indecision.

Review Questions

1. What are four reasons people raise objections?

2. What five steps for handling objections were explained in this chapter?

3. What are two reasons for changing the objection statement into a question?

4. Why should an attempt to close come at this point in the sales process?

5. What is one good way to increase your ability to handle objections?

6. When is the best time to close?

7. What are nine common buying signals?

8. What behaviors indicate that your prospects feel mental ownership of a home?

9. What is one recommended way to handle requests for concessions?

10. What should you do if the prospect wants an outside expert to see the home?

11. What should you do when prospects start selling one another?

12. What are six approaches to a closing?

13. What are some advantages of using the minor point close?

14. What is the basic concept behind the assumptive close?

15. What gamble is involved in asking the client to buy?

16. What are six general guidelines to closing?

17. What should you do after the decision to buy has been made?

18. Why is it recommended that you not sit around and visit after you complete a sale?

Discussion Questions

1. Why do you feel that people raise objections in the sales process?

2. What can you add to this chapter's technique of handling objections?

3. Why is closing an important part of handling objections?

4. What are some additional buying signals you have noticed in yourself or others?

5. What other technique might you use to close a sale, in addition to those mentioned in the chapter?

6. Of the types of closes presented, which are you the most comfortable and most uncomfortable in using? Why?

Situation

Choosing the Right Close

The Kirks are first-time buyers. They seem to like one particular property you have shown them but appear hesitant to make an offer. In your judgment, the property meets their needs and they are well qualified for it. How do you go about closing?

What Now?

Samuel Paul and Charlie Dee believe that 6339 Travis Drive is best of all the properties you have presented to them. They have just agreed that an offer should be submitted. What should you do now?

Presenting the Offer and Negotiating Counteroffers

Key Terms
· Closing
· Counteroffer

Presenting the Offer

After the agent has obtained an offer from the prospects, the sales process moves closer to completion, but it certainly is not finished. If an agreement cannot be reached between buyer and seller, there is no sale. And if there is no consummated sale, the agent probably won't get paid!

The first objective of this chapter is to provide guidelines for presenting the buyer's offer to the seller. The second objective is to present other guidelines for negotiating counteroffers. Like so much of the material in this text, these ideas are effective and may be personalized for individual situations.

Most salespeople feel a strong urge to leave the prospective buyer and immediately call the seller with news of an offer to buy. This could be the biggest mistake in the sales process. Presenting a prospect's offer is a delicate and sometimes touchy part of selling. Following are some ideas to use in increasing your effectiveness in completing the sale.

Plan the Presentation

Analyze the Offer
In selling, there is no substitute for effective planning, and this is certainly true in the offer stage. Take some time to review and analyze the prospect's offer. What are its strengths and weaknesses? How well qualified is the buyer? How can it be presented in the best, most positive manner? To what parts of the offer is the seller most likely to object? Answers to these questions are important to consider. Don't misinterpret this suggestion, however, as you should not unnecessarily *delay* contact with the seller. After

Figure 12.1 / Checklist for Presenting the Offer

SELLING AGENT

1. Have I reviewed the offer to make sure I understand it as the buyer intended?

2. Is the offer completely and accurately filled out?

3. Is the offer signed by the buyer?

4. Did I collect the earnest money (if applicable)?

5. Have I contacted the listing agent?

LISTING AGENT

1. Have I reviewed the offer and do I understand it?

2. Do I have complete information ready for the seller (closing cost statement completed, current financing terms, and so on)?

3. Have I worked out the presentation plan with the selling agent?

4. How do I contact the seller?

all, the seller may accept another offer ahead of yours. At the same time, do not rush in unprepared, because many details must be taken care of before presenting the offer.

These preliminary tasks are presented in this chapter. They are also condensed into a one-page checklist in Figure 12.1, so that you can review them easily before you present an offer. You may want to add more duties to the checklist.

Review with Other Agent

If another agent is involved, both need to review the offer to buy and make sure everyone understands the details. The offer must be checked to ensure that it is written correctly and completely. All supplemental material needs to be prepared. An updated seller's closing cost statement reflecting current financing also must be prepared. After all, most sellers are less worried about sales price than they are about net equity. The only way the seller can decide correctly to accept or reject this offer is to be able to see the bottom line.

Another key preparatory area is in updating market activity. If several comparable properties are now for sale or if other listings have sold recently, this information must be conveyed accurately to the sellers. Most transactions do not occur in a vacuum; instead, they reflect the current marketplace. The interaction of supply and demand must be reported to the sellers so everyone can make an informed decision.

One important and often neglected area in preparing for the offer presentation concerns the relationship between the agents involved in the sale. Listing and selling companies and the agents involved in the transaction need a clear understanding of the role each should play. Nobody wins if the listing and selling agent work against each other. After all, both parties want the same thing—a fair price and a smooth closing. The agents need to resolve all questions about who is going to present the offer, who is going to do most of the explanation of the offer, and so forth, before they are in the presence of the seller. Any conflict between salespeople in the presence of the seller or buyer can decrease the chance of obtaining acceptance of and agreement to the offer. Plan this in advance.

Contact the Seller

Present any offer in person whenever possible. When the listing salesperson calls the seller, the seller wants to know all the details of the offer immediately. To eliminate this problem, have a secretary or salesperson in your office make the call to schedule a visit with the seller because these people honestly can say they have no knowledge of the offer. Avoid phone discussions of details unless there is no other alternative.

Work to Maintain Control

One of the most difficult aspects of presenting an offer is maintaining control. Because of the pressures sellers feel, many want to take charge of the situation. Although there is no best way to present an offer or to maintain control, there certainly are some methods that are better than others.

One approach is to outline on paper a proposed plan of presentation. This will provide a clear understanding of how to progress in explaining the offer. Share your planned method with the seller. This way both of you know the sequence of topics for discussion, which should prevent jumping from one point to another. Many successful salespeople will begin the presentation by pointing out one or two good things about the offer. Presumably, there is something encouraging, such as the price offered or possession date. Emphasize this early to set a positive tone to the offer in the initial stages of the presentation, rather than immediately "doing battle" in the difficult areas of negotiation. Such an approach helps keep the presentation on track. Figure 12.2 provides an example.

Bring the Seller Up-to-Date on the Marketplace

As mentioned before, the pressure to immediately answer the seller's question, "How much?" is strong when reviewing an offer. Before reaching this point, you should update the seller on what is going on in the real estate marketplace. If sellers feel offers are unrealistic, they have made a decision. Then you must try to persuade them to evaluate the offer objectively. If you present all pertinent facts beforehand, the seller may judge the offer fully informed.

You cannot be faulted for giving the seller accurate and current marketplace information even if it is bad. Although the initial reaction may be to "shoot the messenger" because of the bad news, you have a professional responsibility to the seller to deliver the

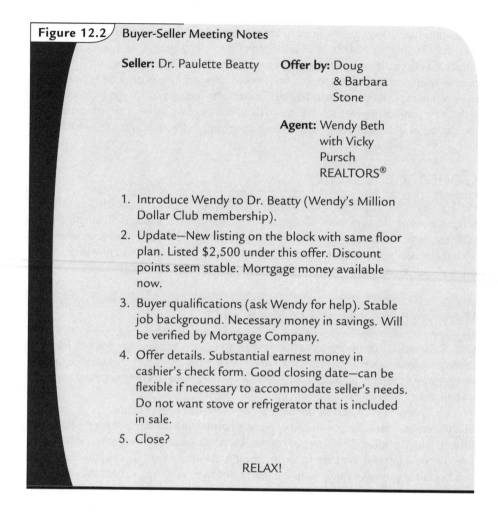

Figure 12.2 / Buyer-Seller Meeting Notes

Seller: Dr. Paulette Beatty   **Offer by:** Doug & Barbara Stone

Agent: Wendy Beth with Vicky Pursch REALTORS®

1. Introduce Wendy to Dr. Beatty (Wendy's Million Dollar Club membership).

2. Update—New listing on the block with same floor plan. Listed $2,500 under this offer. Discount points seem stable. Mortgage money available now.

3. Buyer qualifications (ask Wendy for help). Stable job background. Necessary money in savings. Will be verified by Mortgage Company.

4. Offer details. Substantial earnest money in cashier's check form. Good closing date—can be flexible if necessary to accommodate seller's needs. Do not want stove or refrigerator that is included in sale.

5. Close?

RELAX!

message. What the seller decides to do about the offer is up to him or her. You cannot control the reaction. What you can control is researching the present status and reporting it.

Personalize the Offer

Everyone likes to feel special and unique. The "average person" is always someone else when it comes to our problem. Successful salespeople recognize this and generally attempt to personalize their service when presenting an offer. There are several ways to accomplish this. One way is to tell the seller something about the buyer. Experienced agents talk about owners choosing to sell on more flexible terms or for a lower price because they "liked the buyers."

Telling something about the buyer also serves another purpose. It helps the seller determine the financial qualifications of the prospective purchaser. Knowing the buyer is ready, willing, and able is important. This does not mean you publicly review the buyer's specific income history, but you confidently and correctly inform the seller about the person behind the offer.

Personalizing the offer involves at least one other technique: taking the viewpoint of the seller as you interpret and review the offer. Looking at the proposal to purchase with the owner's interest in mind will keep you sensitive to the seller's feelings. Respecting the seller's particular situation ensures that you keep him or her on your side. At this time, sellers must feel you are sympathetic to their needs and that you have their best interests at heart. In many cases, the sellers are the people paying you! Your obligation as an agent is to your principal, and this commitment needs to be obvious now more than at any other time in the sales process.

Answer All of the Seller's Questions

Almost inevitably during the presentation of an offer, the seller will have questions. Answer these questions as completely and accurately as possible. Although all consumers deserve answers to their questions, in the negotiation phase of a sale, unanswered questions can be particularly dangerous.

If the salesperson lacks the necessary information to answer a question, the temptation is to delay answering. One delay tactic is to say, "I'll look into it and let you know"; another is to fail to recognize or attempt to answer the question. Either way, the unanswered question represents an unknown to the seller. Human nature will cause people to worry about and dwell on unknowns. The anxiety can cause the seller to delay a decision to sell or, even worse, back out of the sale. Keeping the sale together is explored in the next chapter, but at this point, it's important to answer the seller's questions.

Close the Sale

Obviously, the purpose of informing the seller about the offer is to consummate a sale. Chapter 11, "The Closing Stage: Making the Sale and Keeping It Together," suggests some techniques to use for effective **closing**. In addition to those ideas, there are at least two more good suggestions unique to presenting an offer to buy.

Selling Peace of Mind

In this approach, you point out that with the acceptance of the offer, the selling is over. The seller can relax and proceed with his or her other business. No more prospective buyers and agents will be going through the property on showings. There will be no need to wait anxiously for any more offers. Many sellers are eager to reach this point, and appealing to them in this way can help the sale.

Converting the Seller into a Buyer

With this technique, you are pointing out the consequences of rejecting this offer. Propose a hypothetical situation in which the seller has repurchased his or her own property for an amount over the price offered by the prospective buyer. Did the seller make a "good buy" in doing this? By asking the owner to consider his or her decision, you may increase the chance of helping the owner make a correct choice.

Keep Cool!

An owner is often under pressure and stress when attempting to sell. This problem can compound when an overexcited salesperson becomes involved in the situation. The seller needs you to maintain an interested, yet detached, perspective. If you allow yourself to be pulled into the seller's problems on an emotional level, your objectivity is diminished, as is your ability to offer clear, accurate, professional service.

The successful salesperson should make allowances for the behavior of an owner under pressure and be careful not to react personally to anger or abusive actions. Remember, the goal is not to win the battle and lose the sale. The customer is served best by an agent who presents the offer on a well-planned, clear-headed level.

Negotiating Counteroffers

Sometimes when a seller rejects an offer to buy, an agent can persuade him or her to make a counteroffer. Although not as good as an agreement, the **counteroffer** is certainly better than a refusal to negotiate. You must convey to the seller the significance of a decision to counter. In most instances, a counter kills the original offer and allows the buyer to withdraw completely with no obligation.

When this situation occurs (as it commonly does), there are some guidelines to consider. The suggestions on closing, presenting the offer, and other selling techniques are still valid, but negotiating counteroffers is slightly different. Because of this difference, some additional ideas are presented to handle the task.

Keeping Personalities Out of the Negotiations

The earlier section about presenting the offer mentioned the importance of personalizing the offer. In the counteroffer stage, you still should address the real needs of the people involved. Avoid getting into a personality conflict, however. When the seller starts believing the buyer is trying to steal the property, and the buyer firmly is convinced the seller is equally unrealistic, the transaction is in trouble. The sale of the real estate can become secondary to the parties' desire to outdo one another. Do your best to present the interests of each in the most positive manner. If each side feels the other is earnestly and sincerely attempting to negotiate reasonably, the salesperson's job is much easier.

The agents involved must keep their own biases out of the negotiation. Remember your role is that of an adviser and envoy, not a final decision maker. This is not *your* transaction; you are involved only as a negotiator. Keep your perspective clear.

Deal Only with the Differences

When an offer is presented, and the seller counters, rarely will the objections involve the entire contract. Usually only specific parts of the offer are considered unacceptable. The successful salesperson will keep the negotiations focused on the points of difference. Be careful not to re-initiate discussion of points already agreed upon, as doing so will risk changing these points again, thus further complicating the negotiations. Just lead the buyer or seller away from this situation if it develops.

Concentrate on Real Needs

The areas of negotiation in most real estate transactions are well established: price, possession date, personal property, and financing terms. Ideally, the buyer and seller see eye-to-eye on all four of these points, but this rarely happens, at least in the initial negotiation stages. The parties are unlikely to feel equally vehement about all of the four points, however. The salesperson's task is to help the client determine the priorities of the negotiation. Helping people see which aspect is the most important and critical for them gives insight into an area where some compromise may occur. This can be done only with a clear understanding of their most important needs.

For example, a seller may need a flexible closing date because of uncertain moving plans. If the buyer can accommodate on that point but needs a minimal down-payment structure, maybe each party can help the other side to everyone's benefit.

Zero In on the Offer

In the middle of the negotiations, a buyer or seller often will attempt to delay making decisions. This delay may be at a conscious or unconscious level, but the salesperson should anticipate and be prepared to deal with it. For example, some sellers discuss how another family seemed to like the house and may want to make an offer. Another example is when the buyer rationalizes that other suitable properties may be available, even though this person has seen the entire inventory for sale for the last two years and this is the best one so far. The salesperson needs to help the person make decisions on the property under consideration. This must be done in a positive manner, or the strategy can backfire on the agent. If buyers or sellers feel pressured, they will psychologically (if not physically) run away from the decision making. The fact remains that the property may be sold or the offer withdrawn, and the individuals losing the sale will blame the salesperson partially—if not totally—for the loss. The buyer or seller is served best when the agent helps him or her concentrate on the offer at hand and make decisions on its merits alone.

Attempt to Balance the Differences

Negotiations are a give-and-take process. All involved parties must be willing to make some concessions to insure a successful sale. This is especially true in the area of counteroffers, when each party has taken a different stand on one or more issues. Salespeople must be aware of the delicate nature of the sales process at this time and keep things in balance. This can be accomplished by remembering the lesson learned as a child on the see-saw; recall the description of this technique in Chapter 6, "The Listing Presentation." If children on a see-saw were different in weight, some change or shift had to be made in order to move. In dealing with counteroffers, the parties involved also must be willing to make some adjustments, or the sales process is stopped.

By asking each party to meet the other halfway, you ensure that no one has an advantage. Both can "win" if the transaction occurs. Another value of meeting halfway is that subsequent ill feelings will be less likely to arise because each party conceded the same amount. The "amount" is not necessarily a dollar figure, but rather give-and-take on both sides.

If the parties cannot split on a particular point, often they still can accomplish the same goal in a slightly different way. The buyer and seller can agree to divide the demands so that each side wins some. Perhaps the buyer gets a lower sales price while the seller gets the desired financing. The result is a closed sale because each party split the areas of difference. Buyer and seller both have reason to be happy with the sale. This strategy is based upon the assumption that neither buyer nor seller is starting the negotiations from an unrealistic position.

Remain Positive

The buyer and seller may exhibit many behaviors during the stressful negotiation process. It is crucial for the salesperson to maintain an attitude of positive enthusiasm at this time. Nothing can compound the problems more than the agent showing anger, frustration, or disgust to the other parties. Serve as a positive force, with professional interest and encouragement.

You will also find it challenging to remain persistent in your negotiating efforts. One of the marks of a professional salesperson is the ability to keep trying with a sale that everyone else has given up on. There is a difference between being pushy and persistent, but automatically quitting when conflicts appear unresolvable is no way to assure success. Keep positive and keep trying. It may be hard to accomplish this at times, but much success comes from strategy.

Figure 12.3 summarizes the counteroffer plan techniques discussed in this section.

Presenting offers and negotiating counteroffers can be a difficult part of selling for the unprepared agent. Consider these suggestions and adapt them to fit your individual needs. They will increase your success in reaching agreement between the parties involved in a sale.

TECHNOLOGY *IN ACTION*

Visit http://www.gostarpower.com to learn good negotiating tips with common scripts and ways to overcome objections buyers have. This Web site offers a script of the day that is excellent for real estate agents. By subscribing to this Web site, you will receive daily suggestions for overcoming common objections buyers and sellers may have during negotiations.

Counteroffer Plan   **Figure 12.3**

1. Keep personalities out.

   It is not in anyone's best interest to try and "get the best of" anybody.

2. Negotiate the differences.

   Avoid reopening points already agreed upon.

3. Center in on *real* needs. What is in the best interest of your client? Which of the following are critical to each party?

   Price

   Possession date

   Personal property terms

4. Concentrate on *this* offer.

   Don't let the client stray away from the here and now.

5. Split the differences.

   Keep it balanced.

6. Maintain a positive approach.

   Keep Your Cool!

Summary

Presenting a prospect's offer to a seller is a delicate and often touchy part of the real estate sales process. To increase your effectiveness in presenting offers, you should plan the presentation in advance, attempt to maintain control throughout the presentation, bring the seller up-to-date on the marketplace, personalize the offer, answer all of the seller's questions, close the sale, and maintain composure throughout the sales process.

If a seller refuses to accept an offer, the salesperson should suggest that the seller make the buyer a *counteroffer.* When negotiating counteroffers between buyer and seller, a salesperson should keep personalities out of the proceedings, deal with the specific differences only, concentrate on the real needs of both parties, zero in on the offer, attempt to split or balance the differences, and remain positive during the negotiations.

Review Questions

1. Why is it never a good idea to telephone the seller immediately with details of an offer to buy?

2. What are some important questions to consider when planning your presentation of an offer?

3. What should you do with the offer if there is another agent involved in the transaction?

4. How do you assist the seller in seeing the bottom line of any offer?

5. What is one good approach to help maintain control of the presentation?

6. What is the advantage of presenting one or two good points about the offer's terms first?

7. Why is it wise to present all the pertinent facts before answering the "how much" question?

8. What is meant by personalizing the offer, and what is one approach you can use to do it?

9. What are two reasons for telling the seller something about the buyer?

10. What is the reasoning behind answering all of the seller's questions as completely and accurately as possible?

11. What is the "selling peace of mind" approach to presenting an offer?

12. How does the technique of "converting the seller into a buyer" work?

13. Why is it so important to remain cool during consideration of the offer?

14. What is the significance of a decision to entertain a counteroffer?

15. What are six guidelines to help you present a counteroffer?

16. What are some examples of a seller's stalling behavior that the agent should anticipate and be prepared to assist with?

17. If the parties cannot split a particular point, what other way can they accomplish the same thing?

18. Why is it so important that the salesperson maintain a positive attitude of enthusiasm during the negotiations?

Discussion Questions

1. What is the role of the salesperson working with the buyers when the listing agent presents the offer to the sellers?

2. What material should you take with you when presenting an offer?

3. Why is it crucial to keep buyer and seller personalities out of the negotiations?

Situation

Familiar Forms

Bob Newell is a well-known real estate teacher and trainer. When instructing students how to present an offer, Bob teaches that sellers should not be confronted by any new forms when the actual offer is brought to them. Explain the reasoning behind this and how it can be accomplished.

Stress Management

Bob and Lisa Feather are two of your nicest and kindest friends. Upon presenting an offer to them for the sale of their family ranch (a distress sale), they become uncharacteristically critical of you and the offer. How do you react to this?

Keeping the Sale Together

Key Terms

- Abstract/title company
- Appraisal
- Closing
- Earnest money contract
- Escrow agent

The Salesperson's Responsibilities

The inexperienced salesperson may relax after the offers and counteroffers are completed, but merely reaching an agreement does not guarantee that the sale will be consummated. Many details remain to be handled before a smooth ownership transfer occurs. This chapter looks at some of the things a salesperson needs to be aware of and take care of to complete a sale.

Review the Earnest Money Contract

After an agreement has been reached by the buyer and seller, it must be committed to writing. The form most commonly used for recording the agreement is called an **earnest money contract**, or in some areas, a purchase agreement, purchase money offer contract of sale, purchase binder, or some similar term. The completed, signed form establishes a legal contract outlining the specifics of the contract and calling for the earnest money to be held in escrow. Sometimes several offers and counteroffers are made during negotiations, resulting in a messy looking contract as changes are made and initialed. To avoid missing a detail such as an initial or a changed figure that might jeopardize the sale, a new contract should be prepared. The agent(s) involved in the sale must make certain that the contract accurately reflects the agreement between the parties. The experienced professional knows the importance of thoroughly and carefully reviewing all points of this legally binding instrument with both the buyer and the seller.

This careful review will ensure that the contract accurately records the correct names, legal descriptions, terms, and so forth. All negotiated areas should be reviewed.

Both buyer and seller have certain obligations after signing this contract, and they need to understand them clearly.

Remember that a licensed real estate salesperson or broker may not give legal advice. This can be done only by an attorney. Be careful to stay within your boundaries in this area, and do not hesitate to seek help with the document and your understanding of the document if you have any uncertainty at all. No purpose is served in denying yourself the need for help at this important stage of the sale.

The salesperson needs to make enough copies of the contract so that all the parties involved receive one. Of course, buyer and seller each need a copy, as well as the lending institution and title insurance or abstract company involved. If the buyer and seller are represented by attorneys, copies should go to them as well. Taking so much time on the contract may seem wasteful to the uninformed, but time and effort can be saved in the long run (to say nothing of the sale!) by doing a complete and thorough job on it.

Process the Earnest Money

In most real estate transactions, earnest money is collected right after all parties sign the contract. The salesperson must see that this money gets to the proper **escrow agent**— a person or firm that holds the money—as soon as possible. Of course, everyone involved in the sale needs to know and agree about this; most contracts stipulate clearly who the escrow agent will be. Many buyers believe that their earnest money check will simply be held by the escrow agent, when actually the check usually needs to clear the bank before the contract becomes valid. Make certain the prospective buyer is aware of the need to have sufficient funds in the bank account at the time of check writing.

In some states, a sale can be threatened because of disagreement over which escrow officer or **abstract or title company** will handle the transaction. In states where the listing agency handles the escrow and closing, this point is not important. However, keep in mind that this point of negotiation is between buyer and seller. They may have no preference and will turn to the salespeople involved for guidance. No personal bias should be allowed to jeopardize the best interest of the buyer and the seller.

Help the Parties Fulfill Terms of Agreement

As mentioned earlier in this chapter, both buyer and seller have certain responsibilities and tasks to perform for the actual sale to occur.

Buyer's Role

In many situations, the buyer must make a loan application. The effective salesperson will get a last-minute update on the local money situation. The salesperson must have current information to find the best combination of interest rate, loan charges, and services. After the lender has been selected, a loan application appointment should be made as soon as possible. Many salespeople will accompany the buyer for this appointment. Whether or not you attend, check with the loan officer before the appointment to determine what information the potential borrower needs to bring. For example, balances and account numbers of loans and savings accounts are common to every application, and

Figure 13.1	Closing Checklists

For Buyers

1. Send out change-of-mailing address notices.

2. Give notice to landlord (if applicable).

3. Obtain utility deposit refunds:
   (a) Water (b) Gas (c) Electricity (d) Telephone

4. Cancel old insurance policies and start new ones.

5. Make arrangements for moving, including time and date.

6. Arrange new furniture/appliance deliveries.

7. Return keys to the old property; pick up keys to the new property.

8. Obtain records from the children's old school, and enroll them in the new school.*

9. Obtain medical records; locate new doctor, dentist, and so on.*

10. Have banking and credit history transferred.*

For Sellers

1. Send out change-of-mailing address notices.
2. Coordinate moving arrangements.
3. Complete repairs and inspections.
4. Obtain utility deposit refunds:
   (a) Water (b) Gas (c) Electricity (d) Telephone
5. Change insurance policies.
6. Give keys to property to buyer.

*If new to the area

time can be saved if the buyer brings this information to the first meeting with the lender. Charge and credit card numbers and the amount of debt associated with those cards also will be needed in most cases. Verification of income history is also required, and if the buyer is self-employed, certain financial statements or tax returns may be needed. Help the buyers make this a less difficult experience by making sure they know what will be expected of them in advance of the appointment.

Other details, such as a new insurance policy and utility deposits, must be taken care of and may be forgotten by the excited buyer. The experienced salesperson realizes the buyers' tendency to overlook some of these and should be prepared to guide and remind the buyers. Many agents provide the buyer and seller with a checklist, such as the one in Figure 13.1, to make sure no activity is neglected. Expand and adapt these lists to fit your needs as situations arise.

Seller's Role

The seller also has certain responsibilities. Relocation arrangements have to be completed, and the present mortgage holder should be informed of the intended loan pay-off. If certain repairs are stipulated in the earnest money contract, they need to be made. Sellers sometimes have a tendency to drag their feet on these tasks. The attempt to postpone the sales process actually may be an unconscious refusal to leave the property, especially if owning it has been a positive experience. Whatever the cause for delay, the salesperson needs to see that sellers uphold their end of the bargain.

Agent's Role

The time lag between signing an earnest money contract and transfer of ownership can vary. In some sales, the time will be only a few days, and in others, it may be several months. The salesperson has a responsibility to keep current on the progress. Checking with the loan officer regarding buyer qualifications, following up on the **appraisal**, and verifying that inspections have been made, all represent important activities that must be scheduled into the salesperson's timetable. If you fail to monitor this process thoroughly, the closing date may arrive only for you to discover that something was left undone.

However, do not overdo this follow-up by checking details to the point of alienating others involved in the sale. A salesperson can do more harm than good by excessive intervention. After all, your sale is not the only item on the schedule of the loan officer, escrow agent, and appraiser. They all will appreciate your helping make the sale smooth and easy for them, as well as for the buyer and seller. Keep a progress report on the sale. Then if a request for information comes into your office when you are away, anyone can scan the file or folder's contents and give an accurate report.

Keep Everyone Informed

Salespeople should not only keep up-to-date on the progress of the sale but also keep the other involved parties informed. Because the need for a coordinated effort exists among many people, someone must serve as a communications center. The salesperson can often best assume this role. For example, from a purely logistical point of view, the lender, title company, survey team, and appraiser must know about each other's activities.

Even more important is the salesperson's responsibility to keep the buyer and seller current. People have a natural tendency to experience a period of self-doubt after a major decision has been made. This feeling becomes compounded when a person is left in limbo. No news may be interpreted as bad news by the anxious buyer or seller. A surprised and unsuspecting salesperson may be caught off guard by a buyer or seller developing "cold feet" about the sale. One effective way to counteract this tendency is by keeping people informed. Positive news of the progression toward closing often has a way of exciting and remotivating the buyer and seller about the upcoming sale. By taking the time to contact the two most important parties to the sale on a regular basis, the salesperson also can answer any questions that may have come up. This duty may be shared between two salespeople if more than one is involved. These two professionals need to show respect and support of each other's efforts during this important period. "Keeping the fences tight" between the agents and/or agencies is wise, given that there may be future business with the other office or licensee down the road.

Another benefit is the reminder of the salesperson's interest and service all the way to a successful close and beyond. This may be the single most important thing a salesperson can do to hold the sale together between contract and closing.

Be Prepared to Close

The actual transfer of real estate ownership can be a reasonably simple process if everything has been handled properly in anticipation of the transfer. Both buyer and seller need to be ready and prepared to close. This preparation begins by helping them to understand what actually takes place at the closing. Salespeople use the term "closing" so often they may assume that the buyers and sellers will know what to expect, but many of them do not. Both parties need to completely understand what will happen at the **closing** (the time of actual ownership change where a deed is delivered and title passes).

Prevent Last-Minute Surprises

Veteran closers can tell many horror stories about difficult closings. Many bad experiences could have been eliminated by some preclosing planning. The problems that occur at closing often surface because the buyer and seller have to confront something unexpected or unpleasant. Their reaction to this negative surprise is natural and can be anticipated. Closings are not the time for negative surprises! In fact, many buyers and sellers are nervous about this last big step. This confusion and frustration may lead to one or both parties refusing to complete the sale.

Some of this trouble can be eliminated by the knowledgeable salesperson. For example, check with the closing officer a day in advance to verify the closing costs for the buyer and seller. The actual costs can be compared with the estimate prepared at the time of contract signing. If the figures vary, the reason can be determined and explained to the buyer or seller *before* closing. This same strategy can be used with any questionable aspects of the closing.

Most salespeople like to accompany their customers to the closing. If there is any problem regarding transportation, offer to pick them up and take them. This eliminates the chance of "missing person(s)" and delayed completion.

Maintain Low, but Visible, Profile

During the actual explanation and signing of the necessary documents, most closers prefer that the salesperson stay out of the way. This means the salesperson should allow the closer to handle the closing, with the agent being supportive but definitely in the background. Competition for the attention of the buyer or seller at this time is distracting and slows down the process. This agent-closer relationship needs to be understood by both parties before the actual closing occurs. Keep in mind that at this time, it's the closer's turf, not the salesperson's.

Often the transfer of ownership needs to be expedited. Expediting can be facilitated if the buyer has money wired from the bank or brings a cashier's check to closing rather than a personal or company check, which has to clear before funds can be disbursed. In some situations, a set of keys to the property should be ready to present to the buyer at closing. Be certain that you thank *all* parties concerned for their help in making the sale. Remember the importance of ending each close on a positive note if at all possible. Express your sincere appreciation for the buyer's confidence in you. Reassure buyers of their value and importance to you and ask to be of further assistance and service. At this point, you can begin asking for help in developing future business. Do the same thing for the sellers if you worked for them.

Follow Up after Closing

Completing a close is not the same as completing a sale. The experienced salesperson recognizes the need to follow up after the sale. How this is done varies with the situation and the salesperson's preferences, but remember how important it is. Some salespeople feel that follow-up means actually participating during the move in. Others will arrive at the end of the hectic first day with a covered dish for supper, or if you cook like I do, have a meal delivered! A good plan is to stop by after the new owners have been in the property for a short time. This gives you a chance to see if any problems have arisen that you can solve and to reaffirm that they have not been forgotten. Remember that your next sale with these particular folks begins as soon as this one ends!

The idea behind these activities is to remind buyers of your interest in their satisfaction. This plan can work with sellers equally well. It is easy to check with sellers and see how they are. Or you can follow up and make sure each party receives all the documents due from the sale. Anything you can do to be of service after the sale is a pleasant surprise to both buyer and seller and may lead to more business in the future. Some firms have a post-sale evaluation form that is sent out to solicit feedback on the service provided. It is fun to hear the good things we did, but constructive to learn how we can do better.

The Sales Process Revisited

Looking back at Chapter 1 and its explanation of the sales process illuminates an important concept: The process is circular and unending. Following up after closing should restart the cycle. At this point, ask the sellers or buyers for permission to use their names as references. New prospects will appreciate an opportunity to give former customers a call and verify your qualifications. Of course, this should be done only with the former customer's permission.

Another effective way to build future business from a successful sale is by asking for a letter of recommendation. Suggest that your buyers or sellers write a letter, such as the one in Figure 13.2, to your broker expressing satisfaction with your services if, in fact, they are satisfied. Use your success to build on success.

July 11, 2006

Mrs. June Jones, Owner ABC Realty

Dear Mrs. Jones:

At the request of your sales associate Kara Mackey, I would like to express my reaction to the service she provided during our recent purchase of a new home in your area. During the past twelve years, my company has transferred my family four times. In all the moves, we have never had a real estate agent who was more considerate than Ms. Mackey. Her professionalism and true concern for our well-being were a pleasant surprise.

In the event we ever need a real estate agent in the future or know of anyone who does, rest assured we will not hesitate to call upon or recommend Ms. Mackey. She is an asset to your firm and to her profession.

Sincerely,

Rhonda Kay

Figure 13.2   Sample Letter of Recommendation

The successful real estate salesperson will build future sales on each present and past sale. There is no better advertising medium in the world than a satisfied customer. Remember that your past customers can become your future business. As their needs change, they may need your professional services again. In today's highly mobile society, the odds are in your favor that new owners will sell their property within five years. Develop a plan to contact them on a regular basis. A simple note, such as the example in Figure 13.3, or inclusion in your newsletter mailing list will keep your name and offer of service before former customers. This will enable the sales process to function in a cycle as you build a satisfying career as a professional real estate salesperson.

TECHNOLOGY *IN ACTION*

Many real estate companies and agents are using transaction management systems that are integrated into the Web. These software providers and transaction management systems allow all parties involved in the transaction the ability to log into the site with a username and password to check on the closing status. On such vendor can be found at http://www.settlementroom.com. This vendor offer a new service for real estate transactions. Buyers are always available to check on the status of their closing, find out if the appraisal has been completed, where the title work is, and so forth. Sellers can also look up information from the transaction management platform with the agent, broker, and others involved. E-mails and alerts can also be set up so everyone involved can keep the transaction running smoothly.

July 14, 2006

Dear Rhonda:

I want to sincerely thank you for the trust and confidence you placed in me when you were looking for a home. This opportunity to be of service to you was a pleasure to me, and I truly believe you will enjoy your new residence.

If I can ever be of help to you or anyone you know with real estate needs, please don't hesitate to call on me.

Thank you again for your confidence.

Sincerely,

Kara Mackey, Sales Associate

Harrington Realty

Figure 13.3   Sample Follow-Up Note

Summary

After an agreement has been reached between buyer and seller in the real estate sales process, the salesperson must ensure that the terms of the sale are committed to writing in the form of an *earnest money contract.* In addition, the salesperson must see to it that the earnest money is turned over to the proper *escrow agent* as soon as possible and that all parties to the transaction fulfill the terms of the sales contract.

The salesperson should remain fully informed on the progress of the closing process and should promptly share this information with both buyer and seller. Further, the salesperson should be able to avoid last-minute complications by preparing in advance to close the transaction and ensuring that both parties understand what will happen at the closing.

After the sale is completed, the salesperson should follow up with both parties to remind them of his or her interest in their satisfaction and desire to serve them again in the future.

Review Questions

1. What are the responsibilities of the salesperson to keep the sale together?

2. Whose responsibility is it to make sure the earnest money contract accurately reflects the agreement between the parties?

3. How many copies of the earnest money contract does the salesperson need to make?

4. What happens to a buyer's earnest money check?

5. What is the purpose of the salesperson getting a last-minute update on the local money situation?

6. Why should the salesperson check with the loan officer before the loan application appointment?

7. What is the advantage of keeping a progress report on details of the sale?

8. What is one effective way to combat a buyer or seller developing "cold feet" about a sale?

9. How can an agent eliminate the possible delay caused by a "lost" person at closing time?

10. What is a good suggestion to the buyer to help expedite closing?

11. What are some suggestions for follow-up after the closing?

12. What are some ways to build future business from a successful sale?

13. What is the single best advertising medium?

14. When does the sales process end?

Discussion Questions

1. In addition to the activities mentioned in this chapter, what other things must a salesperson do to ensure a sale actually is consummated?

2. Why is it important to "keep the customer sold" between the time of the agreement and the actual ownership transfer?

3. How can you prepare your buyer or seller for the actual closing?

Situation

Value of Satisfied Customers

Pat Nover is a highly skilled salesperson in real estate. She attributes her long-term success to repeat business and referrals from satisfied clients. How can a salesperson get the maximum results from his or her previous customers?

A Follow-Up Plan

You have been given the task of developing a follow-up plan to ensure all the buyers and sellers using your company's services are not forgotten after a few weeks or months. How can this be done effectively?

Chapter

14

Broker Selection and Legal Awareness

Key Terms

- Blockbusting
- Less favorable treatment
- Market allocation
- Minority
- Price fixing
- Redlining
- Steering

What to Look for in a Broker

A beginning salesperson must select the correct broker. Remember, the factors important to one person are not automatically the same for another person. There may be many good brokers in any given marketplace but not all of them may be proper for a particular individual. In general, some points cannot be ignored in choosing a sponsoring broker.

Following are some suggestions that have been well received through the years. They are not absolutes; rather, they should stimulate your thinking about important considerations in this important choice. In some states, you can finish your prelicensing education and sit for the state exam on an "inactive status" before a broker selection must be made. This is a good idea for many people because it reduces the stress of making a broker choice in order to move forward with a licensing goal. Having completed all the requirements except broker selection also makes the person more attractive to the brokerage community. In my many years of teaching and practicing real estate, I have talked with hundreds of people who were going get their license, but never followed through with the plan.

Throughout the material on broker selection, the term broker-manager will be used. In some offices, the manager and broker are the same. In others, a principal or sponsoring broker will have an office manager or sales manager overseeing the operation. The potential agent needs to know the organizational structure and may want to visit with both the manager and broker to get a better perspective of the company.

Hiring the Best Broker

Most new salespeople were employees in other areas before entering the real estate field. As presented in an earlier chapter, the majority of salespeople are not employees but independent contractors. This status creates a different set of relationships. These differences are evident in the selection process as well. Rather than hoping some broker will "take you on," reverse the way you look at selection. Your task is not so much to sell yourself as to be satisfied that you are associating with a company that best suits your needs. The suggestion is not to become overly impressed with yourself but to avoid picking automatically any broker just because that company will "have you." A positive self-image is appropriate at all times but especially when choosing a broker. Do not pick a broker based upon ease but rather on a correct "fit" for you. And keep in mind that what is a good relationship as a starting salesperson may not be the same criteria you will use a few years down the road.

Here are some specific ideas for you to consider:

Select an area you desire to work. This may be a geographic area such as your general neighborhood if you plan to be in residential property, or it can be all properties south and west of your town within one hour if you want to be in rural property. Selection can also be based on type of property (commercial raw land, resort property, and so on). Plan to pick some area that interests you and become experienced in it. The days of the generalist who knows about all phases of real estate are fast diminishing. Specialists are the rule. Keep in mind that you can always expand your areas of expertise after you have mastered a particular segment. Start small and grow versus starting too large and having to shrink.

Investigate your chosen area. You may find that less than 10 and probably only 4 or 5 brokers will dominate a particular aspect of real estate in your area. You should visit with *all* these companies before making any choice. Comparative shopping is the sign of an astute consumer, and it is a good idea in broker selection as well.

Be frank and honest during the interviews. Most office managers and brokers are experienced "people" people. Adopt an attitude of addressing truthfully where you are going in your career and what you can offer the firm. Then ask what the company can do for you. Acknowledge that you plan to look at several companies. The more successful offices will welcome your comparison, knowing they will look good relative to others.

Plan for your interview. There are certain common areas of discussion in most interviews. You will want to know certain things about the company under consideration, and the organization will want to know some things about you. Anticipate the questions you will ask and be asked and think through what you will say and how you will word it. After each interview, review your performance and modify or improve for the next one. Develop a checklist of important questions to ask and points about yourself that you want covered. Practice before and after each interview will increase the chances of both parties (interviewer and interviewee) feeling good about the time spent together. This is an important decision. Put forth the required effort to do a good job. The right company (for you) can greatly enhance your chances of success in the early stages of your real estate sales development.

Investigate the training program. No matter how interested or talented you are, at the beginning, all new salespeople need considerable support and guidance. Most firms recognize this and offer some type of follow-up training to further your prelicensing education. This training support should be an absolute for the vast majority of new salespeople.

But just "some type" of training is not good enough. You need and deserve a well-planned, systematic training program to fill in any "holes" in your real estate education to date. A firm doesn't necessarily need a full-time training specialist to have an effective training program. However, the firm *must* offer something better than an erratic approach. The video programs available today are great *supplements* to face-to-face, hands-on training, but they are not *substitutes* for personal teaching. Ask for and expect specifics on this critical topic. Subjects covered, scheduling, format/techniques used, and people responsible for various topics are examples of questions you need answers to before an intelligent assessment can be made about a particular firm. Veteran salespeople with established track records will view this differently. If you are a relative newcomer to the field, the training offered is one of the most important factors to consider.

Learn about the management team. You deserve accurate and available help when you need it. That first listing presentation or initial purchase offer can be an exciting milestone in a new agent's career, but most people need help at that critical point. Find out what your broker-manager's views are about sales help. The old "sink-or-swim" philosophy is not only questionable but is dangerous from a liability point of view. Investigate your manager's sales record. An outstanding salesperson is not automatically an effective broker or manager of other salespeople, but a manager should have a keen understanding of the demands placed upon a salesperson. The skills necessary for a manager and a salesperson are substantially different, but an important ingredient for an effective real estate office manager or broker is several years' experience as an average or above average salesperson. Whether the manager(s) still sell or not is not so important. What is important is that the management team has the attitude and aptitude to support you.

Keep an open mind about the management team still being active in sales. Qualified opinions are mixed on this topic. Some people think a manager should remain active in selling to stay current. Others view management as a full-time job with nothing left for selling. My own opinion falls in the middle. I see nothing wrong with a broker-manager doing some selling, but *only* if that is not his or her first priority. Administering the office (or having someone competent to do this) *and* supporting the office's agents need to be a higher priority. If the broker-manager *has* to sell all he or she can to keep the doors open, I would be apprehensive about the time available to train a beginning salesperson. Again, this view reflects a newcomer's need and not an established agent's need.

Check the company's track record. What makes this firm so special? That is an important question to get straight in your mind. A company does not necessarily have to be the oldest, biggest, newest, or smallest, but it does need (or have in place a plan to develop) a positive image. Have you ever had to apologize to someone for the public behavior of another person? Do you remember how uncomfortable that made you feel? Before you can sell yourself and your company (virtually one and the same to most consumers), *you* have to be sold on yourself and your organization.

Ask about the company's years in service, overall sales volume, and average volume per agent. You cannot expect a company to offer more than round figures on such topics, but it is important to get a feel for the success potential you could have if you decide to join the firm. A word of caution . . . there is something called the 80/20 rule you must keep in mind. The idea that 80 percent of the sales are done by 20 percent of the people may have merit in the firms you are investigating. That is why it is important to know about the productivity of agents other than the one or two superstars any interviewer will tell you about.

Another aspect of this investigation should center on agent turnover. The stability of a company's sales force is a good indication of agent satisfaction. A company with limited turnover isn't necessarily superior, but that low turnover is a healthy sign.

Discuss company policies. Many readers may think the most significant policy point to discuss is commission splits. Although important, commission split is only *one* factor and may be not even close to the most important. For example, which would you prefer . . . a 10 percent commission on a sale of $100,000 or a 1 percent commission on a sale of $1,000,000? The gross income to you might be the same but what about sales expenses, advertising programs, required versus volunteer floor duty, referrals, showing policies, and resolution of disputes? The list could be several pages long. There is no "right" answer, but a company must have policy procedures defined and committed to writing. You should also review the company manual before choosing a firm. If office brokers-managers are reluctant to allow this, remind them that they are free to check your references. Why should you not be able to review what you have been told? Supporting the company you represent in the critical area of how business is to be conducted is very important. After joining the organization, it is really too late to dispute company policy from a selection perspective. You should become aware and then comfortable in advance with how the firm is run, or don't join that team.

Check the office environment. Meet with the other agents in the office. Not only can you get some verification of what the broker-manager has told you, but you also can get a feel for your potential peers. Some offices are open and friendly, and other offices are more reserved. One is not better than the other, but one may be more comfortable for you. Sitting with and listening to agents as an observer will give you some important insight. Spend several sessions in any office that interests you to get an idea of the match between you and the group. As you grow as an agent, what is important in this area will change, but initially feeling comfortable among your peers is significant.

Certainly these points are not all you must consider, but they will get you thinking about what is important *to you* in your choice of broker. Add to the list those issues you feel need discussing and clarifying to your satisfaction. Figure 14.1 is a condensed checklist of the points made in this section.

Broker Selection Checklist   **Figure 14.1**

1. Select a market area.
2. Investigate the area for broker activity.
3. Meet with several companies before choosing.
4. Plan for your interview. Be frank and honest and expect the same during your visits.
5. Ask questions about:
   (a) Training Programs
   (b) Management Support
   (c) Company Track Record
   (d) Company Policies
   (e) Office Environment

Legal Awareness

Whatever broker selection decisions are made, the real estate salesperson should be aware of certain laws regarding equal opportunities. The intent in providing some information on these topics is not for debate purposes. They are *laws,* not suggestions. Each area merits an entire chapter, if not a complete book. Therefore, the condensed form found here is only a starting point in your awareness and understanding of such legislation. Local and state laws vary, but federal laws prescribe minimum standards. By participating in your local Board of REALTORS® updates, you can keep current in local practice and avoid problems. The Code of Ethics of the National Association of REALTORS® states that real estate agents shall be informed of issues that affect real estate. This awareness clearly extends to the laws.

Fair Housing

The major goal of federal fair housing laws is to provide a single unbiased housing marketplace where personal preference and financial abilities dictate selection.

You have seen the Equal Housing Opportunity sign posted in real estate offices (see Figure 14.2). The purpose of posting such a sign is to make consumers aware of the office's commitment to do business in accordance with the law. Some points to review of the Federal Housing Act of 1968 (and subsequent amendments) include the following:

- The term **minority** can be any group or person that has been discriminated against due to race, religion, color, sex, familial status, handicap, or national origin. Remember, in this case, minority does not refer to a number or percentage but is based on the treatment rendered.
- **Steering** is an attempt to guide people toward or away from an area due to one of the seven factors listed in the first paragraph of this list. It is not appropriate

Figure 14.2 / Equal Housing Opportunity Symbol

for a salesperson to pick any area to show on the basis that a person might "fit in" better. Remember, personal preference and financial ability are the criteria.

- **Blockbusting** is sometimes known as panic selling. This situation centers on inducing people to move or sell due to the possible threat (or fact) of minorities moving in. The old adage "there goes the neighborhood" has no place in the practice of a professional real estate salesperson.
- Another term, **less favorable treatment**, deals with the quality of service offered. Failure to offer full and equal support or service to all persons regardless of the seven criteria stated earlier is a violation of the law.
- Failure to make mortgage loans or insurance available to a particular area due to minority integration is known as **redlining**. Although not directly involved in lending or insuring, a real estate person definitely is involved in helping individuals apply for both in many situations.

Equal Credit Opportunity

This federal legislation adds age and marital status to the seven minorities as points against which discrimination is disallowed. This law primarily addresses the role and responsibility of a lender, but the salesperson should have a basic understanding.

Truth in Lending

The intent of the Truth-in-Lending Act is to help consumers know the real cost of borrowing money. There is sometimes confusion on the difference between an interest charge and a finance charge. The *true* cost of borrowing money as defined in Regulation Z (an extensive publication series setting up interpretation and compliance guides) is more than the interest charges. The annual percentage rate (APR) also includes things such as loan fees, prepaid interest, and other financing charges. Although the rules are complex, it is important to remember that the use of certain words or phrases in advertising and promotion "triggers" the need to comply with Regulation Z. Real estate salespeople should attend REALTORS® seminars and updates on such a topic whenever they are available to assure compliance with full and accurate disclosure.

Anti-Trust

The philosophy of anti-trust laws is that competition brings out the best products and services for consumers. The supporting theme is that the general public is hurt when competition is reduced by monopolies or illegal agreements not to compete. The Sherman Anti-Trust Act and the Clayton Anti-Trust Act are the most significant pieces of anti-trust legislation. Two key areas for real estate people center on **price fixing** and **market allocation**. Price fixing occurs when competing practitioners agree to charge the same fees for such activities as property management, leasing commissions, and so forth. The general view is that you can charge whatever you desire, but make that choice on an independent basis. Legally there is no such thing as a "going rate" or "common charge" that has been determined collectively. Market allocation deals with dividing up the marketplace between competitors. This is done on the basis of price range, location, or type of property. The end result is a reduction in competition, which is illegal. Be aware that local Boards of REALTORS® publish, and have as written policy, statements about the errors in anti-trust.

Deceptive Trade Practices

This area of law centers on false, misleading, deceptive . . . (you can use many adjectives), actions on the part of a licensed practitioner. States vary in the specifics of their particular laws, but most hold it illegal to give false or misleading representations about products *or* services being offered for sale. Note that this law pertains to products or services. Some states have adopted deceptive trade practice laws to apply specifically to real estate. Be sure to confirm and understand the exact nature of the law in your particular locale.

Becoming aware of the various local, state, and federal laws that affect your role as a real estate salesperson is an important strategy to pursue. The brief description presented here is not enough to qualify anyone. The intent is to call attention to these major areas; you should become knowledgeable about the legislation regarding licensees and follow it appropriately.

TECHNOLOGY *IN ACTION*

Many good resources are available for risk reduction and management for brokers to use at sales meetings from http://www.hud.gov, http://www.epa.gov, and your own local and state real estate commission Web site. Many of these Web sites offer downloadable PDF files for real estate brokers or agents to print out and use. Be sure to check out the frequently asked questions and myths and facts portions of these Web sites.

Summary

Selecting a sponsoring broker is an important decision. Much of the success a salesperson can anticipate will depend on the selection of the correct broker for his or her needs and circumstances. Certain key points to consider include broker activity in your chosen market area, a strong training program, management support, company background and policies, and the overall office climate or environment. Such a major decision needs to be based upon well-thought-out factors and should not be done quickly or carelessly.

An awareness of certain federal legislation affecting the real estate practitioner is also vital. Particular state or local laws need to be investigated completely. Some of the federal laws include Fair Housing, Equal Credit, Truth-in-Lending, Anti-Trust, and Deceptive Trade Practices. Attendance at local Board of REALTORS® seminars on such topics will help keep the practitioner current and on the right side of the law on these issues.

Review Questions

1. Why is broker selection so important?

2. What merit does a licensee's personal opinion have regarding Fair Housing?

3. Why is an investigation into an office's policies important?

4. How important is it that these policies be committed to writing?

5. Why is a company's previous track record important to consider in your selection?

6. Where can you find out more about legislation affecting licensees?

7. Why should a person meet and get to know the other salespeople in an office before making a choice of offices?

8. Why should a person talk to several brokers before making a choice for sponsorship?

9. What is the intent of Fair Housing legislation?

Discussion Questions

1. Should the broker be active as a salesperson?

2. What additional factors should be considered in broker selection?

3. Why should a licensee become knowledgeable on local as well as federal legislation affecting real estate?

4 What are some important topics that in your judgment must be included in any effective training program?

Situation

No More Newcomers

You have been asked to list a property in your market area. The seller has been cooperative regarding pricing at market value with good flexible terms. It will easily be your best listing of the year and is quite salable. At the last moment, after the listing form has been signed, the seller says: "By the way, I don't want any of those foreigners that are moving in here to try and buy this house. There are too many of those kind of newcomers in the neighborhood now."

How do you respond?

Keeping It in the Family

Alexis Welch is a student of real estate soon to become licensed. Her sister, Angela Rodriguez, is a very successful commercial real estate broker in the same town where Alexis hopes to practice as a residential salesperson. Angela wants Alexis to join her one-person commercial office and expand the company's offerings into the home market. What counsel might you offer Alexis about this opportunity?

Glossary

A

Abstract/Title Company. A company responsible for searching the public records to help determine the quality of a title that is being transferred. Often issues an abstract of title or title insurance policy. May also serve as closer.

Advisory Close. A purchasing decision based on input from a third party.

Afford Amount. Amount a person feels comfortable investing in real estate.

Amortization. Scheduling a loan over a period of years, during which both principal and interest are payable in periodic installments.

Amortization Table. A table that shows breakdowns of principal and interest payments over the period of the loan.

Appraisal. An estimate of fair market value, generally for the purpose of helping a lending institution determine how much it will loan on a property.

Appreciation. A valid increase in fair market value of a property or area based on comparable sales.

Assumptive Close. Sometimes called the "not if, but when" close. A confident view held by the salesperson that he or she will be able to help the prospect. This should be exhibited from first contact with the prospect.

Attitude Learning. Behavior representative of feeling or conviction that is acquired through experience, practice, or exercise.

B

BIKE Approach. The Belief, Involvement, Knowledge and Enthusiasm technique that has proved helpful in dealing with personal motivation problems.

Blockbusting. Panic selling causing people to sell property because minorities are moving in.

Buying Motive. The prospect's reason for looking for property to purchase.

Buying Signals. Buyer behavior that may indicate that he or she has reached a decision.

C

Call-in Sheet. A form designed to help the salesperson obtain qualifying information from a caller.

Career Apparel. Identical clothing selected by a firm and worn by all salespeople for the purpose of company identity.

Centers of Influence. Individuals who are well respected and influential in the community, such as doctors, lawyers, teachers, and shop owners.

Client Records. Records dealing with information about specific clients and their needs and preferences. Must be continually updated in a systematic manner.

Close. An attempt to get a positive decision from a prospect.

Closing. The appointment at the title or abstract company during which the papers are signed to transfer ownership of the property.

Closing Cost Statement. A form that, when completed by the agent, displays the approximate cost to the buyer or seller of completing the transaction.

CMA. See *Competitive Market Analysis.*

Code of Ethics. Professional standards followed by all REALTORS®.

Cognitive Learning. An intellectual process by which knowledge is gained about perceptions or ideas.

Cold Call. Unsolicited personal visits to property owners to offer service and gain visibility.

Commercial Facilities. Retail stores, banks, restaurants, law offices, doctors' offices, and similar facilities accessible from a particular neighborhood.

Commission. A fee paid for the marketing service rendered by the real estate company. Commission is established at the time the listing agreement is signed.

Communication. The transmission and reception of thoughts, ideas, feelings, and attitudes in the manner intended.

Competitive Market Analysis. A chart of information regarding properties for sale, properties that have recently sold, and properties that were listed but did not sell in a specific area.

Composition of Income. A record-keeping system to determine which of a person's efforts generate the most dollar return.

Consumer Behavior. The behavior consumers display in searching for, purchasing, using, and evaluating products, services, and ideas that they expect will satisfy their needs.

Counteroffer. An alternative offer made by the seller to the buyer to replace the original offer made by the buyer.

Credit Report. Fee paid to local credit reporting service to obtain credit history. Helps the lending institution determine borrower's qualifications. There are additional fees if credit is out of town.

D

Deed of Trust. An instrument used to establish a mortgage lien on the property purchased with the money borrowed in the note.

Deed of Trust to Secure Assumption. Instrument used when a buyer is purchasing a seller's equity and assuming an existing mortgage. This instrument would, under specific conditions, allow the current seller to take up payments again in the event the buyer should stop making payments and be in default.

Demographics. A study of the characteristics of populations to identify certain market segments.

Discount Points. An added loan charge by the lender to make the yield on the loan competitive with other investment options. One point equals 1 percent of the amount to be loaned.

Distractions. Competing obstacles that hinder effective communication.

Distress Advertising. Advertising that creates the impression of a problem as the reason for selling.

E

Earnest Money. Money placed in the possession of a third party by the buyer to be applied to the purchase price when the sale is completed, or forfeited if the buyer defaults.

Earnest Money Contract. The form that, when completed and signed, establishes a legal contract outlining the specifics of a transaction and placing the earnest money in the possession of the escrow agent.

Escrow Agent. The person or firm that holds the earnest money.

Escrow Fee. Fee paid to the escrow agent for handling the transaction and seeing that all terms of the earnest money contract are carried out.

Expired Listing. A property previously under a listing contract that has terminated and now represents a possible listing for another agent.

Explain-and-Request Method. A technique used in qualifying, where the salesperson explains to prospects the need to ask qualifying questions and then requests permission to ask the questions.

F

Fair Market Value. The price a ready, willing, and able buyer would pay for a property he or she chooses to buy when not forced to do so.

Farming. A planned, systematic method of developing prospects in a defined area.

Filing Fees. Charges for filing and recording releases that clear the title to the real estate being sold.

Floor Duty. The time assigned to an agent to handle the incoming telephone calls in the office.

Follow-up Note. Handwritten message from an agent that thanks customers for their business.

Four Ps. The interaction of price, promotion, product, and place in explaining marketing.

FSBOs. For Sale By Owner. An unlisted property being marketed by the owner.

G

Goal Chart. Chart that displays the accomplishment of a salesperson's sales goals.

Goal Setting. The practice of deliberate behaviors that continually gauge a person's effectiveness, thus moving him or her toward predetermined objectives.

Government Structure. The manner in which the governing body of a city or municipality is set up and operated.

H

Hierarchy of Needs. A theory of motivation that assumes various stages of needs ranging from the most fundamental needs to the very elaborate, highly individualized needs.

Housing Developments. Areas of new homes or businesses under construction or in the planning stage.

I

Inattention. Failure to listen to another person's message.

Independent Contractor. A salesperson who is more independent than an employee; this agent is basically in business for himself or herself, is responsible for payment of taxes, and receives no employee benefits from the broker.

Institutional Advertising. Ads run for the purpose of building the image of a company rather than to promote a specific property.

L

Lead. A suggestion of potential business furnished by an individual.

Listing Agent. The particular salesperson responsible for obtaining a listing and through whom all contact with the seller should probably be made.

Listing Agreement. The printed form that, when completed and signed, establishes a legal contract employing a broker as agent to sell real estate on the owner's terms within a given time, for which the broker will be paid a commission.

Listing Presentation. The presentation made by an agent to a prospective seller to obtain a contract to place the property on the market.

Listing Presentation Kit. A package of material devoted to assist a salesperson in covering all necessary points during a listing presentation.

Loan Origination Fee. A fee charged by the lending institution for processing the loan. Generally explained in terms of points. One point equals 1 percent of the loan.

M

Machine-Gun Approach. A sales technique that involves giving many responses to a prospect's objections, rather than dealing with the root of the objection. Not recommended.

Mail-out. Promotional piece that agents mail to homeowners or prospective purchasers.

Market Allocation. Dividing up a marketplace with the intent to reduce competition.

Market Area. Geographical area that an agent selects to farm.

Market Segmentation. The dividing up of the total marketplace into smaller groups with common characteristics.

Marketing. The performance of business activities that direct the flow of goods and services from producer to consumer or user.

Mass Marketing Message. Communication to a large audience of people with an attempt to individualize the message.

MGIC/PMI Charges. Appraisal and insurance policy fees paid to a mortgage insurance company. This insurance protects the lender in case of default and allows the buyer to make less than a 20 percent down payment.

Mini-Decision Approach. Closing technique in which the agent asks prospects to make small decisions about a property that lead to a decision to buy.

Minor Point Close. Sometimes called the "either/or" close. Based on a choice between alternatives.

Minority. Anyone discriminated against due to race, religion, color, sex, or national origin.

MLS. See *Multiple Listing Service*.

Monitoring. A technique that involves recording the number of calls received from ads placed to determine advertising effectiveness.

Mortgagee's Title Policy. An insurance policy issued to the lending institution making the loan. It protects the lender in the event that a bad title causes any loss. Generally issued in conjunction with a title insurance policy to the buyer.

Multiple Listing Service. A subscription service through which brokers share each other's listings for a predetermined-commission split.

N

Note. A written agreement stating a debt and the terms for repayment.

O

Open-Ended Question. A question for which some explanation beyond a yes or no answer is required.

Open House.   A property that is for sale being held open for public inspection.

Owner's Title Policy.   An insurance policy against unknown liens, encumbrances, or defects in the title to the real estate being transferred. Generally paid by the seller for a one-time charge for a policy value in the amount of the sales price. The policy cost is set by the state board of insurance and is good for as long as the buyer keeps the property. (The policy cannot be transferred to another owner.)

P

Perception.   An individualized interpretation of reality.

Personal Motivation.   An inner drive that provides direction toward the accomplishment of individual goals.

Personal Preparation.   The preliminary work a salesperson should do prior to prospecting. The preparation deals with getting the individual salesperson ready to sell.

Prejudice.   Faulty interpretation of information.

Previewing.   Looking at a property prior to showing it to a client.

Price Fixing.   The establishment between competitors of a standard charge or fee for services.

Product Advertising.   Advertising designed to promote a specific property.

Product Knowledge.   The specific information a salesperson must have about real estate and the community in which he or she practices.

Professionalism.   Drive to be the best you can be in spirit, character, and behavior.

Promotional Aids.   Items, such as business cards and signs, used for personal advertising in the real estate business.

Promotional Costs.   The expenses associated with advertising and other means of gaining exposure to potential prospects.

Prospect.   Someone an agent has determined is in need of his or her services.

Prospect File.   Collection of names and addresses of prospects that an agent assembles or purchases.

Prospecting.   Methods of locating buyers or sellers.

Psychographics.   An attempt to better understand consumers based upon their set of values and the impact those values have on buying behavior.

Public Facilities.   Facilities such as libraries, golf courses, and swimming pools that may be used by a client moving into a community.

Public Services.   Services such as utilities, public transportation, fire protection, and police protection available to residents of an area.

Q

Qualify Amount.   Amount people should invest in real estate based on average for the market area.

Qualifying.   Determining a client's needs and financial strengths and weaknesses.

R

Real Estate Developments.   Areas of new construction within your target market.

Recording Fees.   Fees paid for recording a transaction and making it a matter of public record. (States name of new owner, any new mortgage, liens, and so forth.)

Redlining.   Failure to make insurance coverage or mortgage loans available to a particular area due to minority integration.

Reference Aids.   Printed resources available to real estate people to provide helpful information.

Referrals.   Prospective clients generated through recommendations of past clients and other individuals.

Restrictions.   Copy of the building and deed restrictions placed on the property by the developer and previous owners.

Reverse Advertising.   Advertising designed to focus on the problems related to a piece of property and promote the problem as an asset to specific prospects.

Rider Sign.   A small sign displaying an agent's name and telephone number, usually placed below the company's larger For Sale sign.

S

Sales Chart.   Statement of status of each property an agent is handling.

See-Saw Technique. An attempt to provide a balance between the caller and the agent, as both parties give and receive information.

Selling. The basic art of influencing another person to help him or her make decisions that solve problems to the benefit of all parties.

Shopworn Property. Property that is on the market much longer than comparable properties and that projects the image that something is wrong with the listing.

Showing. Presenting properties to clients.

Showing Agent. The particular salesperson presenting the property listed for sale.

Showing File. Brief, informal list of homes shown to prospects and prospects' reactions to the properties shown.

Sponsoring Broker. The licensed real estate broker who agrees to be responsible for the actions of the salesperson. The broker is assumed to have greater knowledge and experience in real estate.

Stair-Step Close. Relatively small decisions made, leading up to a major decision.

Steering. Guiding people toward or away from certain areas because of minority status.

Survey. An examination of the property by a licensed professional surveyor to determine exact boundary lines. Fence lines, easements, and encroachments also may be shown.

Suspect. Someone who may be in need of an agent's services.

Switch Sheet. A listing of comparable alternate properties in which a client may be interested if he or she is uninterested in the original property.

T

Target Market. The particular group of people an agent wants to reach with a specific message.

Tax Account Approach. Technique of opening a separate savings account into which a salesperson deposits a portion of each commission check; it is used to pay taxes when due.

Tax Certificates. Statements from all concerned taxing agencies showing the current tax status of the property being sold.

Telephone Image. The image projected by a salesperson over the telephone.

Termite Inspection. Statement of search and findings by a licensed exterminator as to the condition of the house regarding termites or other wood-destroying insects.

Time Management. The practice of deliberate behaviors that generate planned, structured use of your time to receive maximum benefit from the time.

Transfer Fee. Charge by the lender when buyer assumes existing mortgage. This fee changes the records held by lender over to the buyer's name.

U

Urgency Close. A close based on the need for an expedient decision. Should be used only when need for urgency is factual.

W

Warranty Deed. The instrument that conveys the title.

Index

A

Abstract company, 198
Accounting software, 32–33
Act, 31–32, 36
Action close, 177
Adobe® Photoshop, 32
Advertising
　classified, 105–107
　communication by, 100, 102
　direct mail, 113
　function of, 102–103
　Internet and web, 112–113
　magazine, 112
　outdoor, 112
　reverse, 109
　techniques for effective,
　　107–112
　types of, 103–104
Advisory close, 177
Afford amount, 142
Agency image, 102
Agent Online, 36
Agents
　explaining role of, 88
　follow-up letters from,
　　204, 205
　letters recommending,
　　202, 203
　listing, 86
　printed information on, 92
　responsibilities of, 197–202
　reviewing offer with,
　　186–187
　role of, 200
　showing, 86
　traits of successful, 8–9
Alternative close, 176
Anti-trust laws, 215
Appraisals
　explanation of, 94, 181
　following up on, 200
Appreciation, 46
Assumptive close, 177

Attitude learning, 100
Attorney fee, 181
AutoPlay, 34–35

B

Banks, 43–44
Behavior learning, 100
Ben Franklin close, 177
BIKE approach, 52–54
Blockbusting, 214
Bookkeeping software, 32–33
Brokers
　checklist for choosing, 213
　guidelines for choosing,
　　209–212
Broker's fee, 94
Budgeting, 26
Budget worksheet, 27
Burnout, 52
Buyers
　communicating with,
　　99–100
　converting sellers to, 189
　decision making by, 159
　DVDs for, 154, 160
　handling objections from,
　　169–172
　motivations of, 145
　referrals from, 67
　role of, 198–199
　types of objections from,
　　167–169
Buying signals, 172–175

C

Calendar software, 32
Call-in sheet, 118, 119
Cellular phones
　checklist for purchasing, 30
　explanation of, 28, 29
Census information, 50
Centers of influence (COI)
　explanation of, 68

　follow-ups with, 70–72
　leads from, 69–70
　potential, 68–69
Classified advertising. *See also*
　Advertising
　examples of, 106, 108, 110
　guidelines for, 105–107
　paying attention to
　　competitors', 111
Closing
　being prepared for, 201–202
　buying signals for, 172–175
　checklist for, 199
　follow up after, 202
　guidelines for, 178–179,
　　182, 189–190
　techniques for, 175–178
Closing costs
　estimate of, 180
　preparing information on,
　　92–94
　terms used for, 181
　web site information on, 182
*Code of Ethics and Standards
　of Practice* (National
　Association of Realtors)
　testing on, 14
　text of, 15–21
Cognitive learning, 99
Cold calls, 45–46
Commercial facilities, 43–44
Communication. *See also*
　Advertising; Telephone
　techniques
　advertising as means of,
　　100, 102
　agent's role in, 200–201
　barriers to, 101
　with consumers, 99–100
　elements of, 100
Competitive market analysis
　(CMA)
　examples of, 47, 97

explanation of, 45
as negotiating tool, 86, 87
use of, 46, 50
Computers, 26, 28
Contact management
software, 31
Counteroffers. *See also* Offers
negotiating, 190–192
plan for, 193
Credit reports, 181
Customers. *See* Buyers

D
Database software, 32
David Knox Productions,
154, 160
Deceptive trade practices, 215
Decision making, 159
Deed of trust, 94, 181
Deed of trust to secure
assumption, 94
Desktop publishing, 32
Digital photography, 29030
Digital voice recorders, 34–35
Direct mail advertising, 113
Distractions, 101
Drip marketing
campaign, 126
DVDs
for buyers, 154, 160
Interactive, 34–35

E
Earnest money, 197, 198
Earnest money contract, 197
e-books, 34
Education. *See also* Training
advertising classes and, 111
investing time in, 54
web sites for real estate, 53
8 Steps to Buying a Home
(David Knox
Productions), 154
Enthusiasm, 123
Equal credit opportunity, 214
Equal housing opportunity,
213
Escrow agent, 198
Escrow fees, 94, 181

Excel (Microsoft), 140
Expired listings, 77–78
Explain-and-request method,
136–137

F
Fair housing, 213–214
Fair market value, 86
Farming
checklist for, 76
choosing area for, 70,
73–74
explanation of, 70
information gathering for,
74–75
strengthening contacts for,
75–76
FHA qualifying formula, 144
Filing fees per release, 94
Financial situation, 139–140
Floor duty
explanation of, 118
guidelines for, 118–124
Flow charts, 5
Follow-Up Note, 71
For sale by owner (FSBO),
76–77
Four P's, 3
Free Reports, 46

G
Goal charts, 58
Goal setting
explanation of, 57
guidelines for, 57–59
Goldmine, 31–32, 36
Government structure, 44
GPS (global positioning
systems), 29

H
Houses of worship, 43
Hwang, Haley M., 10

I
Image
in advertisements, 108–109
telephone, 119–123
Inattention, 101

Income, 12, 13
Inspection fees, 181
Instinctive learning, 99
Institutional advertising,
103, 104
Interactive CDs, 34–35
Interactive DVDs, 34–35
Internet. *See also* Web sites
advertising on, 112–113
home viewing on, 29,
31, 150

J
Jump drives, 35

L
Leads, 69–70
Learning, 99–100
Legal issues
anti-trust laws, 215
deceptive trade
practices, 215
equal credit
opportunity, 214
fair housing, 213–214
truth in lending, 214–215
Less favorable treatment, 214
Letters
follow-up, 71, 204, 205
recommendation, 202, 203
returning a favor, 72
Listing agents, 86
Listing presentation kit
checklist for, 91
contents of, 92–94
explanation of, 90, 92
Listings
guidelines for, 86–90
importance of, 83–86
notes to property owners
near, 85
Loan application fee, 181
Loan discount fees, 94
Loan origination fee, 181

M
Machine-gun approach, 170
Magazine advertising, 112
Map Point, 33, 73

Market allocation, 215
Marketing
  characteristics of real
    estate, 7
  explanation of, 3
  factors influencing, 4–5
  sales vs., 3
  tools for, 10
Market niches, 40
Marketplace
  bringing seller up-to-date
    on, 187–188
  gaining market knowledge
    on, 41–44
  learning history of,
    45–48
  making decisions about,
    39–41
McCarthy, E. Jerome, 3
Microsoft Excel, 140
Microsoft Outlook, 31, 32
Microsoft Publisher, 32
Microsoft Streets and
  Trips, 33
Mini-decision approach, 159
Minorities, 213
MLS® system, 126
Money (Microsoft), 32–33
Monitoring, 107
Mortgage policy, 181
Multiple Listing Service®
  (MLS®), 25

N
National Association of Real
  Estate Boards, 14. *See
  also* National Association
  of REALTORS®
National Association of
  REALTORS®
  *Code of Ethics and
    Standards of Practice,*
    15–21
  establishment of, 14
  *Profile of Homebuyers and
    Sellers,* 8
National Do Not Call Registry,
  127–128
Note, 94, 181

O
Objections
  checklist for, 171
  methods for handling,
    169–172
  resolving, 179
  types of, 167–169
  valid, 169
Offers. *See also* Counteroffers
  contacting seller about, 187
  maintaining control in,
    187–190
  negotiating, 190–192
  presenting, 185–187
Open-ended questions, 122
Open House Invitation, 78
Open houses, 78–79
Outdoor advertising, 112
Oversell, 178

P
PDF files, 33
Perception, 101
Personal management
  goal setting and, 57–59
  personal motivation and,
    51–54
  self-discipline and, 51
  time management and,
    54–57
Personal motivation
  BIKE approach to, 52–54
  explanation of, 51–52
Peterson, Cheri, 10
Photo-editing software, 34
PMI (private mortgage
  insurance) Fee and
  Appraisal, 181
Podcasts, 34
Portable hard drives, 35
Prejudice, 101
Preparing Your Home to Sell
  (David Knox
  Productions), 160
Presentation software, 33–34
Previewing checklist, 152
Price fixing, 215
Prices
  in classified ads, 105–106

helping sellers determine
  realistic, 87–88
using competitive market
  analysis to help set, 86–87
Pricing Your Home to Sell
  (David Knox
  Productions), 160
Problem solving, 52
Procrastination, 55
Product advertising, 103–104
Professionalism, 13–14
*Profile of Homebuyers and
  Sellers* (National
  Association of
  REALTORS), 8
Properties. *See also* Showing
  properties
  mental ownership of, 173
  previewing, 152–153
  reexamining, 172–173
  shopworn, 87
  specific details about,
    173–174
Prorations of Taxes and
  insurance, 181
Prospect Information
  Form, 141
Prospecting
  advertising as method
    for, 102
  centers of influence as
    source of, 67–70
  developing system for, 66–67
  explanation of, 66
  farming method of, 70, 73–76
  open house method of, 78–79
  overview of, 65–66
  for sale by owners and
    expired listings, 76–78
  satisfied customers as
    source of, 67
Public facilities, 43

Q
Qualifying
  afford amount vs., 142,
    144–145
  buying motives and, 145
  explanation of, 133–134

FHA, 144
information checklist for,
    137–141
method for, 136–137
reasons for, 134–135
showing properties to
    further, 151–152
timing for, 135–136
VA, 142, 143
Quality amount, 142
Quarterly Goal Chart, 58
Questions
    changing objections into,
        170–171
    open-ended, 122
Quicken (Intuit), 32–33

R
Radio advertising, 112
Rationalization, 55
Real estate, 7
Real estate developers, 44
Real Estate Marketing
    Assistant, 32
Real Estate Settlement
    Procedures Act
    (RESPA), 181
Reassurance, 174
Recommendation letters,
    202, 203
Recording fees, 181
Redlining, 214
Referrals, 67
Regulation Z, 215
Religious institutions, 43
Residents
    getting acquainted with,
        74–75
    strengthening contact with,
        75–76
Restrictions, 181
Reverse advertising, 109, 110
Rider signs, 84
Risk reduction, 216

S
Sales
    advantages and
        disadvantages of, 11–13

characteristics of, 7,
    202, 204
explanation of, 6–7
marketing vs., 3
overview of, 5
professionalism in, 13–14
Sales process
    responsibilities during,
        197–202
    review of, 202–204
Satisfied customers, 67
Schools, 42
See-saw technique, 122
Self-discipline, 51
Sellers
    advertising to satisfy, 103
    converted to buyers, 189
    explaining role of, 88–90
    gaining information
        from, 111
    presenting offers to, 187, 189
    role of, 200
    during showings, 154, 156
Selling
    explanation of, 6–7
    oneself, 10–11
    piece of mind, 189
Setbacks, 52
Shopworn property, 87
Showing agents, 86
Showing properties
    checklist for, 161
    guidelines for, 152–160
    limiting choices for, 157
    making appointments
        for, 153
    reasons for, 149–152
    websites for scheduling and
        tracking, 125
Smart phones
    checklist for purchasing, 30
    explanation of, 28–29
Software
    accounting and
        bookkeeping, 32–33
    calendar, 32
    contact management, 31
    database, 32
    desktop publishing, 32

PDF, 33
photo-editing, 34
presentation, 33–34
specialty, 34–35
types of, 30, 31
word processing, 33
Specialty software, 34–35
Stair-step approach, 159,
    176–177
Steering, 213–214
Survey, 181
Surveys, 94
Switch sheet, 118

T
Tablet PC, 26, 28
Target market, 104
Tax certificates, 94
Technology. See also Internet;
    Web sites
    budget for, 26, 27
    cellular vs. smart phone,
        28–29
    computers and, 26, 28
    digital photography and,
        29–30
    DVD, 34–35, 154, 160
    making the most of, 36
    overview of, 25–26
    software types and, 30–35
    web sites and, 35–36
Technology classes, 36
Telephone image, 119–123
Telephone techniques
    general guidelines for,
        126–128
    overview of, 117
    for placing calls, 124–126
    for receiving calls,
        118–124
Television advertising, 112
Termite inspection, 94
Time management
    explanation of, 54
    guidelines to improve,
        54–57
    qualifying and, 134
    during showings, 156–157
Title company, 198

Title policy, 94
Top Producer®, 26, 31, 32, 36
Total closing costs, 181
Training. *See also* Education
    elements of effective, 211
    ethics, 14
    online technology, 36
    web sites for real
        estate, 53
Transaction management
    systems, 204
Transfer fee, 181
Truth in lending, 214–215

V
VA Entitlement Form, 142
VA qualifying, 142, 143
Virtual tours, 31

W
Warranty deed, 94
Web sites
    advertising on, 112–113
    for census
        information, 50
    for closing cost
        information, 182
    for David Knox
        Productions, 160
    for goal-setting
        approaches, 59
    for handwritten fonts, 70
    for loan calculators, 140
    for Map Point, 73
    for National Do Not Call
        Registry, 127
    for negotiating tips, 192
    for online technology
        classes, 36
    personalized, 34–36
    for real estate courses, 53
    for Real Estate Settlement
        Procedures Act
        information, 182
    for risk reduction, 216
    for scheduling and tracking
        property showings, 125
    for school information, 42
    for spreadsheets, 140
    for transaction management
        systems, 204
    for Web site marketing, 116
Word-processing software, 33
World Wide Web. *See* Internet;
    Web sites